Empowering Communities with Media Literacy

CRITICAL ISSUES FOR LEARNING AND TEACHING

Shirley R. Steinberg
General Editor

Vol. 19

The Minding the Media series is part of both the
Peter Lang Education list and the Media and Communication list.
Every volume is peer reviewed and meets
the highest quality standards for content and production.

PETER LANG
New York • Berlin • Brussels • Lausanne • Oxford

Vitor Tomé and Belinha S. De Abreu

Empowering Communities with Media Literacy

The Critical Role of Young Children

PETER LANG
New York • Berlin • Brussels • Lausanne • Oxford

Library of Congress Cataloging-in-Publication Data

Names: Tomé, Vitor, author. | De Abreu, Belinha S., author.
Title: Empowering communities with media literacy: the critical role of young children / Vitor Tomé and Belinha S. De Abreu.
Description: New York: Peter Lang, 2023.
Series: Minding the media: critical issues for learning and teaching; Volume 19 | ISSN 2151-2949
Includes bibliographical references and index.
Identifiers: LCCN 2022016567 (print) | LCCN 2022016568 (ebook)
ISBN 978-1-4331-9509-9 (hardback) | ISBN 978-1-4331-9508-2 (paperback)
ISBN 978-1-4331-9506-8 (ebook pdf) | ISBN 978-1-4331-9507-5 (epub)
Subjects: LCSH: Community and school—Portugal—Lisbon. | Media literacy—Study and teaching (Preschool)—Portugal—Lisbon. | Media literacy—Study and teaching (Primary)—Portugal—Lisbon. | Citizenship—Study and teaching (Preschool)—Portugal—Lisbon. | Citizenship—Study and teaching (Primary)—Portugal—Lisbon. | Digital media—Portugal—Lisbon. | Computers and literacy—Research—Portugal—Lisbon.
Classification: LCC LC221.4.P8 T66 2023 (print) | LCC LC221.4.P8 (ebook) | DDC 370.11/50946942—dc23/eng/20220622
LC record available at https://lccn.loc.gov/2022016567
LC ebook record available at https://lccn.loc.gov/2022016568
DOI 10.3726/b19399

Bibliographic information published by **Die Deutsche Nationalbibliothek**.
Die Deutsche Nationalbibliothek lists this publication in the "Deutsche Nationalbibliografie"; detailed bibliographic data are available on the Internet at http://dnb.d-nb.de/.

© 2023 Peter Lang Publishing, Inc., New York
80 Broad Street, 5th floor, New York, NY 10004
www.peterlang.com

All rights reserved.
Reprint or reproduction, even partially, in all forms such as microfilm, xerography, microfiche, microcard, and offset strictly prohibited.

Dedication

We would like to dedicate this book to the children, parents, and community of Caneças who without their initial interest would not have moved this project forward.

Table of Contents

Foreword ix
Preface xi
Acknowledgments xv

Chapter 1 Introduction 1
Chapter 2 Empowering Digital Citizens 13
Chapter 3 Want a Community Project? Dive in the Context First! 47
Chapter 4 Preparing Teachers to Work with the Greater Community 59
Chapter 5 The Community in Action – From Printed School Newspaper to Video News Services 119
Chapter 6 A Never Ending Project 171
Chapter 7 Lessons Learned and Moving Forward 183

Appendix A: Workshop Sheet of the "Digital Citizenship Academy" Project 189
Appendix B: STEAM/Media Literacy Workshop – structure of the final report 191
Appendix C: Workshop evaluation form for preschool children_A 193
Appendix D: Workshop evaluation form for preschool children_B 197
Appendix E: Workshop evaluation form to be filled out by primary school children 199

Appendix F: Workshop evaluation form to be filled out by teachers   201
Appendix G: Initial questionnaire for parents   203
Appendix H: Initial questionnaire for teachers   211
Index   219

Foreword

I was delighted to be invited to write the foreword to this book. I have been aware of the innovative research that Vitor Tomé, his colleague Belinha De Abreu and his collaborators have been undertaking for some years and am pleased that the outcomes of this exciting project are now being shared in these pages. It is my view that the 'Digital Citizenship Academy' project offers a number of important insights into how schooling can be transformed in the 21st century, insights which are outlined below.

Firstly, the project offers a vision of how schools can engage with the challenges posed by the fourth industrial revolution, in which new skills and knowledge will be needed as technology transforms every aspect of our lives. When children in classrooms today leave school to join the employment market in the years ahead, jobs will be very different in many cases due to advances in artificial intelligence, cloud computing, nanotechnology, and so on. Preparation for a world of work and leisure in which technology is integrated into the fabric of everyday life requires a focus on transferable skills that will enable people to be digitally literate, flexible, innovative, creative and able to work across inter-disciplinary and inter-sector teams. These skills are particularly critical, as future generations will need them in order to meet the global challenges that lie ahead in areas such as environmental change, mass immigration, food security, and so on. The emphasis in the 'Digital Citizenship Academy' project on science, technology, engineering and mathematics

(STEM) is, therefore, vital in this context. However, this approach does not ignore the significant role that the arts and humanities play in ensuring citizens have rich and fruitful cultural lives. In this book, you will find wonderful examples of how children in the project developed digital literacy and STEM knowledge and skills through engagement with the arts, such as the creation of an orchestra in which children played instruments they had made in order to interpret Mozart's 'Turkish March' piano sonata. This, alongside many other examples, demonstrates the power of offering a curriculum in which interdisciplinary learning is facilitated through making.

Secondly, the 'Digital Citizenship Academy' project offers an example of research collaboration in action. Academics, teachers, parents, children and wider community members were all actively engaged in the project, each having an important part to play. The participatory approach of the research project was designed to ensure that even very young children could play an important part in the quest for knowledge about learning in the digital age. The co-production of knowledge in such collaborative research projects ensures that the insights gained can inform everyday community practices in meaningful ways.

Thirdly, the project provides a clear example of how professional learning for teachers can be designed in a manner that emphasizes iterative, collaborative learning over time. Having networked communities of professionals who are given the time and opportunity to take risks and reflect on processes and outcomes can lead to lasting changes in practice. Such an approach also respects the agency of teachers, placing them in the driving seat of transformations in schooling rather than being the passive recipients of ready-formed curricula and pedagogy.

In 2020, the world faced a major challenge with the onset of the COVID-19 pandemic. However, the 'Digital Citizenship Academy' project team managed to continue their collaboration throughout the lockdowns, demonstrating their impressive commitment to this community-based action research project. It is clear that this work is unstoppable. Just like a snowball growing larger and larger as it rolls down a mountainside, I have no doubt that this project will continue to grow and flourish in the years ahead. For now, I am sure that you, as I did, will enjoy reading about its progress to date in these pages.

Professor Jackie Marsh
Maker{Futures}—https://makerfutures.org
University of Sheffield, UK

Preface

Who are you in the digital space? Who are we? What are students using for technology and how do they engage with digital environments? Do they know how to analyze information or practice citizenship online? These are a few questions which inspirited the work you are about to read.

Distinguishing the digital work from the real world is important and needed for people to function in our society, but they are both intertwined. One cannot speak of Digital Citizenship without thinking about what it is to be a citizen. Understanding how these ideas work together is in many ways what led us to this work in Digital Citizenship and Media Literacy. Here are some worldwide statistics about children, youth, and teens and their consideration of media environments:

- Young adults (18–34) today are more distrusting of the media than older adults and report less trust in media than adults their age 20 years ago (Fioroni, 2021).
- More than half of children have a social media profile by the age of 13; and by the age of 15, almost all have one. WhatsApp, which has gained popularity among teenagers, is used by 62% of 12- to 15-year- olds, Facebook (69%), Snapchat (68%) and Instagram (66%) (Ofcom, 2020).
- A 2016 report claims that 80% of middle schoolers couldn't tell the difference between a native ad and editorial content (p. 10) and 93% of college

students didn't realize that they were reading information put out by industry PR (p. 5) (Stanford History Group, 2016).

In a graduate class, a first-grade teacher commented that she felt that her little ones were too small to think about online Digital Citizenship. However, the reality is that her students are already in those spaces, and in their everyday lives are learning how to be real-world citizens by when they are taught to say "please," "thank you," "may I," etc. In fact, beyond that we look at citizenship when we see how students interact with each other and we correct their behavior or teach them societal cues. As researchers in the UK stated, "the rise in Internet use by children and young people has called into question the impact that it has both on their development and on their ability to act on character virtues, including, in particular, their honesty and compassion" (Harrison and Polizzi, 2021).

This initial teaching and guidance translates well when students are online, with the only significant difference being they are facing a computer screen. We are often reminding our students, as they get older and become teenagers, that they are that there are real people on the other side of that screen. There are feelings, sentiments, hurts, worries, and much more that go on with the person who is on the receiving end of messages that are transmitted by the digital display. They, people, are real. The screen acts as a barrier in effect, holding back the reality of what is going on. This lesson is the hardest to teach. Research and other data can talk about effects and so forth, but it is in the everyday practical application that change can be most valuable. Whether it is a parent who is correcting their child, a teacher who is fostering digital competency, or an everyday individual who takes on the role of being an upstander versus a bystander, we all participate in the creation of a digital citizen. In the online world this tenet seems to be more easily forgotten.

In the 1960s, a Canadian academic, Marshall McLuhan, wrote in his book *Understanding Media* that "the medium is the message." McLuhan had predicted that technology and media were growing at a rapid pace and that schools needed to adapt techniques for students to learn and process the information they were receiving, by, at that time, only television and radio. Fast forward to 2021 and beyond, and technology is the main staple of people's information diet. As we look at our classrooms, libraries, and other places where our students can be found, there is an obvious pattern of students plugged in and educators trying to get their curriculum out to students in various modalities. There is a digital disconnect that is real and one that completely separates belief from practice.

Parents worry about how and where their children might be exploited online, Students want to know why their favorite tools are constantly being monitored, taken away from them, or limited--- and not by just a little, but by extreme amounts. They question why education is not keeping up with their own technology preferences. They ask why they are not allowed to become digital leaders online, as if they are being prevented from stepping up and stepping into that realm of possibility. They are often right on this point. They want to know why teachers and administrators aren't seeing the possibilities of how they can lead with technology and do better. In fairness to all, it is because educators have seen much more of the opposite, but it is also because students are still learning what it looks like to be a good citizen offline –never mind online. This point brings me back to where we started.

In the mix, we have had a pandemic that has shown us the capacity to which our lives can continue through interactive apps and programs, in spite of restrictions put in place to keep us distanced. We have lived by these restrictions for over two years, and in doing so, we have begun to see the strain of being "on" all the time. The screens are tiring and have also changed how we engage both online and offline. Many educators say that we may be teaching how to actually have social norms while our students have lost their essence behind a screen and a mask. This point is still unfolding and, without a doubt, will be researched and discussed much more in the future.

In the meantime, we are left with what we know and what has been exposed by the media relative to digital tools. Of significance, we have been confronted with Facebook's own abhorrent relationship with teens and young adults released through leaked documents that digital tools are damaging to those students who are most susceptible and most vulnerable. Consider what Frances Haugen's, the Facebook whistleblower, in testimony at the Senate hearing in October of 2021 stated regarding Facebook when she said,

> "I'm here today because I believe Facebook's products harm children, stoke division, and weaken our democracy. These problems are solvable. A safer, free-speech respecting, more enjoyable social media is possible. But there is one thing that I hope everyone takes away from these disclosures, it is that Facebook can change, but is clearly not going to do so on its own" (Hao, 2021).

Our social media is a part of our social stratosphere and it is also a part of discourse as a community engaged in civil society online as well as offline.

Whether it is first grade, kindergarten, or high school, we are finally at the point where we acknowledge that technology is wide sweeping and here to stay. The pandemic in particular has shown us this most clearly. No longer is it possible to sit back and hope it will pass it by; nor is it feasible to think that students will become digital, media, or information literate through the mere fact that they have technology. It isn't osmosis. Frankly, it would be better for all of us if parents, teachers, administrators, and the general public would stop sharing the idea that digital natives means digitally savvy. It doesn't quite work that way which is why we continue to have the discussion on Digital Citizenship.

Being digital is a practical experience. Stepping away is not educationally sound and certainly does not benefit the digital society as a whole especially when we are considering what the next step will be in the process of digital evolution. This book, our story, is about looking at the evidence and seeing the purposeful implementation of Media Literacy education in conjunction with Digital Citizenship.

References

Fioroni, S. (2021, September 21). Skeptics or cynics? Age determines how Americans view the news media. *Knight Foundation*. Retrieved: https://knightfoundation.org/articles/skeptics-or-cynics-age-differences-in-how-americans-view-the-news-media/?utm_medium=email&utm_source=the-sift&utm_campaign=the-sift-sept27-2021&emci=6cf5aba7-a51f-ec11-981f-0050f271a1a2&emdi=b14f4e22-be1f-ec11-981f-0050f271a1a2&ceid=7505070.

Hao, K. (2021, October 5). The Facebook whistleblower says its algorithms are dangerous. Here's why. *MIT Technology Review*. Retrieved: https://www.technologyreview.com/2021/10/05/1036519/facebook-whistleblower-frances-haugen-algorithms/?utm_source=pocket-newtab.

Harrison, T., & Polizzi, G. (2021, May). A cyber-wisdom approach to digital citizenship education. University of Birmingham. *The Jubilee Centre for Character and Virtue*. Retrieved: https://www.jubileecentre.ac.uk/userfiles/jubileecentre/Final%20PDF%20Cyber%20Wisdom%20Report%20v2.pdf

Ofcom. (2020). *Children and parents: Media use and attitudes report 2019*. Retrieved: https://www.ofcom.org.uk/__data/assets/pdf_file/0023/190616/children-media-use-attitudes-2019-report.pdf.

Stanford History Education Group. (2016). *Evaluating information: The cornerstone of civic online reasoning*. Retrieved: https://sheg.stanford.edu/upload/V3LessonPlans/Executive%20Summary%2011.21.16.pdf.

Acknowledgments

A project of this large scale could not go on with the support and encouragement from the various groups of people, colleagues and organizations.

We thank the following organizations and institutions for their financial and community support:

- Calouste Gulbenkian Foundation (Portugal)—Gulbenkian Knowledge Program
- Science and Technology Portuguese Foundation (SFRH/BPD/77874/2011)
- Directorate-General of Education (Ministry of Education, Portugal)
- Autonoma University of Lisbon
- Agrupamento de Escolas de Caneças
- Câmara Municipal de Odivelas
- União das Freguesias de Ramada e Caneças
- Centro Protocolar de Formação Profissional para Jornalistas
- RVJ-Editores (Castelo Branco, Portugal)
- Centro de Formação Leonardo Coimbra (Associação Nacional de Professores)
- Sindicato dos Jornalistas
- Associação Literacia para os Media e Jornalismo

Their support made this research possible on both a large and small scale, boosted by the support of the distinguished colleagues Isabel Silva (Autonoma University of Lisbon), Miguel Crespo (CIES-ISCTE-University Institute of Lisbon), Valentina Valente (Escola Afonso de Paiva - Castelo Branco) and Morgana Bordalo Santos (Catholic University of Lisbon).

We would like to thank our families, who have watched us working on this book as well as throughout the many years of trainings, data collections, as well as presenting on this topic around the world.

- Vitor in particular would like to thank: Mónica Gomes, Beatriz Tomé, João Almeida, Margarida Tomé, Rita Almeida. They are the backbone and the inspiration for the work that is here.
- Belinha would also like to thank her family, in particular her husband, sister, brother-in-law, and mom who have shared with her in this journey of Media Literacy education.

We would like to thank our colleagues from the various Media Literacy and Digital Citizenship communities around the world.

We would also like to thank the students, parents, and community leaders we have met during the time period of this project. This book is 100% dedicated to you and your efforts.

Lastly, we would like to thank the group at Peter Lang Publishing, Dani Green and Patty Mulrane, our editors, who accepted this initial project and worked with us throughout the pandemic to make this work come to fruition.

CHAPTER 1

Introduction

This book describes the evolution of the project currently named 'Digital Citizenship Academy'[1], an ongoing community-based research project on Digital Citizenship Education, whose main participants are preschool and primary school teachers, students, and those students' relatives, as well as many other community members. The project envisioned the following objectives:

- Infuse Media Education into the preschool and primary school curricula;
- Identify sense-making practices aimed at formal, non-formal and informal learning contexts;
- Contribute to the selection of learning outcomes to assess the development, by children and young people, of Media Literacy competencies;
- Inform policymakers and other entities responsible for the definition of public policies in Digital Citizenship Education for democratic participation;
- Implement a Media Education project in a local community in Portugal that is replicable at national and international levels;

---

1 This is the name of the project since November 2019, following funding from the Calouste Gulbenkian Foundation, since when the project was started in 2015, it was called "Digital Citizenship Education for Democratic Participation" and was then funded by a post-doctoral fellowship funded by the Science and Technology Portuguese Foundation, from the Ministry of Science, Technology and Higher Education.

- Contribute to the development of social and emotional skills, in children aged 3–9, in terms of communication and problem solving, creating conditions for them to intervene through the media and acquire the ability to implement entrepreneurial strategies.

The research project started in March 2015, in Odivelas Municipality (north of Lisbon, Portugal), with 145,000 inhabitants, representing the second-highest population density in the country (5,424 inhabitants / km^2). Half the population (51%) only completed basic education (9 years) and one-fourth concluded only primary school (four years). School-age population accounts for 11% of the total population (total youth population is 15%), and 16% of the total population are immigrants. The activities are currently centered on the Parish of Ramada and Caneças, with around 35,000 inhabitants, and more specifically at the Caneças School District (which includes 10 schools, from preschool to primary school), located in the village of Caneças, a community of 12,000 inhabitants.

Since 2016, four teacher training courses have been implemented, one in Digital Citizenship (2016), one in Media Education (2017/18) and two in Media Literacy and STEAM—Science, Technology, Engineering, Arts and Mathematics (2020). As part of these trainings, dozens of activities were planned, implemented and evaluated, involving 79 teachers and more than one thousand children and families from several schools in the area of the Parish Union.

Following the first training, in 2016, the project was based at the Artur Alves Cardoso School, which includes the Artur Alves Cardoso Kindergarten and Artur Alves Cardoso Primary School. There was a total of 10 teachers and 200 students who played a central role in this intervention project. These schoolteachers and their students created a printed school newspaper (and have published nine editions since December 2016), produced a video news service by and with children (2018), as well as produced an online school newspaper and a YouTube channel (2020).

In 2021, the Portuguese Ministry of Education published a book of practices in Media Literacy and STEAM, created by the children and teachers involved in the project and organized by the research team. The book contains plans for the implementation of practices, the methodologies and resources used in the implementation of these practices, as well as observation and evaluation tools of these practices, often jointly created by teachers and researchers.

In six years of uninterrupted activity, the project has been referenced in book chapters, scientific articles and in international conferences in several European countries, the United States, Brazil and Australia. It has led the Caneças School District to become a member of the Council of Europe Democratic Schools Network. Along the way, the project received funding in 2019 from Portugal's most important cultural foundation, the Calouste Gulbenkian Foundation, which will allow for activities to be developed until December 2022.

However, the full scope of the project, based on all the data collected, all the activities developed, the intervention plan developed in 2016 and reformulated in the following years, is still an untold story. It is for all of these reasons that this book has come to fruition. Further, this book allows for all participants to have a voice, first and foremost the children, and including the teachers and members of the research team.

We analyze the path taken from Media Literacy to STEAM using the editions of the student-developed school newspaper 'O Cusco' (The Busybody). Through this school newspaper, we understand the natural evolution of the project, according to the interests of the children and teachers, but also of the families.

1.1 How Is This Book Structured?

This book is structured in seven parts to frame the research and the model by which we created and developed the project. We begin with Chapter 1 which introduces the project, its objectives, its evolution over the years, and its structure in terms of content.

In Chapter 2 we define key concepts, frame the project within the international models of citizen training, as well as the educational policies of Portugal, and justify the need for the project and the strategy of community-based action research projects.

Chapter 3 explains how the project was planned in 2014, proposed to several municipalities, and after selecting one municipality, how it was presented to schools and their communities. It also explains how the instruments used to collect data from children and their parents were produced and validated, as well as teachers' longitudinal data collection, and the questionnaire applied in 2016 at the beginning of the first of three teacher training courses that the project has involved thus far.

Chapter 4 describes precisely these three training courses held between 2016 and 2020, focusing on the training plans, the work developed by teachers, their students, parents and the community. It further explains the evaluation of the work developed, and the evaluation of the training course itself. The final part of the chapter summarizes the results of the training and explains the role of these courses in terms of the continuity of the project that will continue at least until December 2022.

Chapter 5 explains how the project's 2014 design was remodeled in March 2016, after the first teacher training. It was further changed in light of the results of the analysis of the data collected from teachers, children and parents between January and June 2016. The resulting plan was based on this data and the needs identified in the context itself so that an intervention plan was designed in the community, with the collaboration of all stakeholders. The chapter also mentions how this plan was implemented, evaluated, and gradually improved according to the needs and interests of the community.

In Chapter 6, the evaluation of the project is provided, detailing two international strategies for analyzing projects of this type. This is followed by a presentation of the reasons behind the continuity of the project, which was supposed to end in February 2018. The current sustainability plan is presented, and summarized resources and methodological strategies shown that can make the project replicable, with acknowledgment that this will not be feasible without necessary adaptations to the context, as any project requires.

Chapter 7 summarizes the lessons learned and explains how the project will be replicated in the countryside of Portugal, namely in Proença-a-Nova Municipality, which has a total of 7500 inhabitants, but has been losing population over the last 40 years due to emigration as well as the rural exodus from the countryside to the shore of Portugal.

1.2 A Journey from Media Literacy to STEAM

In January 2016, the board of the Caneças School District agreed to provide facilities for continuous and ongoing teacher professional development training course entitled "The importance of social media in the democratic participation of children and young people." This course was accredited for teachers of preschool education, primary school and special education. Twenty-five teachers participated, creating and implementing Media Education and Digital Citizenship activities with their students and involving families and the community.

The program ended in March and all the teachers were invited to join the project "Digital Citizenship Education for Democratic Participation," where this training was integrated. Eight teachers, all from Escola EB Artur Alves Cardoso, accepted the challenge and continued to develop activities with their students. Simultaneously, the research team collected data, interviewing parents, children, teachers and other elements of the school and educational community (Tomé and Abreu, 2016; Tomé, 2016).

In December 2016 the school newspaper was born. "O Cusco," loosely translated as "The Busybody," was a name chosen and voted by the school children, whose front page was entitled "Being a Digital Citizen" (Photo 1.1). Digital Citizenship is a theme that the children discussed with their families and the community. In 2017, three more issues of the newspaper were published in print, as the representation of the community pointed out this need so as to not exclude anyone. Each issue of the newspaper was centered on a theme prepared by the preschool and primary school teachers.

Photo 1.1: First edition of 'O Cusco' (12/2016)

The headlines of the 2017 issues included: *For a School Without Violence, How Children Imagine Playgrounds, A Letter to the Minister of Education Comes Out* (Photo 1.2).

Photo 1.2: Editions 2, 3 and 4 of 'O Cusco' (2017)

All were testimony to the willingness of children to participate and even intervene socially through the media. The project, funded by the Science and Technology Portuguese Foundation (FCT)[2], ended in February 2018. However, the March 2018 headline of 'O Cusco' left no doubt: "Cusco is Already on TV" (Photo 1.3). Teachers and students had produced the school's first video news story, "Telecusco," as the children named it.

In the meantime, the teachers attended the accredited continuing education course "Media Education and School Newspaper in the Promotion of Reading and Writing," taught by a researcher who continued to collaborate with the school. The school was creating ties with national research projects such as "Media Literacy and Journalism" (Portuguese Journalists' Union, Directorate-General of Education, CENJOR – National Training Center for Journalists) or international ones such as "Digital Citizenship Education" (Council of Europe).

---

2 FCT is the Portuguese public agency that supports science, technology and innovation, in all scientific domains, under responsibility of the Ministry for Science, Technology and Higher Education.

Photo 1.3: Issue 5 d' "The Cusco' (2018)

In June 2018, "O Cusco" was once again dedicated to preschool education with the headline: "The School We Always Dreamed Of" (Photo 1.4). Educators, children, parents and community members created the model of the school that the children wanted in the future. This was another example of intervening for change, not only through the production of the model whose production had followed the STEAM methodology, but also of intervening through the media, and in this case the school newspaper, which was already commonly used among primary school children (Tomé, Lopes, Reis and Dias, 2019; Tomé, 2019).

Photo 1.4: Issue 6 of 'O Cusco' (2018)

This work was a perfect fit for another collaboration that began in 2016, and which has been growing progressively, with the direction and several researchers of the European Cooperation in Science and Technology (COST) Action titled "The digital literacy and multimodal practices of young children" (DigiLitEY), a project funded by the European Commission that involved researchers from 36 European countries, Brazil and Australia.

This collaboration helped to create the Media Literacy pathway to STEAM, which would take shape in March 2019 as the Knowledge Science Academies Program. At that time, a group of children, from 3rd and 4th grades, had already visited the studios of the Autonoma University of Lisbon, where they rehearsed the second video news service of 'O Cusco', an activity that made the second headline of the only edition of the newspaper published in 2019: "Telecusco arrives in Lisbon" (Photo 1.5). The following paper was dedicated to the roller car race (baptized "Os Arturinhos") that teachers, students' families, and the community organized near the school.

Photo 1.5: Issue 7 of 'O Cusco' (Cusco)

The school year at the Caneças School District was now organized in semesters, so the next edition of the newspaper 'O Cusco', published in January 2020, reported the beginning of the "Digital Citizenship Academy" project, which had begun in November 2019. The newspaper's last page also reported that Caneças School District was one of the three Portuguese schools to join the Council of Europe's Democratic Schools Network, having been represented at the meeting in Florence, Italy by teacher Elisabete Monteiro, from Artur Alves Cardoso School.

Photo 1.6: Issue 8 of "O Cusco" (2020)

The headline of the January 2020 edition was dedicated to an interview with the Director of Caneças School District, Fernando Costa, under the title: "The Most Important Thing is the Students" (Photo 1.6). To continue to fulfill this mission, it was necessary to invest in teacher training, this time in Media Literacy and STEAM, which was foreseen in the project as a cornerstone.

The teacher training in STEAM and Media Literacy was first scheduled for March 2020. However, due to the lockdown which ensued because of the Covid-19 pandemic, this timeframe had to change. Therefore, the training was postponed to September of that year, and made fully accessible online instead of face-to-face. Although there were several setbacks, including quarantined teachers and students, and a second lockdown in January 2021, teachers and students managed to plan, implement, and evaluate STEAM and Media Literacy activities, two of which were mentioned in the headlines of issue 9 of "O Cusco," published in July 2021 (Photo 1.7).

Photo 1.7: Issue 9 of "O Cusco" (2021)

The activity mentioned above consisted of the planning and creation of a vegetable garden in the school space, by preschool children, their teachers and families. Together they prepared the soil, created a sprinkler irrigation system, built a scarecrow, and chose the crops. They produced lettuce, cabbage, strawberries, and cilantro. The vegetable garden creation process was followed by a photoshoot, which allowed the creation of a video that was made available on the YouTube Channel "O Cusco." The children also produced three other videos related to the transformation of products from the garden, such as strawberries (which became strawberry smoothies), cabbage (which became soup) and lettuce (which became salad).

The second activity consisted in the creation of a model about the regulation of human and vehicle traffic patterns around the school. First, the children studied the rules of road safety. Then, they went outside school to check if these rules, as well as the signage and lighting conditions or other conditions were in accordance with what they had studied. The students found that this was not the case and that, in fact, street lighting, crosswalks, parking places and speed bumps were missing. As a result, they created a 3D scale model in which they presented their solutions and wrote to the local government claiming that there was an urgent need to fix these problems.

This work was comprehensive and detailed for all involved – from the children to the educators, as well as the community and researchers. The integration of the different curriculum which embedded Media Literacy, STEAM, as well as other literacies was of significant importance to the outcomes that were needed in order to empower the community and students in a digital world.

References

Tomé, V. (2016). Cidadania na era digital: um projeto-piloto de formação de crianças dos 3 aos 9 anos em contexto formal e informal de aprendizagem. *Revista Educação e Cultura Contemporânea, 13*(31), 372–403. Available at: http://goo.gl/ULH0zR

Tomé, V. (2019). Usos de tecnologias analógicas e digitais na formação de cidadãos ativos: um percurso com crianças dos 3 aos 9 anos, seus professores, pais e comunidade local. *Revista Educação e Cultura Contemporânea, 42*, 432–469. Available at: http://periodicos.estacio.br/index.php/reeduc/article/viewArticle/5895

Tomé, V., & De Abreu, B. (2016). Developing digital citizenship in children aged from 3 to 9: a pilot project in the Portuguese region of Odivelas. *Special Issue of the Journal Media Education: Studi, Ricerche, Buone Pratiche, 7*(2), 215–233. Available at: https://goo.gl/lBfIQw

Tomé, V., Lopes, P., Reis, B., & Dias, C. P. (2019). Active citizenship and participation through the media: A community project focused on preschool and primary school children. *Comunicação e Sociedade, 36*, 101–120. Available at: http://dx.doi.org/10.17231/comsoc.36(2019).2347

CHAPTER 2

Empowering Digital Citizens

This chapter provides the scientific background of the project currently named 'Digital Citizenship Education Academy'. We start by defining the key concepts, namely Digital Citizenship Education, Media Literacy, and Science, Technology, Engineering, Arts and Mathematics, hereinafter referred to by the acronym STEAM—concepts used throughout the project with the school and community. The chapter also refers to the role attributed to Media Literacy and STEAM in four international models of citizenship education, as well as by the current Portuguese educational policy. It finally explains, with scientific rationale, why the project is focused on very young children and why we chose to create a community-based participatory project.

2.1 Digital Citizenship Education, Media Literacy and STEAM

Being an active and responsible citizen implies the development of a set of lifelong competencies both online and offline, and at various levels, from local to global. The model "Competences of Democratic Culture" (Council of Europe, 2016, 2018a), for instance, consisting of 20 items, and better known as the "butterfly model," is organized into four areas:

- **Values**
  - o Valuing human dignity and human rights
  - o Valuing cultural diversity
  - o Valuing democracy, justice, fairness, equality and the rule of law
- **Attitudes**
  - o Openness to cultural otherness and to other beliefs, world views and practices
  - o Respect
  - o Civic-mindedness
  - o Responsibility
  - o Self-efficacy
  - o Tolerance of ambiguity
- **Skills**
  - o Autonomous learning skills
  - o Analytical and critical thinking skills
  - o Skills of listening and observing
  - o Empathy
  - o Flexibility and adaptability
  - o Linguistic, communicative and plurilingual skills
  - o Co-operation skills
  - o Conflict-resolution skills
- **Knowledge and critical understanding**
  - o Knowledge and critical understanding of the self
  - o Knowledge and critical understanding of language and communication
  - o Knowledge and critical understanding of the world: politics, law, human rights, culture, cultures, religions, history, media, economies, environment, sustainability.

According to the model, which integrates a set of learning outcomes and whose application has been tested in formal learning contexts, the competence items are teachable, learnable and this learning is measurable. Knowing that the model is valid for both the offline and online context, which together form the citizen context, as we focus on the development of competences in the digital world.

We understand Digital Citizenship Education according to the following definition:

> The ability to positively and competently engage with technologies (create, work, share, socialize, investigate, play, communicate and learn); participating actively and responsibly (values, skills, attitudes, knowledge and critical understanding) in communities (local, national, global), at all levels (political, economic, social, cultural

and intercultural); being involved in a lifelong learning process (in formal, non-formal and informal context); continuously defending human rights and human dignity (Frau-Meigs, O'Neill, Soriani and Tomé, 2017, pp. 11–12).

2.1.1 Media Literacy

Media Literacy is the result of Media Education activities and consists of the set of knowledge, skills and abilities needed to participate in contemporary society, through access, analysis, critical evaluation and reflective and creative production of media messages in a wide variety of formats and languages (Buckingham, 2003; Hobbs, 2016). This production is valid only when associated with a structured dissemination, through multiple channels, enhancing participation, social intervention, and social reflection.

There is no doubt of the need for Media Literacy education in formal and informal learning contexts. If there were any doubts, they have been dispelled with the growth and dissemination of misinformation and disinformation (Wardle and Derakhshan, 2019), more recently dubbed "infodemic" (Nielsen, Fletcher, Newman, Brennen and Howard, 2020), or "disinfodemic" as UNESCO (2020) recently called it.

Media Literacy is not the answer to misinformation, but is only one dimension of a needed global response, with which new laws and policies will be created to respond to emerging challenges, with a focus on science, communication technologies, and better mechanisms to detect false information and strategies to protect the public (Heath, 2021).

As UNESCO (*idem*) states, Media and Information Literacy is a key competence that contributes to access to information, freedom of expression, digital security and privacy protection, as well as to the prevention of extremism and combating hate speech and inequalities. Media Literacy today should aim at "transmedia literacy," that consists in the development of seven areas of competencies listed:

1. Production of multiformat media messages (e.g. from conception to reformulation and technical aspects)
2. Management of the interrelationship (individual and collective) with the media and its contents
3. Performative (e.g., problem solving, strategic thinking, creativity, and performance art)
4. Media and technology use (e.g., consumption, participation, and use of digital social networks)

5. Narratives and aesthetics (e.g., reconstructing narratives and expressing worldviews)
6. Risk prevention, ideology, and ethics (e.g., being reflective and critical of the media and one's own productions)
7. Informal learning strategies (e.g., learning by doing, problem solving, through simulations, games and others) (Scolari, 2018).

Media Literacy results from a process developed throughout life that Jolls (2008) called the "empowerment spiral." This process must begin at birth (Gonnet, 1999) and continue throughout life, and is therefore a function of the family, the school, non-governmental organizations, the state, and supranational institutions such as the European Commission, the OECD or UNESCO.

Although Media Literacy's importance is finally receiving recognition, the truth is that there are several challenges that have arisen in its development path. In particular, overcoming the traditional school resistance to change, the integration of formal, non-formal and informal learning contexts, or the implementation of a Media Education with a critical and cultural logic and not only focused on the practical and technical use of media. Other challenges are the bridging of several digital gaps and the necessary initial and continuing teacher training on which this book is also focused (Tomé, 2015).

2.1.2 STEAM

The English acronym STEAM (Science, Technology, Engineering, Arts and Mathematics) is an evolution of the STEM methodology, whose implementation in schools in the United States of America dates back to the beginning of the century (Catterall, 2017). It designates a project-based learning methodology, unstructured and open at the beginning, gradually evolving into research processes aimed at designing solutions and solving problems from which products result (Diego-Mantecón, Blanco, Ortiz-Laso and Lavicza, 2021).

By linking the arts to STEM, STEAM opens up a transdisciplinary space that spans the areas between, across, and beyond traditional disciplines, paving the way for creativity (Liao, 2016). Combining disciplines traditionally taught separately, STEAM projects explore real-world problems, enhance learning from experience, and given their character of informal social interaction, promote the realization of flexible learning, with peers and with mentors (Vuorikari, Ferrari, and Punie, 2019).

STEAM, when integrated into the curriculum, promotes students' cognitive development, but also develops emotional and spiritual domains, improving students' critical thinking and problem-solving skills, and enhancing their creativity (Setiawan and Saputri, 2019). Schools can offer potential growth in the areas of STEAM/STEM through Makerspace activities whereby students are encouraged to respond to challenges that appeal to their interests, and then making plans, presenting projects, and creating products (Khor, 2017).

Makerspaces can be created in libraries, museums or other community spaces, and the very methodologies of creation and making, while pedagogical, are also applicable in informal spaces. Making and problem-solving promote working as part of a community, which is a key life skill because it involves sharing and cooperation, both online and offline, contributing to sustainable development (Vuorikari et al., 2019).

Media Literacy and STEAM have a central aspect in common: using technologies, namely digital technologies (Jorge, Tomé and Pacheco, 2019), first as toys, but gradually to communicate and learn, and later to work. In other words, there is a transversal use of digital technologies, from birth and throughout life, individually and as part of a community, in formal and informal environments, always preparing individuals for that which the whole society is responsible.

This preparation has positive effects at the primary school level, namely at four levels: creativity, critical thinking, design-thinking and digital skills (Bower, Stevenson, Falloon, Forbes, Hatzigianni, 2018). In formalized education, STEAM should start in preschool education through a focus on transformative pedagogies that prepare children to participate in the digital society. As a STEAM contribution, Makerspaces take into account five central aspects (Marsh, Wood, Chesworth, Nisha, Nutbrown and Olney, 2019):

1. *Interest*—technologies evolve very fast, which changes the opportunities they offer to children and the motivations that lead them to use these technologies, so it is essential that children can choose topics or problems based on their interest (*"maker agency"*).
2. *Community*—without prejudice to the child's interest, in a logic centered on the individual, it is important to realize that *Makerspaces* are not based on individual agendas or personal improvement, but on a participative, democratic vision of common interest, which serves as a basis for the development of socio-cultural practices.

3. *Prior knowledge*—the child's prior knowledge, which comes from home, is central, as well as the relationships he establishes with his peers, so it mobilizes the cognitive, affective, creative, and relational areas, which considerably increases learning potential.
4. *Play*—Play is fundamental in *Makerspaces*, as it involves cognitive processes linked to creativity, such as problem solving, metacognition and creative practices. The activities that children develop there (e.g.: movement, expressions, drawing, photography, models, cultural tools or objects) allow them to communicate their meanings and perspectives towards the world.
5. *"Postdigital maker play"*—it matters not to separate digital activities from those that are analog, because that boundary no longer makes sense.

2.1.3 Why Media Literacy and STEAM together?

The work developed by Marsh et al. (2019) involves children attending preschool education and those attending the first years of primary school. Thus, a Media Literacy and STEAM project aimed at these two levels of education is justified in itself, but also to ensure curricular and pedagogical continuity between the two levels, eliminating inconsistencies in curriculum and pedagogical content regarding the transition phase between these two levels (OECD, 2017).

Further, it was justified that the training be developed within the 'Digital Citizenship Academy', not least because the efficacy of digital workshops, following project work, has already proven effective in other countries, such as Italy (Tomé, Falconi and Mendes, 2019). Moreover, it is a natural approach to achieving a central objective of the project: to develop social and emotional skills, in children aged three to 12 years, in terms of communication and problem solving, creating conditions for them to intervene through the media and acquire the ability to implement entrepreneurial strategies.

2.2 Media Literacy and STEAM-Empowering Digital Citizens

The competencies associated with Media Literacy and STEAM are central in international models focused on the implementation of Digital Citizenship Education, such as the Council of Europe's "10 Digital Domains" (Richardson and Milovidov, 2019), the "Key Competences for Lifelong Learning" (Council of the European Union, 2018), the "global competence" (OECD, 2018a, 2016) and the "global citizenship" (UNESCO, 2015a).

2.2.1 Council of Europe—10 Domains of Digital Citizenship

In 2016, taking the 'Competencies of Democratic Culture' model (Council of Europe, 2018a) as a reference, the Council of Europe created a project focused on Digital Citizenship Education, which defined 10 key domains, organized into three groups that are related to Media Literacy and STEAM:

- **Being online**—Access and Inclusion; Learning and Creativity; Media and Information Literacy.
- **Well-being Online**—Ethics and Empathy; Health and Wellbeing; e-Presence and Communications.
- **Rights online**—Active Participation; Rights and Responsibilities; Privacy and Security; Consumer Awareness (Council of Europe, 2018b).

Although Media (and Information) Literacy is one of the 10 domains, it does not end there, since the domains are not impermeable and overlap. Media Literacy implies knowing how to access media (Access and Inclusion), learning about and from media, and expressing oneself through media (Learning and Creativity), ethically putting oneself in the position of the Other (Ethics and Empathy), protecting one's well-being (Health and Well-Being), managing one's presence and communicating effectively (e-Presence and Communication).

Media Literacy is related to social intervention through media (Active Participation), respecting the law and assuming your responsibilities (Rights and Responsibilities), protecting your personal data and implementing safety procedures (Privacy and Security), and understanding, for example media financing models (Consumer Awareness).

The STEAM methodology is also related to each of the domains, as it is an inclusive methodology (Access and Inclusion) which enhances learning by doing and is focused on creative freedom (Learning and Creativity), and is also associated with the use of media and technology (Media and Information Literacy). It is based on the relationship of cooperation and collaboration with others (Ethics and Empathy) and therefore implies well-being (Health and Well-Being) of the participants and effective communication, within and outside the group (e-Presence and Communication).

The STEAM methodology aims at sustainable development and solving real problems through social intervention (Active Participation), and respecting legislation (Rights and Responsibilities). Finally, it implies data management (Privacy and Security) and, at least in some cases, inherently teaches consumption, since the resources used have costs (Consumer Awareness).

These 10 domains are central to the Recommendation of the Committee of Ministers of the Council of Europe (2019a) for the development and promotion of Digital Citizenship Education, which can contribute, among others, to "creating greater educational opportunities in the science, technology, engineering and mathematics (STEM) fields for girls and women and ensur[ing] that all citizens benefit fully from the digital revolution." Further, the 10 domains are considered the foundations of the concept of Digital Citizenship and the appropriate way to develop democratic culture skills in the digital environment.

The Committee of Ministers' document recommends that member states review their legislation, policies, and practices in order to structure, implement, and evaluate Digital Citizenship education in formal and informal learning contexts, involving all relevant actors, creating resources, ensuring initial and ongoing training of teachers and other education professionals, articulating the strategy between the public, private, and social sectors, and between these and international institutions, such as the Council of Europe or others. It then mentions the principles to be taken into account when implementing Digital Citizenship Education. The Recommendation was reinforced, days after it was signed, by the Ministerial Declaration on Education for Citizenship in the Digital Age and endorsed by the ministers of education for the 50 states that are part of the 1954 European Cultural Convention. We summarize their commitment here:

1. Ensuring the development of digital skills from a very early age, in order to prepare citizens for higher education, the world of work, and life in society;
2. Ensure that learners make ethical and responsible use of digital tools, taking advantage of opportunities while minimizing risks, developing strategies for communication and well-being, creativity and social participation, seeking to limit the environmental effects of technologies;
3. Develop students' critical thinking by helping them distinguish fact from opinion and reject stereotypes, hate speech, cyberbullying, and other violence;
4. Provide Media Literacy to develop the ability to critically analyze information and promote active, creative and responsible participation in the digital environment;
5. Take into account each student's learning abilities and special needs;
6. Implement strategies to evaluate the results of Digital Citizenship education (Council of Europe, 2019b).

We should note that both documents mentioned, the Recommendation and the Ministerial Declaration, clearly refer to the importance of states contributing to the achievement of the commitments made under the United Nations Agenda on Sustainable Development Goals 2030, in particular for Goal 4, on quality, inclusive and equitable education throughout life. This is also a clear commitment of the Council of the European Union.

2.2.2 Council of the European Union—8 Key Competences for Learning

Media Literacy and STEAM are also highlighted in the model of key competencies for lifelong learning defined by the Council of the European Union (2018) organized into eight areas:

1. Reading and writing (Literacy competence)
2. Linguistics (Multilingual competence)
3. STEM + Arts (Mathematical competence and competence in science, technology, engineering)
4. Digital (Digital competence)
5. Personal, social, and well-being (Personal, social and learning to learn competence)
6. Citizenship and values (Citizenship competence)
7. Entrepreneurship (Entrepreneurship competence)
8. Social participation (Cultural awareness and expression competence)

Competence 3 refers to "the acquisition of competences in science, technology, engineering and mathematics (STEM), taking into account their links with the arts, creativity and innovation." In other words, this is what we have been referring to by the English acronym "STEAM." Competence area 4 is to "increase and improve the level of digital competences at all levels of education and training, for all segments of the population," and is then subdivided into areas such as information and data literacy, communication and collaboration, digital content creation, security and problem solving (Vuorikari, Punie, Carretero and Van den Brande, 2016).

As with the 10 domains of Digital Citizenship, defined by the Council of Europe, there is a close relationship between the key competences for lifelong learning, because a citizen cannot participate actively in activities following the "making" methodology if he or she does not have reading, personal, or citizenship skills. One cannot be focused on solving a real problem if they don't have entrepreneurial or social participation skills.

2.2.3 OECD—Global Competence and Learning Compass

The Organization for Economic Cooperation and Development (OECD), which has been assessing how 15-year-olds apply their math, reading, and science skills in real-life situations through the *Programme for International Student Assessment* (PISA) since 2000, decided in the 2018 study (OECD, 2018a) to measure the "global competence" of 15-year-olds. Essentially, the study measured the extent to which these students are prepared to live in today's globalized and interconnected world. Global competence is the multidimensional capability that consists of the mobilization of knowledge, skills, attitudes, and values, to act in the following four dimensions:

1. Examining local, global and cross-cultural issues ("refers to globally competent people's practices of effectively combining knowledge about the world and critical reasoning whenever they form their own opinion about a global issue").
2. Understanding and evaluating other people's perspectives and ways of seeing the world ("highlights that globally competent people are willing and capable of considering global problems and other people's perspectives and behaviors from multiple viewpoints").
3. Interact openly, appropriately, and effectively within different cultures ("describes what globally competent individuals are able to do when they interact with people from different cultures").
4. Advocate for collective well-being and sustainable development "focuses on young people's role as active and responsible members of society, and refers to individuals' readiness to respond to a given local, global or intercultural issue or situation" (OECD, 2018a).

The 2018 study, whose results were presented in October 2020, applied two data collection instruments: *i)* a test measuring knowledge and cognitive skills; and *ii)* a self-report questionnaire focusing on students' cognitive and social skills and attitudes regarding the four dimensions of global competence. Information was also collected from schools and teachers about activities that can prepare students for global competence. Data collection on values will be carried out by the OECD in subsequent studies.

It is not our goal here to analyze the results of the study, but we will highlight recommendations associated with those results. First of all, there is continuity, because skills such as critical thinking, problem solving and Media Literacy were needed before and continue to be needed, as reading, writing and counting are and have been. What must change is the frequency of addressing the dimensions of global competence, which cannot be sporadic, but must be systematic (OECD, 2020).

It is then necessary to adapt the existing curriculum to integrate global competence, which implies training teachers in global education. It is also necessary to create, validate, and provide resources for pedagogical approaches such as "cooperative learning" and "project-based learning" in which students have to deal with real-world situations.

Students should plan, organize, and investigate global issues, making decisions and solving problems. They should participate in pedagogical activities that emphasize multiple perspectives, role-playing, and simulations. And all these activities should be developed across areas such as mathematics, science, languages or history, always keeping in mind the defined learning outcomes. This perspective, recommends the OECD, implies the development of an inclusive and culturally comprehensive curriculum.

However, changing the curriculum is not enough. It is necessary to change the school culture, so that diversity and mutual understanding between cultures is at the heart of all aspects of school life, from what the Council of Europe calls a 'whole-school approach' (Huber and Reynolds, 2014; OECD, 2020, p. 179; Raulin-Serrier, Soriani, Styslavska and Tomé, 2020, p. 8).

The OECD believes that a concerted and clear action to develop the global competence of citizens is key to achieving the Sustainable Development Goals 2030. It is in this sense that, as part of its global project *Future of Education and Skills2030*, it has created the Learning Compass 2030, a tool that points out the competencies that students need to "attain learning objectives and also to contribute to individual and collective well-being, including at the global level" and not only at an individual level (OECD, 2020, p. 198).

The learning compass is characterized by the following aspects:

1. It views a learner (in relation to peers, teachers, parents, and communities) as someone who has the will and ability to positively influence his or her own life and that of the world, to set goals, reflect, and bring about change.
2. To act in the world, a learner needs to develop competencies, composed of knowledge, skills, attitudes, and values, to realize his or her potential and

contribute to the well-being of their communities, but also of the global community.
3. To contribute to this overall well-being, a leaner must have skills that are key prerequisites ("core foundations"), namely literacy and numeracy, digital and data literacy, physical and mental health, social and emotional foundations.
4. A learner also needs to develop three transformative competencies to act and shape the future of the world (adding value, reconciling tensions and dilemmas, taking responsibility), which are developed through a cyclical learning process.
5. This cyclical iterative learning process, which allows for continuous improvement in intentional and responsible thinking and action, has three phases (anticipation-action-reflection):
    o In the first phase (anticipation), the student evaluates the consequences of his actions;
    o In the second (action) the student manifests the desire and ability to act in order to contribute to the global welfare;
    o In the third (reflection) the student reflects on the process in order to improve his future actions for the well-being of the individual, society and the environment.

Since 2018, the OECD has been developing a study focused on social and emotional skills, which are based on the "Big 5" model (OECD, 2018b), which seeks to measure the level of children in the following dimensions:

- Open-mindedness—Tolerance, Curiosity, Creativity
- Task Performance—Self-Control, Responsibility. Persistence
- Emotional regulation—Stress Resistance, Optimism, Emotional Control
- Communication—Sociability, Assertiveness, Energy
- Collaboration—Empathy, Trust, Cooperation
- Composite skills—Critical Thinking, Metacognition, Personal Effectiveness.

This study, which involved a total of 10 regions in nine countries (including Portugal), will have a second phase in the triennium 2021–2023, and is mentioned here because the "Digital Citizenship Academy" project includes a task that consists in the study of social and emotional skills, having collected data through a questionnaire survey in 2020 (pre-test), and with new data collection planned at the end of the school year 2020/2021 (post-test).

The OECD's work is aligned with others, such as the Council of Europe's Digital Citizenship Education and Key Competences for Lifelong Learning.

Its assumptions and goals are, therefore, articulated with Media Literacy and STEAM methodology, as well as with the Sustainable Development Goals 2030, whose achievement involves the implementation of a global education, which does not have a consensual definition, but we adopt here the one from the Council of Europe (2019c):

> Global education is an education perspective which arises from the fact that contemporary people live and interact in an increasingly globalised world. This makes it crucial for education to give learners the opportunity and competences to reflect and share their own point of view and role within a global, interconnected society, as well as to understand and discuss complex relationships of common social, ecological, political and economic issues, so as to derive new ways of thinking and acting. (p. 21)

This global education perspective is the basis of UNESCO's *citizenship* education model, called *Global Citizenship Education*, which we refer to in the next section.

2.2.4 UNESCO—Global Citizenship Education

The Education for Global Citizenship model (UNESCO, 2015a) is intended for educators, curriculum development practitioners, policy-makers and others associated with the education sector, whether working in formal, non-formal or informal learning settings. It is a model that presents content and learning objectives for four age groups (5–9, 9–12, 12–15 and 15–18), but needs to be further adapted, with national and, possibly, regional authorities creating guidelines for its implementation. The UNESCO document, whose main aim is to contribute to the four pillars of learning (to know, to do, to be and to live together) considers three base domains and types of key learning outcomes, as follows:

1. **Cognitive**—Acquiring knowledge and understanding of local, national, and global issues, as well as the interconnectedness and interdependencies of different countries and populations, critical thinking and analytical skills.
2. **Socio-emotional**—Feeling of belonging to a common humanity, sharing values and responsibilities based on Human Rights, as well as attitudes of empathy, solidarity and respect for differences and diversity.
3. **Behavioral**—Acting effectively and responsibly at local, national, and global levels towards a more peaceful and sustainable world, as well as motivation and predisposition to undertake the necessary actions.

As the models of the Council of Europe, the Council of the European Union and the OECD refer the UNESCO proposal points out a set of factors that can contribute to the success of global education, including its long-term, sustained and holistic inclusion in curricula, so it is important to invest in the initial and continuing training of teachers. The dimensions of global citizenship (local, national, global) should be reinforced in each school year, but also in non-formal and informal learning contexts. The process can start at a pilot level and be consistently scaled up, which requires monitoring and evaluation of the process, which should be continuous and assured by experts.

According to UNESCO (2015a), inclusive, participatory and learner-centered practices are central, in order to involve students in the teaching-learning process. Given its broad scope and the pursuit of meaningful learning, global citizenship education requires "a sophisticated range of teaching and learning practices, some of which include project-based learning, participation projects, collaborative work, experiential learning and service learning" (pp. 13–14).

In summary, the four models presented in this subsection are prospective in relation to the comprehensive training of citizens prepared to act for individual, social and global welfare. This training should begin in infancy and continue throughout life, being closely associated with the informed use of technologies, in their multiple uses, whether *online* or *offline*, whether in formal, non-formal or informal contexts.

The models are descriptive rather than prescriptive, which means that they are global, need to be adapted to the context, are competency-based, and therefore are dependent upon the breaking down of traditional and artificial barriers between disciplines. The models show a particular commitment to the fact that training processes should make an essential contribution to the achievement of the 17 Sustainable Development Goals defined by the United Nations for 2030.

They are also inclusive models, meaning that they involve all learners, regardless of their needs or their culture. They are models that clearly refer to the importance of Media Literacy and STEAM, or at least project methodologies focused on real issues, and associated skills such as communication, collaboration, cooperation, critical thinking, active participation and social intervention.

The four models also refer to the need to invest in global education, in a systematic way, adapting curricula, changing school culture, and changing the national legislation itself because this is a task for all sectors and entities in society. Finally, they are dependent upon an evaluation of the activities developed and the progress made, as well as regular monitoring and evaluation of all training processes, with the aim of improving them.

2.3 Media Literacy and STEAM in Current Educational Policy in Portugal

In May 2019, the Ministry of Education of Portugal and three institutions with intervention on four continents—African and Asian (Community of Portuguese Language Countries—CPLP), American (Organization of Ibero-American States for Education, Science and Culture—OEI) and European (Council of Europe, CoE)—organized, in Lisbon, the conference *Education, Citizenship, World: Which School for Which Society?*, in which the Director-General of the Directorate-General for Democracy of the Council of Europe, Snežana Samardžić-Marković, concluded her intervention by holding up the National Strategy for Citizenship Education (NSCE) (Ministério da Educação, 2017a) and referring (Samardžić-Marković, 2019):

> This strategy is a good example for all our European neighbors and beyond across the Atlantic and the Mediterranean. I hope that our partners will disseminate this good experience and continue to spread the knowledge and implementation of our European Reference Framework for Democratic Culture Competencies, which is also part of this National Strategy for Citizenship Education.

The existing link between the National Strategy for Citizenship Education - NSCE and the Reference Framework of Competences for Democratic Culture (Council of Europe, 2018b) was thus publicly reinforced, although the team responsible for its elaboration had also analyzed many other documents from international entities (European Union, UN/UNESCO) and several documents produced in Portugal (e.g. NSCE).

NSCE proposed the operationalization of Citizenship Education from pre-school education to the end of compulsory education, through the subject of Citizenship and Development, which takes on a transdisciplinary character at primary school (grades 1 to 4) and as an autonomous subject in the 2nd (grades 5 and 6) and 3rd cycles (grades 7 to 9), to be transversal to all subjects and training components in secondary education. However, as the international models propose, the formation of citizens is not the task of a single subject or curriculum, but of the whole school, the school community and the local community.

In short, the document is clearly in line with what the international models propose, starting right away with the proposal that the Citizenship and Development curriculum component be implemented following a whole-school approach. The alignment with the models goes deeper in the objectives that underlie the proposed approach, which we mention here in relation to what we wrote above in terms of the models:

1. Integrate citizenship (the skills of democratic culture and lifelong learning, as well as the dimensions of global competence and global citizenship) in the curricula, in a sustained manner and not with one-off practices, extending these practices to non-formal and informal learning contexts, joining with the local, national, and global community;
2. Increase the training offerings in Citizenship Education, Digital Citizenship, Democratic Culture Skills, Global Citizenship and in the dimensions of Global Competence, at the level of initial and ongoing teacher training, focusing on active methodologies (e.g. project work) and inclusive ones, which also allow for the development of personal and social skills;
3. Adapting activities and projects to the context, to the specificities of the students, and to the priorities of the school and education communities, in order to better involve families and other elements of the communities in a sustained process that aims at the well-being of each individual and of the local, national, and global communities, something that can only be assessed if the whole process (planning, implementation, monitoring, and evaluation) is widely and effectively implemented.

Citizenship Education is composed of 17 domains, organized into three groups, the first being mandatory at all levels and cycles of schooling. The second is only compulsory in two of the three cycles of basic education, while the third is optional and can be applied in any year of schooling. The media section is integrated in the second group, however, as we stated when we approached international models, we believe that Media Literacy can assume some transversality in relation to the other domains, in the three groups.

Let us focus, for example, on the first group, which includes transversal and longitudinal learning such as Human Rights, Gender Equality, Interculturality, Sustainable Development, Environmental Education and Health. Without in any way wanting to question the individuality and coherence of each domain, we understand them as circles that are not concentric, but that have overlaps between them. For example, the right to express one's opinion is linked to the media, as is interaction with other cultures. Online wellness is part of health. Environmental issues are discussed through the media, as are others such as gender equality.

Questions like these can arise within specific classes at the preschool, primary school, and secondary school levels. At the school level, Citizenship Education implies the existence of "an open and free climate for active discussion of decisions that affect the lives of all members of the school community" (*idem*, p. 10) and the implementation of practices that include "real experiences of participation" (*idem*, p. 10). This implies an open school culture which teaches attitudes, values, rules and principles, and puts them into practice in everyday life, allowing students to learn through experience.

The school is in connection with its community, with other communities, with other schools, and with other cultures. These entities become a network, designing and developing "projects based on the needs, resources and potentialities of the community" (*idem* p. 11). We believe that STEAM methodology projects assume a central role here, because NSCE is designed with a humanistic-based curriculum, which is flexible and adaptable to the context, and is also inclusive, sustainable, and stable with a transversal logic. Its curriculum areas, without exception, contribute to the development of different areas of competence (Figure 2.1).

This is our reading of the 'Student's Profile by the End of Compulsory Schooling' (SPECS) (Ministério da Educação, 2017b), the reference document that guides decision-making in curriculum organization and management in Portugal, as well as "the definition of strategies, methodologies and pedagogical-didactic procedures to be used in teaching practice" (*idem*, p. 5).

Understanding and defending values such as freedom, responsibility and integrity, excellence and demand, curiosity, reflection and innovation, as well as the importance of exercising citizenship by participating socially, the student develops skills in ten areas. This process is integrated, coherent, based on principles such as inclusion, flexibility and adaptability, sustainability and empathy, and it is through this pathway that the student becomes progressively competent to "make free and informed decisions about natural, social and ethical issues, and to carry out a civic, active, conscious and responsible participation" (*idem*, p. 6).

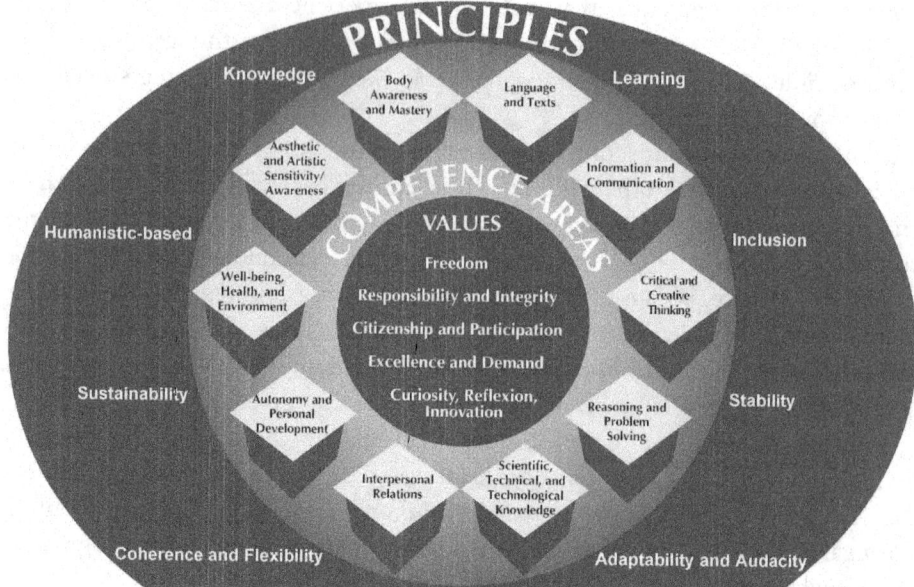

Figure 2.1: Conceptual Framework for the Students' Profile by the End of Compulsory Schooling (Ministério da Educação, 2017b, p. 11)

We now focus on the ten areas of competencies, which are based on ethical values which "comprise competences understood as complex combinations of knowledge, skills and attitudes that allow effective human action within diverse contexts" (*idem*, p. 6). The areas of competences are complementary to the curricular areas in that they are dependent upon a transdisciplinary curricular operationalization, which necessarily has implications.

The authors of SPECS define each area, presenting the competences associated with, along with the learning outcomes. An analysis of the associated competences by area shows that STEAM projects which also focus on Media Literacy are likely to contribute to the development of many, if not all, of the competences explained in the document, as we see at the end of Chapter 4 ("4.3.3.2 Results Analysis in Light of the National Educational Policy").

In line with this observation, we highlight some aspects of the "vision of the student" defined in the document. At the end of compulsory education, young people should be able to master "multiple literacies so that he can critically analyse and question reality, evaluate and select information," to be someone who "acknowledges the importance and the challenges offered by Arts, Humanities, Science and Technology for the social, cultural, economic and environmental sustainability," who continuously learns and exercises his/her "social intervention," who values "human dignity," "cultural diversity" and who rejects "all forms of discrimination" (*idem*, p. 10).

SPECS also refers to the need to adapt "educational action to the purposes" of the profile and skills of each student, which implies "changes in pedagogical and didactic practices" (*idem*, p. 23), at least at seven levels, which we summarize here, through a lens focused on Media Literacy and STEAM.

Thus, it is essential to organize "intra-school or extra-school projects," focused on real global issues, adapted to the "daily life of the student," and to the "sociocultural and geographical environment," which involves the integration of transdisciplinary content, the "critical use of the different information resources as well as the ICT," and the "experimentation of techniques, tools and different kinds of work" in order to allow each student to make choices, confront points of view, solve problems and make decisions based on values. Projects and "cooperative learning activities" should be valued in the "assessment of learning" (*idem*, p. 31).

We conclude here this brief and partial approach to educational policy, focusing on the SPECS and on the NSCE, according to its relations with Media Literacy and STEAM. Yet, we do not do so without mentioning other documents and/or legalities, which we do not analyze here, and which were addressed in the training workshops.

Two of these documents, "Essential Learnings for basic education" (Ministério da Educação 2018a) and for "Essential Learnings for secondary education" (Ministério da Educação, 2018b), define the knowledge, skills and attitudes that each student should be able to mobilize at the end of each school year, for each component of the curriculum and each subject area. It also presents examples of strategic teaching actions (to be developed by teachers), as well as learning outcomes associated with each of the proposed actions.

Other key documents are the curriculum for basic and secondary education (Decreto-Lei nº 55/2018) and the legal regime of Inclusive Education (Decreto-Lei nº 54/2018). The Pupils' Profile is also at the basis of the Schools' Autonomy and Curricular Flexibility Project (Despacho n.º 5908/2017), which gives schools the possibility of managing up to 25% of the curriculum. Its application began as a pilot project in the 2017–2018 school year and is currently widespread in primary and secondary schools.

2.4 The Urgency of Focusing on Very Young Children

Young children's online practices had been largely ignored over the last decade by policymakers in many countries (Holloway, Green and Livingstone, 2013), and only 12% of approximately 1,200 research projects identified included children under the age of seven, while only 20% included the perspectives of teachers and 13% of parents (O'Neill and Staksrud, 2014). The scenario has considerably changed in recent years, namely through relevant projects such as EU Kids Online and Global Kids Online, but it was an identified need when we started the project, in 2015.

Children, even those from underprivileged families, were already, and still are, living in rich digital environments (Chaudron, 2016), using digital platforms, especially mobile ones, even before learning to speak (Hooft Graafland, 2018; Jorge, Tomé and Pacheco, 2018; Kotilainen and Suoninen, 2013). Over half of the 3–4 year-olds in the United Kingdom use tablets as well as one-third of the children under five-years-old (Marsh, 2014). In the UK, by the age of two, most children are using a tablet or a laptop (Sefton-Green et al., 2016). A study in four European countries showed that amongst children under five-year-old, 60% use digital technologies and 23% simultaneously use television, computers and Internet (Palaiologou, 2016). Data collected from 206 families with children aged zero to eight, in 18 countries, showed TV still leading as children's preference, even if rarely referenced during interviews. The tablet is the most popular device among young children, and all of the families use smartphones (Chaudron, 2016).

Television is a factor, as is the increase in the number and the quality of the games they play. Children have more independence in media use and prefer tools that depend less on written text and more on still and moving images. They typically also love to produce and share using multimedia environments because the nature of their activities is increasingly social (Marsh, 2014).

This use increases (in terms of time of use, diversity of devices and activities performed), as they grow from zero to nine years of age (Brito and Dias, 2016; Chaudron, 2016; Danby, Fleer, Davidson, and Hatzigianni, 2018; Marsh, 2014; Palaiologou, 2016; Ponte, Simões, Baptista and Jorge, 2017; Sefton-Green et al., 2016; Slot, 2018) as they start entering pre- and primary school. However, the use happens mostly at home, outside of school (Kumpulainen and Gillen, 2017; Tomé and Domingues, 2014).

Data on young children's digital use and practices are however not enough, since they "do not tell us what such engagement means in terms of the child's learning especially their developing literacy.......their understanding of the world, their understanding of social relationships and indeed what implications such use might have for their education as a whole" (Sefton-Green et al., 2016, p. 9). Children's early experiences of literacy through digital devices are reconfiguring meaning-making as their literacy practices are multimodal. They need to know how to deal with words, images and sounds, both in traditional and digital platforms. Thus, it is a key task for educators and researchers "to understand how young learners make sense of multimodal texts in digital environments, and how they impose order on the juxtaposition of different modes" (*idem*, p. 20).

Children's digital literacies practices are co-constructed across generations (Marsh, 2014), and it is therefore necessary to articulate formal and non-formal learning contexts, i.e., to embed core skills in the school curriculum, such as flexibility, innovation, creativity, and problem solving, as well as helping children's families evolve from family literacy to family digital literacy (Marsh, Hannon, Lewis and Ritchie, 2015).

Digital literacy is "a social practice that involves reading, writing and multimodal meaning-making through the use of a range of digital technologies" as well as traditional technologies that "can involve accessing, using and analysing texts [in a broader sense: text, sound, moving and still image], in addition to their production and dissemination," which implies "the acquisition of skills, including traditional skills related to alphabetic print, but also skills related to accessing and using digital technologies" (Sefton-Green et al., 2016, p. 15), such as "create, work, share, socialise, investigate, play, work, communicate and learn" (Meyers, Erickson, and Small, 2013, p. 356).

Children gradually become more independent in their use, consumption, production, and sharing of media content within digital environments, having a greater opportunity to participate as they grow older (Marsh, 2014). These activities do not mean, however, that children are increasing their social participation. As Livingstone, Kardefelt Winther, Kanchev, Cabello, Claro, Burton, Patrick, and Phyfer (2019, p. 6) purport, even if children "are already enjoying some online opportunities in sizeable proportions," they do not climb the "Ladder of participation" in that "most children do not reach the point where they commonly undertake many of the civic, informational and creative activities online that are heralded as the opportunities of the digital age."

The empowerment of active citizens should then be planned and implemented from birth and throughout life, which requires special attention from the early years of early childhood education, when children begin to understand values and to develop skills in terms of attitudes, skills, knowledge and critical understanding. This development will be key for creativity and entrepreneurship in its various meanings (e.g., business, social, personal), with positive effects throughout life (Ozanus, 2017; Patrinos, 2018) in an increasingly digital society.

Besides being a mental phenomenon, education is also a sociocultural phenomenon (Gee, 2010; Jenkins, 2009), and learning processes are not internalized individually. They are socially distributed, with implications for pedagogy and instruction (Underwood, Parker and Stone, 2013). Being literate as a citizen is not a state that is attained, but is an ongoing, lifelong process. Children learn by watching others, and then mimicking first their parents and siblings, and then extending observation to grandparents, cousins, uncles, and neighbors (Chaudron, 2015). Later, they watch and mimic those at school, within the local community, and then progressively within the world at large. Therefore, we advocate that the preparation of children should follow a community-based participatory-research approach.

2.5 The Importance of Participatory-Research Approach

Between 2012 and 2015 in Portugal, we developed the research project "Online social networks and the new Media Literacy," aimed to understand: (i) what young people (aged 9–16) do in social networks, namely how they communicate (with whom, what, how, and why), how they learn from online peers, how they deal with risks and potentialities, how they relate to other social spheres (family, school, peers …), and what capacities they develop and need to develop; (ii) the relationship of teachers and parents/guardians with social networks and their students/learners through these, as well as their perception of the use of social networks by young people.

Quantitative data were collected from 549 students, 267 of their parents and 150 of their teachers. After data analysis, we structured an interview guide aimed at students and then developed a set of focus groups with 120 students. We also interviewed 20 parents and 20 teachers. Results showed that:

- 90% of students, 75% of teachers and 66% of parents used social media;
- 91% of the students started using social media before the age of 13, and 40% started using it at the age of 8 or before.
- The majority of all groups (80% teachers, 70% parents and 60% students) preferred to share others' content instead of publishing their own content;
- 35% of students stated that they had felt uncomfortable using social media;
- teachers and parents were concerned more with the risks than the opportunities of students in social media;
- teachers and students considered learning via social media, but did not acknowledge a difference between the formal and informal contexts.

The study concluded that there was an urgent need to follow two main recommendations: to empower citizens on Digital Citizenship with a focus on children aged 8 years old and younger, and to achieve this task, it was crucial to research school, family and community contexts (Tomé and de Abreu, 2016). To put the recommendations in practice, the best strategy we have found on the scientific literature was "a planned, systematic approach to issues relevant to the community of interest, [which] requires community involvement, has a problem-solving focus, is directed at societal change, and makes a lasting contribution to the community" (Hills, Mullet and Carroll, 2007, p. 127).

Participatory research is an "umbrella-term" that encompasses a set of designations (Howarth, Mansfield, McCartney and Main, 2020, p. 1) such as "community-based participatory action research project [CBPAR]" (Hills, Mullet and Carroll, 2007, p. 127), "participatory action research [PAR]" (Langhout and Thomas, 2010, p. 60), "participatory action research approach" (Hart, 1992), "participant action research" (O'Toole, 2020, p. 31), "community education projects" (Ford, 2000, p. 7) or "community-service project" (Michigan State University, 2007, p. 2) .

Even if there is no agreement on a common designation, the different designations have a set of characteristics in common, namely "participation, engagement, empowerment, mutual learning, capacity building and fulfillment of both research and action agendas" (Shamrova and Cummings, 2017, p. 401). This means that participatory research is research with the population, not of the population (Schlebbe, 2019), since it includes the individuals in several ways, for instance as co-researchers (Funk, Van Borek, Taylor, Grewal, Tzemis and Buxton, 2012). There are also different levels of participation, as the eight "rungs" of the Ladder of Citizen Participation, developed by Arnstein (1969), explain how more fortunate citizens deprive regular citizens from participating in urban planning. Analyzing it from bottom to top:

- The first two (Manipulation and Therapy) are levels of non-participation, since they do not aim to enable people to participate, but to enable powerholders to 'educate' or 'cure' the participants;
- The levels 3, 4 and 5 (Informing, Consultation and Placation) are degrees of tokenism, in which participants are only apparently involved, because their roles do not allow them to change the status quo;
- The levels 6, 7 and 8 (Partnership, Delegated Power and Citizen Control) are the degrees of citizen power, since participants have a decision-making role, which increases as the higher rungs are attained.

Furthermore, these types of projects are more consensual among researchers and practitioners. Participatory research within communities is associated with a set of core benefits regarding the process, as well as its outcomes, as pointed out by Burns, Coke and Schweidler (2011, p. 8), in Table 2.1:

Table 2.1: Core Benefits of Community-based Participatory Research Projects

Community Participation in …	Results in …
Identifying issues	increased alignment with critical issues experienced from the community, empowers communities to take action and provides motivation to participate in process
Development of study design and proposal submission	increased acceptability of study approach by stakeholders, possibility of funds for community
Planning and/or carrying out recruitment and retention of participation	enhanced recruitment and retention
Development of data collection tools and testing	increased reliability of results; helps identify and better cope with potentially sensitive issues and situations
Development and implementation of the action plan	greater cultural and social relevance to the population of the community, increased likelihood of bringing about lasting positive change
Analysis, interpretation, translation and dissemination of findings	increased validation of results, enhancement of translating findings into action

Participatory research projects shall be organized with two levels of organization in mind: the general level, focused on action, and a specific level embedded on the general one and focused on research. Both project levels shall be leveled as follows (*idem*, p. 5):

Action level

1. Choose a problem
2. Identify resources and solutions
3. Develop a plan
4. Implement the plan
5. Evaluate, and perhaps return to step 1

Research level

1. Identifying a research question
2. Choosing a research methodology
3. Implementing the methodology
4. Analyzing the results
5. Reporting on the results

These types of projects actively engage most, if not all, the community stakeholders (e.g.: decision makers, practitioners, researchers), preferably in all the research phases, from establishing the research questions, to developing data collection tools, to analysis and dissemination of findings (Burns et al., 2011; Glandon, Paina, Olakunle, Peters and Bennett, 2017; Rush and Ritchie, 2003). They also demand a collaborative logic, which is closely related with a "bottom-up community-based approach," meaning that the project arises from the community and aims to gather resources and find a solution to a collective need or to overcome a problem (Ford, 2000, p. 7). However, adequate participatory research projects are not exclusive to bottom-up strategies, since "top-down externally-initiates approaches," when a community need of a project is externally identified, also work: "Often externally-initiated projects provide the impetus for, or lead to the development of, community-based projects" (*idem*, p. 8).

Whatever the case, the success of participatory research projects lies on active cooperation among all stakeholders (e.g.: practitioners, policy and decision makers, and researchers) envisaging the creation of "new knowledge or understanding about a practical issue in order to bring about change" (Hills et al., 2007, p. 127). Participatory research is a reliable strategy to "empower people individually and collectively in specific contexts," equipping them "with a new consciousness of what must be done and how to do it" (Sohng, 1996, p. 93). Practitioners, whether adults or children, research and evaluate their practices, being progressively more able to make decisions about changing their own practices based on the collected evidence (Hills et al., 2007, p. 127). This statement raises doubts, especially when facing the need to develop a Digital Citizenship education aimed at very young children, as pointed out by our 2012–15 research project.

Our study recommendations were in line with those issued by the pan-European project EU Kids Online (Livingstone, O'Neill, and Mclaughlin, 2011), which stressed the need for Digital Citizenship education, including "a new policy focus on much younger children for whom the Internet is an everyday experience" (p. 5), since "children and young people increasingly use the Internet independently of adult supervision, [so] greater emphasis needs to be placed on empowering children to self-govern and manage their online experience" (p. 17).

On one hand, these findings were in line with O'Toole (2020), who concluded that participatory research "may provide unique opportunities to develop respectful, relevant, inclusive and useful research for early childhood and primary education, in spite of the challenges inherent in its non-linear nature" (p. 41). These opportunities are, on the other hand, dependent on an effective youth participation, which Carpentier, Melo and Ribeiro (2019) understand as dealing:

"with inclusion of youngsters in a decision-making process that corrects the weak power base that youngsters have in society (often through the logic of ageism, that leads to the privileging of adults). By allowing youngsters to engage in decision-making processes at an equal footing with adults, this power imbalance is adjusted, and youngsters and adults find themselves in more equalised power relations" (¶ 20)

Designing and implementing a participatory research project on Media Literacy and Digital Citizenship, focused on children, could address the need for the participation of under-10's, which is the highly unrepresented group in a set of 45 projects identified globally, as revealed by an international integrative review developed by Shamrova and Cummings (2017). After identifying more than 29,000 scientific articles, only 242 papers on participatory research met the pre-selection criteria, of which 45 involved youth under the age of 18. Only 9 articles (20%) involved children under 10, and merely 4 articles (8%) effectively involved children under 7 years old.

There is then "a need for more academic work that protects, defends and rescues participation" (Carpentier, Melo and Ribeiro, 2019, ¶ 9), especially youth participation in research projects, which may also be envisaged in eight levels, as Hart (1992) pointed out, based on the work of Arnstein (1969). The rungs of the Ladder of young participation in research projects, using Hart's own words, are organized in two levels of participation:

Non-participation levels

- 6 - Tokenism: "children are apparently given a voice, but in fact have little or no choice about the subject or the style of communicating it, and little or no opportunity to formulate their own opinions" (Hart, 1992, p. 9)
- 7 - Decoration: "occasions when children are given T-shirts related to some cause, and may sing or dance at an event in such dress, but have little idea of what it is all about and no say in the organizing of the occasion" (*idem*).
- 8 - Manipulation: "one example is that of preschool children carrying political placards concerning the impact of social policies on children. If children have no understanding of the issues and hence do not understand their actions, then this is manipulation" (*idem*).

Genuine participation levels

- 1 - Child-initiated, shared decisions with adult: "children (…) incorporate adults into projects they have designed and managed" (*idem*, p. 14).
- 2 - Child-initiated and directed decisions: "children in their play conceive of and carry out complex projects" (*idem*, p. 14).

- 3 - Adult-initiated, shared decision with children: "though the projects at this level are initiated by adults, the decision making is shared with the young people" (*idem*, p. 12).
- 4 - Consulted and informed: When "the project is designed and run by adults, but children understand the process and their opinions are treated seriously" (*idem*, p. 12).
- 5 - Assigned but informed: "Children understand the intentions of the project (…) know who made the decisions concerning their involvement and why, (…) have a meaningful (rather than 'decorative') role" and "volunteer for the project after the project was made clear to them" (*idem*, p. 10).

Even though Hart's model of youth participation stands as an important tool, it is not immune from criticism, namely the possibility of "pseudo participation" when children are briefed by the researchers, or the fact that the model does not apply to all social, cultural and professional backgrounds (Bergold, 2012). The model also suggests a hierarchical Ladder of rungs, with higher rungs superior to lower one. However, as Hart (1992) stated, this does not mean that children should always operate on the highest possible rungs along the project, since they are different from another and they shall have the choice to participate at different levels according to their interest in the different activities.

Inspired or not by Hart's Ladder of participation, a set of alternate models were identified by Schlebbe (2019) such as Treseder's (1997) non-linear model (includes Hart's five participation degrees of participation around a circle), Shier's (2001) Pathway to Participation (a five level model starting from "Children are listened to" to "Children share power and responsibility for decision-making"), Kirby, Lanyon, Cronin and Sinclair's (2003) categorization model (a non-linear model with four levels, namely children make autonomous decisions, are involved in decision making with adults, their views are taken into account by adults, share power and responsibility for decision making with adults).

All the above referenced models are useful to inspire the design of participatory research projects involving children and young people, keeping in mind the specific context and goals. We have followed these guidelines in the design process of a project that envisaged preschool and primary schools as a base for community research and development. The design process is explained in the next chapter, as is the methodological options and the assessment and evaluation options, which are different from the Ladder of Participation, since, as Hart (1992) stated, it "should not be considered as a simple measuring stick of the quality of any programme" (p. 11).

The project design, at both the action level and the research level, the models in which it was based, the way(s) the methodology was implemented, and the analysis and reporting are the focus of this book, in which we examine the development of the community-based project between September 2015 and the end of the 2020–2021 school year.

References

Arnstein, S. R. (1969). A ladder of citizen participation. *Journal of the American Planning Association, 35*(4), 216–224.

Bergold, J., & Thomas, S. (2012). Participatory research methods: A methodological approach in motion. *Forum Qualitative Sozialforschung / Forum: Qualitative Social Research, 13*(1). https://doi.org/10.17169/fqs-13.1.1801

Bower, M., Stevenson, M., Falloon, G., Forbes, A., & Hatzigianni, M. (2018). *Makerspaces in primary school settings – Advancing 21st century and STEM capabilities using 3D design and 3D printing.* Sydney, Australia: Macquarie University. Accessed from: https://primarymakers.com.

Buckingham, D. (2003). *Media education: Literacy, learning and contemporary culture.* Cambridge: Polity Press.

Burns, J., Cooke, D., & Schweidler, C. (2011). *A short guide to community based participatory action research.* Los Angeles: Advancement Project.

Carpentier, N., Melo, A., & Ribeiro, F. (2019). Rescuing participation: A critique on the dark participation concept. *Comunicação e sociedade [Online], 36* | 2019, published online on 20 December 2019. Accessed from: http://journals.openedition.org/cs/1284

Catterall, Lisa G. (2017). A brief history of STEM and STEAM from an inadvertent insider. *The STEAM Journal, 3*(1), Article 5. DOI: 10.5642/steam.20170301.05. Accessed from: http://scholarship.claremont.edu/steam/vol3/iss1/5

Chaudron, S. (2015). *Young children & digital technology: A qualitative exploratory study across seven countries.* Luxembourg: Publications Office of the European Union.

Chaudron, S. (2016). *Young children, parents and digital technology in the home context across Europe: The findings of the extension of the young children (0–8) and digital technology pilot study to 17 European countries.* DigiLitEY Project Meeting, 3., Lordos Hotel, Larnaca, Chipre, 17–18 May.

Council of Europe. (2016). *Competences for democratic culture – Living together as equals in culturally diverse societies.* Strasbourg: Council of Europe.

Council of Europe. (2018a). *Reference framework of competences for democratic culture.* Accessed from: https://www.coe.int/en/web/reference-framework-of-competences-for-democratic-culture/

Council of Europe. (2018b). *Digital Citizenship Education (DCE) – 10 Domains*. Accessed from: https://rm.coe.int/10-domains-dce/168077668e.

Council of Europe. (2019a). *Recommendation CM/Rec(2019)10 of the Committee of Ministers to member States on developing and promoting digital citizenship education*. Accessed from: https://search.coe.int/cm/Pages/result_details.aspx?ObjectID=090000168098de08

Council of Europe. (2019b). *Citizenship education in the digital era Ministerial Declaration*. Accessed from: https://rm.coe.int/coe-declaration-digital-citizenship-english-vf-sur-table-26-11-19/168098fb15

Council of Europe. (2019c). *Global education guidelines – Concepts and methodologies on global education for educators and policy makers*. Lisbon: North-South Centre of the Council of Europe.

Council of the European Union. (2018). *Council recommendation of 22 May 2018 on key competences for lifelong learning*. Accessed from: https://eur-lex.europa.eu/legal-content/EN/TXT/?uri=CELEX:32018H0604(01)

Danby, S., Fleer, M., Davidson, C., & Hatzigianni, M. (Eds.). (2018). *Digital childhoods: technologies and children's everyday lives*. Singapore: Springer.

Decreto-Lei n.º 54/2018. Accessed from: https://dre.pt/application/conteudo/115652961

Decreto-Lei n.º 55/2018. Accessed from: https://www.dge.mec.pt/sites/default/files/Curriculo/AFC/dl_55_2018_afc.pdf.

Despacho normativo n.º 5908/2017. Accessed from: http://www.dge.mec.pt/sites/default/files/Curriculo/Projeto_Autonomia_e_Flexibilidade/despacho_5908_2017.pdf

Dias, P., & Brito, R. (2016). *Crianças (0 aos 8 anos) e tecnologias digitais—Um estudo qualitativo exploratório*. Lisboa: Centro de Estudos de Comunicação e Cultura da Universidade Católica Portuguesa.

Diego-Mantecón, J., Blanco, T., Ortiz-Laso, Z., e Lavicza, Z. (2021). Proyectos STEAM con formato KIKS para el desarrollo de competencias clave. *Comunicar*, 66(XXIX), 33–43. Accessed from: DOI https://doi.org/10.3916/C66-2021-03

Ford, C. (2000). *What we need is ... A community education project – An eight-step guide to running a community education project*.

Frau-Meigs, D., O'Neill, B., Soriani, A., & Tomé, V. (2017). *Digital citizenship education: Overview and new perspectives*. Strasbourg: Council of Europe.

Funk, A., Van Borek, N., Taylor, D., Grewal, P., Tzemis, D., & Buxton, J. (2012). Climbing the "Ladder of participation": Engaging experiential youth in a participatory research project. *Can J Public Health*, 103(4), e288–92. doi: 10.1007/BF03404237. Accessed from: https://pubmed.ncbi.nlm.nih.gov/23618643/

Glandon, D., Paina, L., Alonge, O., Peters, D., & Bennett, S. (2017). 10 Best resources for community engagement in implementation research. *Health Policy and Planning*, 32, 1457–1465. doi: 10.1093/heapol/czx123

Gee, J. P. (2010). *New Digital Media and learning as an emerging area and "worked examples" as one way forward*. New York: MIT Press.

Gonnet, J. (1999). *Éducation et Médias*. Paris: PUF.

Hart, R. (1992). *Children's participation from tokenism to citizenship*. Florence: UNICEF Innocenti Research Centre.

Heath, C. (2021). *Annotated bibliography for online misinformation. Evidence for democracy*. Accessed from: https://evidencefordemocracy.ca/en/research/reports/annotated-bibliography-online-misinformation?fbclid=IwAR00hkSOe3lTtcg1n6eCdHIj6f1G2z2MbS8PsqkoOzWEHWkmqVybGvKEYkc

Hills, M., Mullett, J., & Carroll, S. (2007). Community-based participatory action research: transforming multidisciplinary practice in primary health care. *Rev Panam Salud Publica*, 21(2–3), 125–35. doi: 10.1590/s1020-49892007000200007.

Hobbs, R. (2016). Media literacy. In D. Mastro & J. Nussbaum (Eds.), *Oxford research encyclopedia of communication*. London: Oxford University Press.

Holloway, D., Green, L., & Livingstone, S. (2013). *Zero to eight: Young children and their Internet use*. LSE, London: EU Kids Online. Accessed from: http://eprints.lse.ac.uk/52630/

Hooft Graafland, J. (2018). *New technologies and 21st century children: Recent trends and outcomes*, OECD Education Working Papers, No. 179, OECD Publishing, Paris. Accessed from: http://dx.doi.org/10.1787/e071a505-en

Howarth, C., Mansfield, M., McCartney, C., & Main, G. (2020). *A different take: Reflections on an intergenerational participatory research project on child poverty*. Social Work & Society, 18. Accessed from: http://nbn-resolving.de/urn:nbn:de:hbz:464-sws-2333

Huber, J., & Reynolds, C. (2014). *Developing intercultural competence through education*. Strasbourg: Council of Europe. Accessed from: https://rm.coe.int/developing-intercultural-enfr/16808ce258

Jenkins, H. (2009). *Confronting the challenges of participatory culture: Media education for the 21st century*. New York: MIT Press.

Jolls, T. (2008). *Literacy for the 21st century: An overview & orientation guide to media literacy education—edition 2 featuring CML's five key questions for both construction and deconstruction questions/tips (Q/TIPS)*. Los Angeles: Center of Media Literacy. Accessed from: http://medialit.org/pdf/mlk/ola_mlkorientation_rev2.pdf

Jorge, A., Tomé, V., & Pacheco, R. (2018). Um dia na vida de 3 meninos portugueses com menos de 3 anos. In Claudia Stella e Catherine Ann Cameron (Orgs.), *Psicologia do Desenvolvimento* (pp. 65–74). Curitiba: Juruá Editora.

Khor, R. (2017, 27 Novembro). *A makerspace built by elementary students*. Edutopia. Accessed from: https://www.edutopia.org/article/makerspace-built-elementary-students

Kirby, P., Lanyon, C., Cronin, K., & Sinclair, R. (2003). *Building a culture of participation: Involving children and young people in policy, service planning, delivery and evaluation. Research report*. London, UK: Department for Education and Skills. Accessed from: https://dera.ioe.ac.uk/17522/1/Handbook%20-%20Building%20a%20Culture%20of%20Participation.pdf

Kotilainen, S., & Suoninen, A. (2013). Cultures of media and information literacies among the young: South-North viewpoints. In U. Carlsson & S. H. Culver (Eds.), *Media and information literacy and intercultural dialogue* (pp. 141–162). Göteborg: Nordicom.

Kumpulainen, K., & Gillen, J. (2017). *Young children's digital literacy practices in the home: A review of the literature*. COST ACTION ISI1410 DigiLitEY. ISBN: 9780902831469. Accessed from: http://digilitey.eu

Langhout, R. D., & Thomas, E. (2010). Imagining participatory action research in collaboration with children: An introduction. *American Journal of Community Psychology, 46*, 60–66. Accessed from: https://onlinelibrary.wiley.com/doi/10.1007/s10464-010-9321-1

Liao, C. (2016). From interdisciplinary to transdisciplinary: An arts-integrated approach to STEAM education. *Art Education, 69*(6), 44–49, DOI: 10.1080/00043125.2016.1224873.

Livingstone, S., Kardefelt-Winter, D., Kanchev, P., Cabello, P., Claro, M., Burton, P., & Phyfer, J. (2019). *Is there a Ladder of children's online participation? Findings from three Global Kids Online countries*, Innocenti Research Briefs no. 2019–02, UNICEF Office of Research – Innocenti, Florence.

Livingstone, S., O'Neill, B., & Mclaughlin, S. (2011). *Final recommendations for policy, methodology and research*. EU Kids Online network, London, UK. Accessed from: http://eprints.lse.ac.uk/39410/

Marsh, J. (2014). *Young children's online practices: Past, present and future*. Literacy Research Association Conference, Marco Island, USA. Accessed from: https://www.academia.edu/9799081/Young_Childrens_Online_Practices_Past_Present_and_Future

Marsh, J., Hannon, P., Lewis, M., & Ritchie, L. (2015, June 18). Young children's initiation into family literacy practices in the digital age. *Journal of Early Childhood Research*. Published online before print. doi: https://doi.org/10.1177/1476718X15582095.

Marsh, J., Wood, E., Chesworth, L., Nisha, B., Nutbrown, B., & Olney, B. (2019). Makerspaces in early childhood education: Principles of pedagogy and practice. *Mind, Culture, and Activity, 26*(3), 221–233, DOI: 10.1080/10749039.2019.1655651.

Meyers, E. M., Erickson, I., & Small, R. V. (2013). Digital literacy and informal learning environments: An introduction. *Learning, Media and Technology, 38*(4), 355–367.

Michigan State University. (2007). *Planning your community service project*. Detroit (MI): Michigan State University. Accessed from: https://agrilife.org/d84h/files/2020/09/Planning-Your-Community-Service-Project.pdf

Ministério da Educação. (2017a). *Estratégia Nacional de Educação para a Cidadania*. Lisboa: Ministério da Educação. Accessed from: http://www.dge.mec.pt/sites/default/files/ECidadania/Docs_referencia/estrategia_cidadania_original.pdf

Ministério da Educação. (2017b). *Perfil dos Alunos à Saída da Escolaridade Obrigatória*. Lisboa: Editorial do Ministério da Educação e Ciência. Accessed from: https://www.dge.mec.pt/sites/default/files/Curriculo/Projeto_Autonomia_e_Flexibilidade/perfil_dos_alunos.pdf

Ministério da Educação. (2018a). *Aprendizagens Essenciais—Ensino Básico*. Accessed from: http://www.dge.mec.pt/aprendizagens-essenciais-ensino-basico

Ministério da Educação. (2018b). *Aprendizagens Essenciais—Ensino Secundário*. Accessed from: http://www.dge.mec.pt/aprendizagens-essenciais-ensino-secundario

Nielsen, R. K., Fletcher, R., Newman, N., Brennen, J. S., & Howard, Philip N. (2020). *Navigating the 'Infodemic': How people in six countries access and rate news and information about coronavirus*. Oxford: Reuters Institute for the Study of Journalism & University of Oxford. Accessed from: https://reutersinstitute.politics.ox.ac.uk/sites/default/files/2020-04/Navigating%20the%20Coronavirus%20Infodemic%20FINAL.pdf

OECD. (2016). *Global competency for an inclusive world*. Accessed from: www.oecd.org/pisa/aboutpisa/Global-competency-for-an-inclusive-world.pdf.

OECD. (2017). *Starting strong V: Transitions from early childhood education and care to primary education*. Paris: OECD Publishing. Accessed from: http://dx.doi.org/10.1787/9789264276253-en.

OECD. (2018a). *Preparing our youth for an inclusive and sustainable world – The OECD PISA global competence framework*. Paris: OECD Publishing. Accessed from: https://www.oecd.org/pisa/Handbook-PISA-2018-Global-Competence.pdf

OECD. (2018b). *About the OECD's study on social and emotional skills*. Available at: https://www.oecd.org/education/ceri/social-emotional-skills-study/about/

OECD. (2020). *PISA 2018 results (Volume VI): Are students ready to thrive in an interconnected world?. PISA*. Paris: OECD Publishing. Accessed from: https://doi.org/10.1787/d5f68679-en.

O'Neill, B., & Staksrud, E. (2014). *Final recommendations for policy*. London: EU Kids Online, LSE.

O'Toole, L. (2020). Participant Action Research (PAR) for early childhood and primary education: The example of the THRIECE project. *Problemy Wczesnej Edukacji, 49*(2), 31–44. Accessed from: https://doi.org/10.26881/pwe.2020.49.03

Ozanus, S. (2017). Early childhood as the foundation for tomorrow's workforce, 2017. https://blogs.worldbank.org/education/early-childhood-foundation-tomorrow-s-workforce.

Palaiologou, I. (2016). Children under five and digital technologies: Implications for early years pedagogy. *European Early Childhood Education Research Journal, 24*(1), 5–24.

Patrinos, H. (2018). *The economic case for early learning*. http://blogs.worldbank.org/education/economic-case-early-learning.

Ponte, C., Simões, J. A., Baptista, S., e Jorge, A. (2017). *CRESCENDO ENTRE ECRÃS: Usos de meios eletrónicos por crianças* (3–8 Anos). Lisboa: Entidade Reguladora da Comunicação.

Raulin-Serrier, P., Soriani, A., Styslavska, O., & Tomé, V. (2020). *Digital citizenship education – Trainers' pack*. Strasbourg: Council of Europe. Accessed from: https://book.coe.int/en/human-rights-democratic-citizenship-and-interculturalism/8161-digital-citizenship-education-trainers-pack.html

Richardson, J., & Milovidov, E. (2019). *Digital citizenship education handbook*. Strasbourg: Council of Europe.

Rush, M., & Ritchie, H. (2003). *From seed to success tool kit for community conservation projects*. Department of Conservation, New Zealand. Accessed from: https://www.doc.govt.nz/globalassets/documents/getting-involved/in-your-community/community-conservation-guidelines/seed-to-success-toolkit.pdf

Samardžić-Marković, S. (2019, 28 de maio). Intervenção na Conferência Internacional "Educação, Cidadania, Mundo. Que escola para que sociedade?" (28 e 29 de maio), Pavilhão do Conhecimento. Lisboa: Portugal. Accessed from: https://www.youtube.com/watch?v=TxN_pQKOfv4

Schlebbe, K. (2019). *Participatory research with children: Different degrees of participation*. Accessed from: https://www.youtube.com/watch?v=Pmsj1-0K7Kc

Scolari, C. (2018). *Adolescentes, medios de comunicación y culturas colaborativas. Aprovechando las competencias transmedia de los jóvenes en el aula*. Barcelona: Universidade Pompeu Fabra. Accessed from: https://digital.fundacionceibal.edu.uy/jspui/handle/123456789/247

Sefton-Green, J., Marsh, J., Erstad, O., & Flewitt, R. (2016). *Establishing a research agenda for the digital literacy practices of young children: A white paper for COST action IS1410*. Accessed from: http://digilitey.eu

Setiawan, A. R., & Saputri, W. E. (2019, December, 27). *STEAM Education: background, framework, and characteristics*. EdArXiv. Accessed from: https://www.researchgate.net/publication/338196186_STEAM_Education_background_framework_and_characteristics.

Shamrova, D., & Cummings, C. (2017). Participatory action research (PAR) with children and youth: An integrative review of methodology and PAR outcomes for participants, organizations, and communities. *Children and Youth Services Review, 81*, 400–412. Accessed from: https://www.sciencedirect.com/science/article/pii/S0190740917302086?via%3Dihub

Shier, H. (2001). Pathways to participation: Openings, opportunities and obligations: A new model for enhancing children's participation in decision-making, in line with Article 12.1 of the United Nations Convention on the rights of the child. *Children & Society, 15*, 107–117, doi: 10.1002/chi.617. Accessed from: http://hdl.handle.net/10197/12051

Slot, P. (2018). *Structural characteristics and process quality in early childhood education and care: A literature review*, OECD Education Working Papers, No. 176, OECD Publishing, Paris. http://dx.doi.org/10.1787/edaf3793-en

Sohng, S. S. L. (1996). Participatory research and community organizing. *The Journal of Sociology & Social Welfare, 23*(4), 77–97. Accessed from: https://scholarworks.wmich.edu/jssw/vol23/iss4/6

Tomé, V. (2015). Redes sociais online: práticas e percepções de jovens (9–16), seus professores e encarregados de educação. In Vitor Tomé, Evelyne Bévort e Vitor Reia-Baptista (Orgs.), *Research on social media: A global view*. (pp. 127–335). Lisbon: RVJ-Editores.

Tomé, V., & De Abreu, B. (2016). Developing digital citizenship in children aged from 3 to 9: A pilot project in the Portuguese region of Odivelas. *Special Issue of the Journal Media Education: Studi, Ricerche, Buone Pratiche, 7*(2), 215–233. Available at: https://goo.gl/lBflQw

Tomé, V., & Domingues, I. (2014). A utilização do computador por alunos e professores do 1º Ciclo dentro e fora da sala de aula: um estudo de caso em Portugal. In Educação e Tecnologia: Parcerias 3.0. Luis Rosado, Giselle Ferreira, Márcio Lemgruber, Estrella

Bohadana (Eds.), pp. 265–300. ISBN 978-85-60923-27-4. Rio de Janeiro: Universidade Estácio de Sá.

Tomé, V., Falconi, A., e Mendes, S. (Orgs.) (2019). *App Your School – Experiências e um Manual para Atividades Futuras*. Bellaria Igea-Marina: Centro Zaffiria.

Treseder, P. (1997). *Empowering children & young people. Promoting involvement in decision-making*. London, UK: Save the Children.

Underwood, C., Parker, L., & Stone, L. (2013). Getting it together: Relational habitus in the emergence of digital literacies. *Learning, Media and Technology, New York 38*(4), 478–494.

UNESCO. (2015a). *Global citizenship education: Topics and learning objectives*. Paris: UNESCO. Accessed from: http://unesdoc.unesco.org/images/0023/002329/232993e.pdf

UNESCO. (2020). *Seoul declaration on media and information literacy for everyone and by everyone: A defence against disinfodemics*. Accessed from: https://en.unesco.org/sites/default/files/seoul_declaration_mil_disinfodemic_en.pdf

Vuorikari, R., Ferrari, A., & Punie, Y. (2019). *Makerspaces for education and training – Exploring future implications for Europe*, EUR 29819 EN, Publications Office of the European Union, Luxembourg. ISBN 978-92-76-09032-8, doi:10.2760/946996, JRC117481.

Vuorikari, R., Punie, Y., Carretero Gomez, S., & Van den Brande, L. (2016). *DigComp 2.0: The digital competence framework for citizens. Update Phase 1: The conceptual reference model*. Luxembourg: Publication Office of the European Union.

Wardle, C. and Derakhshan, H. (2017). *Information disorder: Toward an interdisciplinary framework for research and policy making*. Strasbourg: Council of Europe. Available at: https://rm.coe.int/information-disorder-report-november-2017/1680764666.

Wardle, C., e Derakhshan, H. (2019). *Information disorder: Toward an interdisciplinary framework for research and policy making*. Strasbourg: Council of Europe. Accessed from: https://rm.coe.int/information-disorder-report-november-2017/1680764666

CHAPTER 3

Want a Community Project? Dive in the Context First!

This chapter presents the organization of a project initially structured to a 3–year period, but which exceeded the expectations and is now in its seventh year. It can be broken down to four phases:

1. *March 2015 to February 2018*: funded by the Science and Technology Portuguese Foundation, consisted of four subphases:
   (a) preparing a certified in-service teacher training course, producing the collecting data instruments, finding a municipality to collaborate on the project implementation and presenting the project to schools and teachers (Mar–Dec 2015).
   (b) implementing the training, collecting data from teachers, inviting teachers to take part in the intervention process in the community, scheduled for April 2016 through February 2018 (Jan-Apr 2016).
   (c) collecting data from pupils and parents, apart from co-organizing the intervention plan according to the results of data analysis (May-Sep 2016).
   (d) implementing the plan and monitoring its implementation, working together with teachers, the school board, and the local government (Oct 2016 – Feb 2018).

2. *March 2018 to October 2019*: not funded, but active, since the teachers continued working, planning, implementing and developing Media Literacy and Digital Citizenship activities. From this, were produced three new editions of the printed school newspaper and meetings with the researcher on a regular basis. During this year and a half period, the project results were presented nationally and internationally. In addition, the Caneças School District became a member of the Council of Europe's Democratic School Network.
3. *November 2019 to present*: renamed "Digital Citizenship Academy" and funded by the Calouste Gulbenkian Foundation (until December 2022), the project focused on STEAM and Media Literacy, and restarted with two in-service teacher training courses (40 hours each, attended by a total of 29 teachers from preschool, primary school and 2nd cycle). It also included data collection on socioemotional competences (by way of a pre-test and post-test). Teachers and pupils planned, implemented and assessed STEAM/ML workshops related with the community context and aimed, in some cases, to solve local problems.

3.1 Planning the Project

The idea for the community-based research project was conceived in the summer of 2014 because of a set of three factors. First, we were in the final stages of the initial three-year post-doctoral grant (Mar 2012–Feb 2015), in which we had studied the uses, practices, risk perception and associated advantages of digital social networks (e.g., communication and learning) by students (aged 9–16), their parents and their teachers; second, the Science and Technology Portuguese Foundation offered us the possibility to organize and apply for a project to be developed in a second triennium (Mar 2015–Feb 2018); third, the research results from the first triennium, in line with other scientific literature, pointed to the need to intervene with younger children, their parents, and their teachers.

Children were beginning their interrelationship with social media at an increasingly early age (Boyd, 2014), with the average age being eight. However, on the Facebook network, for example, there were five million users who were 10-years-old or younger and 6% of the total users of that network were up to six years old (Lepi, 2013). In Europe, the average age of first access to the Internet was 9 years in 2010, ranging from 7 in Sweden to 11 in Greece. In Portugal it was 10-years-old (Ponte and Simões, 2013).

Our first triennial study surveyed 549 young people (9–16 years old) in 2013 and showed that nine out of 10 had at least one profile on digital social networks, with 91% of those having created it before the age of 13 (the minimum age allowed to have a Facebook profile). Only 26% of 10-year-olds did not have a profile on any network, while 40% were already on the network at age 8 or before (Tomé, 2014). Therefore, it was urgent to start intervening with younger children, in line with the scientific literature, which had identified a gap in research with children and young people. Prior research was focused on ages 9–10 years and older, despite a time in children's lives when they started interacting with the media still on their parents' laps, without the parents recognizing this media relationship, as they viewed the digital equipment their children accessed as if they were toys (Kotilainen and Suoninen, 2013).

It was crucial that we focus our research on the zero to six-year-olds (*idem*) and to create guidelines for parents and other adults to monitor the relationship between children and media, organized by groups: 0–2, 3–4 and 5–8 years (Holloway, Green and Livingstone, 2013). For this reason, our second three-year project focused on very young children, and since we intended to continue working in schools, the way forward would be to work at the preschool and primary schools.

The results of a study initiated in 2012 also pointed to two considerations for a future project. On one hand, children's access to media (also their parents' and even teachers') was not widespread. Only 10% of children did not use digital social networks, and this was especially true among the youngest, reinforcing the existence of digital divides (Tomé, 2014; Ponte and Simões, 2013). On the other hand, among those who did use these networks, access to information was high. However, the critical reception and response to this information was not evident. It was also clear that there was a deficit in terms of reflective, creative and democratic participation through media such as social networks (Steeves, 2014; Tomé, 2014).

There were limitations in each of the three dimensions of Media Education: (i) accessing and using media (skills in hardware, software, programming and security monitoring); (ii) having a critical and reflective sense of media (evaluating content, reflecting on political and economic influences on media, participating in e-governance, dealing with risks and opportunities); (iii) using media and technologies for individual purposes (the right to decide to be connected or not, the right to be forgotten, and the right to privacy, as well as the rights to innovative and creative use of media, to use media for entertainment, and to use media for learning and work purposes) (UNESCO, 2014).

Contributing to bridge these digital gaps by working with preschool and primary school children became a key reason for the project we applied for in September, which aimed to create conditions for the development of skills of critical analysis and reflective production of media content (Buckingham, 2009; Ministério da Educação e Ciência, 2011; UNESCO, 2011), in traditional and digital media, by children and young people, in a process involving several contexts:

- The family context: for example, parents are the people with experience and the first interlocutors of children, but research showed that they were mostly afraid of the consequences of their children's use of social media and few had habits of parental mediation (Tomé, 2014);
- The school context (teachers, librarians, students and their peers): teachers used social media a lot, in a personal capacity, and attributed great pedagogical potential to them, but few addressed the critical, reflective and creative use of media with students at school (Tomé, 2014).
- The media context outside the school (traditional and digital media, academia and civil society): more than understanding which projects were developed with the aim of preparing citizens (Pinto, Pereira, Pereira and Ferreira, 2011), it was important to analyze the results of these actions and establish bases of cooperation and continuity between the formal, non-formal and informal learning contexts.

It was necessary to move forward bearing in mind that media studies should go beyond the focus on the individual, focusing also on the community that surrounds him/her. They should embrace a qualitative approach to interrelationships between individuals, with a sociological approach focused on the analysis of distributed competencies—not only on the individual, but on what one does in relation to others, what one creates, how one cooperates, and how one participates (Frau-Meigs, 2014).

In this sense, the project would aim to:

- Enhance the role of the family in raising the level of Media Literacy of children from birth, preparing and providing parents with the means to do so (Tomé, 2014);
- Enhance the role of the school (as early as preschool and primary school), through the continuous training of teachers, the implementation and monitoring of pedagogical activities proposed for national (Ministério da Educação e Ciência, 2014) and international contexts (Ministère de l'Éducation Nationale, 2013; UNESCO, 2011) and intervention with children;
- Enhance the role of the media, academia, and entities outside the school in preparing children for interrelationships with the media (Pinto et al., 2011).

- Take a humanistic approach to the media, thinking of pedagogy in the sense of the formation of the individual child and the citizen (Becchetti-Bizot, 2013).

Once the analysis was completed, it was time to act especially since the shortcomings verified were a reality in Europe, but were even more pressing in Portugal, where this work had yet to be done (Pereira, 2013). The proposed project aimed to understand the use of digital media by children aged two to nine years old, which we believe is only possible in collaboration with preschool and primary school teachers, as well as with the children's families and teachers. The goals of this project were to help:

- Infuse Media Education into the preschool and primary school curricula;
- Identify best practices aimed at formal, non-formal and informal learning contexts;
- Contribute to the selection of learning outcomes to assess the development of Media Literacy competences;
- Inform policy makers and other entities responsible for the definition of public policies in the area of Digital Citizenship Education and democratic participation;
- Implement a localized Media Education project that is replicable at national and international levels.

To achieve the objectives, the proposed project was centered on a set of actions that involved the training of a group of up to 60 preschool and primary school teachers (if possible, 30 in one region and 30 in another region of the country). After this training, the teachers would be invited to assist in the creation of a community intervention project, participating actively as co-organizers. This would be followed by data collection from children in the participating teachers' classes, but also from their parents and/or caregivers.

According to the results of the data collected from teachers, children and parents, a first intervention plan would then be designed, taking into account the political, economic, social and cultural dynamics of the local community, as well as projects and initiatives developed by different actors (e.g.: Policy makers, Academia, media outlets …) in the area of Media Education developed in Portugal and internationally.

Our starting question was the following: To what extent a community-based project can empower preschool and primary school age children in order to become active and effective citizens in the digital era? Considering the results obtained with the first three-year study, as well as the scientific literature, our hypotheses were the following:

- The use of media by preschool and primary school children is part of an international digital culture;
- A concerted action in family, school, and media contexts allows preschool and primary school students to initiate a responsible interrelationship with digital media;
- Preschool and primary school teachers can, with training and monitoring, implement pedagogical activities to prepare children for interrelationship with digital media;
- Families can develop strategies to empower their own and their children's interrelationship with social media;
- Media outlets (traditional and digital), academia and other out-of-school initiatives play an important role in preparing preschool and primary school children for their interrelationship with digital media.

As of the summer of 2014, the planned outcomes of the project to be developed through February 2018 were the following:

1. Characterization of the media diet of children aged two to nine years, as well as their teachers and guardians;
2. Identification of sense-making practices to be developed in schools (with advantages, constraints and ways to overcome them) and publication of a manual of those practices;
3. Identification of sense-making practices to be developed by parents, in order to raise their level of Media Literacy, but also that of their children, and publication of a manual of those practices;
4. Identification of sense-making practices that the media (traditional and digital), academia and civil society can develop in order to contribute to raising the Media Literacy level of children and young people, and publication of a manual of those practices;
5. Organization and publication of a book (available in PDF format) with the results, advantages and constraints found, and how to overcome them in order to create conditions for the project to be replicated, either in other Portuguese municipalities, or in other countries;
6. Publication of scientific articles in international peer-reviewed journals;
7. Creation of a sustainability plan so that local governments, in other regions of the country or internationally, could be able to continue the project after the second triennium.

The methodology to be followed would be mixed, as data collection would be done from documentary analysis, semi-structured interviews and interviews with children, questionnaires (indirect application), participant observation and a logbook of field notes. Data processing and analysis included content analysis (in the *Atlas.ti* program) and quantitative data analysis (in the *SPSS* program).

The application submitted to the Science and Technology Portuguese Foundation was approved in October 2014, and the project began in March 2015. It was then the time to organize the accredited teacher training, and to create the data collection instruments according to the methodology.

3.2 Producing Data Collection Instruments

The organization of data collection instruments involved an extended scientific literature review, after which we decided to use existing questionnaires, adapting them to the Portuguese reality and validating the adapted versions with national experts. In the case of questionnaires aimed at teachers and parents of preschool and primary school children, the most appropriate we found were those applied by Mathen, Fastrez and De Smedt (2015), in the study "Les enfants et les écrans" [Children and Screens], developed for the 'Office de la naissance et de l'enfance,' the reference public institution of the French community in Belgium that implements childhood policies.

The study, about the use of these screens by children from zero to six years old, focused on the representations and attitudes of parents and preschool teachers. In the case of parents, it focused on children's perceptions of screen use, parental mediation strategies, and understanding their attitudes towards screens in the family context. In the case of preschool teachers, given their close relationship with families, the study aimed to understand if there was dialogue with parents regarding the use of screens by children, as well as limits and bans on the use of screens by children, and also to understand the attitudes of teachers, as educational professionals, regarding this issue. Given the studies' objectives, we asked the authors for permission to adapt the questionnaire, which was granted. We then organized a questionnaire for preschool and primary school teachers, which was composed of 27 questions organized into five parts:

- Part 1—Data such as age, sex, years taught, length of service, academic training.
- Part 2—Personal media use in the form of access and the most common Internet activities.

- Part 3—Likert scales to collect data on the teachers' perception regarding: (i) the pedagogical potential of the media, (ii) the use of media in their daily teaching activities (iii) dialogue with students about media; (iv) perception of use by students and their effects; (v) level of knowledge in terms of Internet security.
- Part 4—Likert scales aimed at understanding whether teachers talk to guardians and parents about the use of media by children and, if so, what the most-mentioned medium was.
- Part 5—Possible obstacles to the use of Internet and social media in pedagogical contexts.

Data from parents was collected through a 29-question questionnaire organized in four sections, and very similar to the questionnaire organized for teachers, as follows:

- Part 1—Personal data (and if they had other children attending Kindergarten or primary school).
- Part 2—Personal digital media use and practices (individual context and familiar context).
- Part 3—Likert scales focused on learning potential of the media, dialogue with children on media use and practices, perception of use by children and of media use effects, level of knowledge in terms of Internet security, perceptions of risks and opportunities.
- Part 4—Strategies of parental mediation and eventual talks with teachers about children media use, practices and encouraged/discouraged limits.

Both questionnaires were tested with preschool and primary school teachers, as well as with specialists in the research arena, who were previously presented with the objectives of the research project and the longitudinal perspective that was intended to be implemented. It was also mentioned that the project would allow the collection of qualitative data, from teachers and parents, but also qualitative data from the children themselves, which initiated the creation of an interview script with children.

For the collection of qualitative data from children aged 3–10 years old, we considered as a key resource the questionnaire used in the study "Young Children & Digital Technology: a qualitative exploratory study across seven countries" (Chaudron, 2015), published by the Office of the European Union. This was an exploratory study involving 70 families and was simultaneously implemented in six European Union countries (Belgium, Czech Republic, Finland, Germany, Italy,

UK) and Russia. It was aimed at "testing a new methodology while collecting information on how children between 0 to 8 years old engage with (online) technologies [e.g.: smartphones, tablets, computers and games], on how parents mediate their use, and to identify potential benefits and risks associated with their (online) interactions with new technologies" (*idem*, p. 7). It was, therefore, in line with the objectives of the project we sought to implement in Caneças, so we contacted the coordinator of the study, who authorized us to use the data collection instruments they had used.

This authorization allowed us to upgrade the questionnaire aimed at parents, while making it possible to collect data from children using instruments previously validated and tested in several European countries, which had already been translated into Portuguese by Patrícia Dias and Rita Brito, who would later publish studies based on these questionnaires (Dias and Brito, 2016) but who immediately agreed to provide us with the translated instrument. The interview guide aimed at children was organized in three sections: icebreaker, introduction (family personal data) and interview (children media use and activities developed, skills, parental mediation and family rules).

The data collection instruments were thus organized, but it was still necessary to maintain other records, so a diary was kept in order to register the coordinates from all the participants, as well as to take notes after each contact with parents, teachers, children and community organizations. It was then time to carry out the teacher training and data collection in the field, which would only be possible through partnerships with local government and schools, established through contacts initiated months before.

3.3 Contacting the Local Community, Municipalities and Schools

When our research project started, in 2015, our idea consisted of progressively and effectively involving preschool and primary school teachers and, through them, their students and families, to best reach the community. We started also contacting municipalities, presenting the project and asking for logistical support to implement it, namely introducing the researcher to the school boards, providing facilities to organize a meeting with the school district representatives. We had also asked about the chance of creating conditions to continue the project beyond the post-doctoral scholarship period (2015–2018).

We contacted the municipal counties of Castelo Branco (center north of the Portuguese countryside, near Spain), Grândola (south of the Portuguese countryside), Loures and Odivelas (north of Lisbon), Moita (south of Lisbon) and Oeiras (west of Lisbon). The municipalities of Castelo Branco and Odivelas agreed to participate. In Castelo Branco, the project did not advance because the number of interested teachers was less than the minimum required by the Leonardo Coimbra Training Center, which is part of the National Association of Teachers (Associação Nacional de Professores).

Odivelas Municipality approved the project in a council session held in October 2015. The project was then presented to the school district, in a session held in the Auditorium of the City Hall of Odivelas, on 28th October 2015, in which all the Odivelas schools were represented. Following this presentation the enrollment process was opened to the preschool and primary school teachers of all the schools. Twenty-eight teachers enrolled in the training course until early December, most of them working at the Caneças School District (based in Caneças, a small village of Odivelas municipality). The training was then officially scheduled from January 4th to February 28th 2016, at the headquarters of Caneças School District since the school board agreed on making a room available.

3.4 Collecting Data from Teachers, Children, Families and the Community

To organize the intervention plan of this community-based research project, data from teachers, children, and their families were needed. We first collected data from teachers, through a questionnaire survey applied in January 2016. Data from families were collected between April and June, at Artur Alves Cardoso School, whose teachers agreed to go ahead with the project, after the teacher training course. Children's data were collected in the same time frame as families, through a semi-structured interview.

In the case of teachers, before the start of the first training session in January 2016, 24 out of 25 participants training (10 preschool and 15 primary-school teachers) completed the questionnaire. This data collection made it possible to organize the following sessions according to the teachers' characteristics and interests (see Chapters 4 and 5), and they were also a precious help in interpreting the reports that the teachers produced at the end of the training in February 2016.

It was then necessary to collect data from children and parents to characterize the community, but this collection was dependent on the continuity of the project in the field. In March 2016, we asked teachers about their availability to continue planning and implementing Digital Citizenship activities with their students, but only in April we received the positive responses from eight teachers working at the Artur Alves Cardoso school.

The eight teachers organized themselves into three groups and continued to plan and implement activities (see Section 3.5). However it was necessary to contact the children's parents for two reasons: (i) to invite them to join the project and accept to answer the questionnaire we had organized for them; (ii) to authorize us to interview their children. To contact parents, we needed authorization from the Caneças School District, which we requested and which was granted. However, the contact still depended on the approval of the parents themselves, in the March mid-term meetings. In order to get their approval, we went to the school and requested meeting with the parents to help with the decision making. Although some parents were reluctant, all the groups accepted that we could present the project. This paved the way for us to distribute the interview authorization requests to one of the parents and their children.

We obtained a total of 45 authorizations, but three parents changed their minds and did not authorize their children to be interviewed, while four parents did not attend the scheduled interview. Therefore, we considered data collected from 38 parents and 38 children (22 aged 4–6 years and 16 aged 7–10 years).

All the collected data were processed using the Statistical Package for Social Sciences (quantitative data) and Atlas.ti (qualitative data). Results from the data analysis allowed us to characterize this multidimensional context (see Chapter 5), a crucial task in order to adapt the intervention model accordingly. The intervention model was fundamentally based on teacher training, which we describe in Chapter 4.

References

Becchetti-Bizot, C. (2013). *L'Education aux Médias, un savoir nouvelle*. In Ministère de l'Éducation Nationale. *Médias & Information: on apprend* (pp. 6–7). Paris: CNDP/CLEMI

Boyd, H. (2014). *It's complicated: The social lives of networked teens*. London: Yale University Press.

Buckingham, D. (2009). Media education policy: The future of media literacy in the digital age. In *Media literacy in Europe* (pp. 13–25). Brussels: Euromeduc.

Chaudron, S. (2015). *Young children & digital technology: A qualitative exploratory study across seven countries*. Luxembourg: Publications Office of the European Union.

Dias, P., & Brito, R. (2016). *Crianças (0 aos 8 anos) e tecnologias digitais – Um estudo qualitativo exploratório*. Lisboa: Centro de Estudos de Comunicação e Cultura da Universidade Católica Portuguesa.

Frau-Meigs, D. (2014). *Oral intervention on the European Media Literacy Forum 2014 (27–18 May, 2014)*, Paris: UNESCO.

Holloway, D., Green, L., & Livingstone, S. (2013). *Zero to eight: Young children and their Internet use. LSE.* London: EU Kids Online. Accessed from: http://eprints.lse.ac.uk/52630/

Kotilainen, S., & Suoninen, A. (2013). Cultures of media and information literacies among the young: South-North viewpoints. In U. Carlsson & S. H. Culver (Eds.), *Media and information literacy and intercultural dialogue* (pp. 141–162). Göteborg: Nordicom.

Lepi, K. (2013). *This is how teens are using social media.* Accessed from: https://stemreadings.wordpress.com/2013/07/28/this-is-how-teens-are-using-social-media/.

Mathen, M., Fastrez, P., & De Smedt, T. (2015). *Les enfants et les écrans – Usages des enfants de 0 à 6 ans, représentations et attitudes de leurs parents et des professionnels de la petite enfance.* Louvain-la-Neuve: UCL-Institut Langage et Communication. Accessed from: http://dial.uclouvain.be/handle/boreal:165802

Ministère de l'Éducation Nationale. (2013). *Médias & Information: on apprend.* Paris: CNDP/CLEMI.

Ministério da Educação e Ciência. (2011). *Recomendação sobre Educação para a Literacia Mediática.* Lisboa: MEC.

Ministério da Educação e Ciência. (2014). *Referencial de Educação para os Media para a Educação Pré-escolar, o Ensino Básico e o Ensino Secundário.* Lisboa: MEC.

Pereira, L. (2013). *Literacia Digital e Políticas Tecnológicas para a Educação.* Santo Tirso: DeFacto Editores.

Pinto, M., Pereira S., Pereira, L., e Ferreira, T. (2011). *Educação para os Media em Portugal: experiências, actores e contextos.* Lisboa: ERC.

Ponte, C., & Simões, J. (2013). Comparando resultados sobre acessos e usos da Internet: Brasil, Portugal e Europa. In *TIC kids online Brazil 2012* (pp. 27–35). São Paulo: Comitê Gestor da Internet no Brasil.

Steeves, V. (2014). *Young Canadians in a wired world, Phase III: Life online.* Ottawa: Media Smarts. Accessed from: http://mediasmarts.ca/ycww/life-online.

Tomé, V. (2014). Usos e relações nas redes sociais: um estudo com jovens, seus pais e professores. In *Actas do Congresso Confibercom* (14–16 Abril de 2014). CECS. Braga: Universidade do Minho.

UNESCO. (1982). *Grunwald declaration on media education.* https://dokumen.tips/documents/grunwald-declaration-on-media-education.html

UNESCO. (2011). *Media and information literacy: Curriculum for teachers.* Paris: UNESCO.

UNESCO. (2014). *Declaration on Augmented Media and Information Literacy (MIL) in the Digital era.* Paris: Unesco. Accessed from: http://www.unesco.org/new/en/communication-and-information/resources/news-and-in-focus-articles/in-focus-articles/2014/paris-declaration-on-media-and-information-literacy-adopted/

CHAPTER 4

Preparing Teachers to Work with the Greater Community

This chapter provides an in depth analysis of the three in-service teacher training courses implemented throughout the project, which were focused on Digital Citizenship Education for Democratic Participation (January–February 2016), Media Education and School Newspapers (April–May 2018) and on STEAM and Media Literacy (September–December 2020). The three courses were milestones of the community project "Digital Citizenship Education."

4.1 Training Teachers in Media Literacy and Digital Citizenship (2016–2020)

The first one was centered on exploring core concepts and pedagogical guidelines and best practices in order to empower, motivate and help teachers through planning, implementing and assessing Media Literacy and Digital Citizenship Education activities with their pupils. The second one was more specific, addressing in particular the school newspaper production, because a group of preschool and primary school teachers had started a printed school newspaper in December 2016, making the implementation of this course a crucial need. The third one was associated with the project's name change from 'Digital Citizenship Education for Democratic Participation' to 'Digital

Citizenship Academy', following a funding from the Calouste Gulbenkian Foundation, through the 'Academies of Knowledge' program. The course aimed at planning and implementing Media Literacy and STEAM workshops in formal learning contexts, involving children aged from 3 to 12 years old, along with their relatives and other members from the local community.

The main reasons in-service teacher training in the above-referenced areas is key to education and in which ways and levels it shall be planned and implemented are outlined below.

The need for teacher training in Media Literacy was pointed out by the Grünwald Declaration (UNESCO, 1982), but despite all the efforts made since then, the celebration of the 25th anniversary of the Declaration, from which resulted the Paris Declaration (UNESCO, 2007), showed that the global landscape did not change significantly. The weak or non-existing pre-service and in-service teacher training in Media Literacy was one of the main problems identified by Pinto, Pereira, Pereira and Ferreira (2011) during a national research study on Media Literacy developed in Portugal. The authors recommended a significant investment in teacher training, from preschool to secondary school, and especially in Higher Education (pre-service) and in in-service teacher training centers. Focusing on digital media and social networks, de Abreu (2011) states that "the greater issue for many teachers is that they do not actually know how to use social networking sites and furthermore they do not understand how to tie it in their already full curriculum" (p. 52). Or, they are not able to operate the digital devices and prefer not to use them in order to hide their difficulties from the students (UNESCO, 2015b). Even the Council of the European Union (2012) agrees that "the pedagogical competences of primary school teachers in the teaching of reading and writing, for instance in the pedagogical use of ICT, need to be strengthened," besides "supporting teachers in secondary schools to teach literacy across all subjects and, where relevant, promoting access to expert advice for all teachers" (p. 2).

Among teachers, the question is not whether to use digital media. An Australian research study involving teachers and students from preschool to Year 12 revealed that "screen content is now a part of the seamless flow of a lesson, with YouTube being the far most used resource," but teachers have little time to spend identifying and adapting YouTube content for the classroom, and they need specific help in this task (Cunningham, Dezzuani, Goldsmith, Burns, Miles, Henkel, Ryan and Murphy, 2016).

Apart from the lack of teacher training, there is a lack of research in school contexts involving collaboration among researchers, teachers, media representatives and political decision-makers (Rivoltella, 2007), the lack of educational resources validated by specialists, teachers and students (Tomé, 2008), and an insufficient curricular development as well (Frau-Meigs and Torrent, 2009).

4.2 Digital Citizenship Education for Democratic Participation (2016): The Training Plans Project

The training course "Digital Citizenship Education for Democratic Participation of young people" was structured within the framework of a Module of the Council of Europe's Pestalozzi program in 2012 and was tested with 14 Portuguese teachers from various educational levels in 2013. Following the test, it was improved and adapted for teachers of preschool, primary school, and Special Education teachers, and was accredited in 2014 by the Scientific-Pedagogical Council for Continuous Education, the department of the Ministry of Education which is responsible for certifying trainers and accrediting teacher training in Portugal.

The 25-hour course (6 theoretical and 19 practical) was part of the training offer of the Leonardo Coimbra Training Center. It focused on the importance of children's social participation through media, with a focus on digital media, as well as on the analysis of online hate speech and ways to fight it:

1. Train preschool and primary school teachers in the area of social media and democratic participation and tackling online hate speech;
2. Be aware of practices of young people in social media with a focus on democratic participation;
3. Organize practical activities involving teachers and their students, from 3 to 10 years old;
4. Plan and implement Media Education practices, involving preschool and primary school children, in formal and non-formal learning contexts;
5. Challenge teachers to involve other teachers, children's families and other community members on the implementation of the planned Media Education activities.

The course was open to all of the approximately 300 preschool, primary and special needs education teachers working in the Municipality of Odivelas. In order to start the course, at least 15 teachers were needed. A total of 28 registered but only 25 attended (10 from the preschool, 14 from the primary school and one from Special Education). Nine of these teachers worked at the Artur Alves Cardoso School, where the project would later start, although at the start of the training, this fact had not even been realized.

Fifteen teachers had 20 or more years of service, eight had between 10 and 20, while two had worked for less than 10 years (one did not respond), and their distribution by age is shown in Graph 4.1:

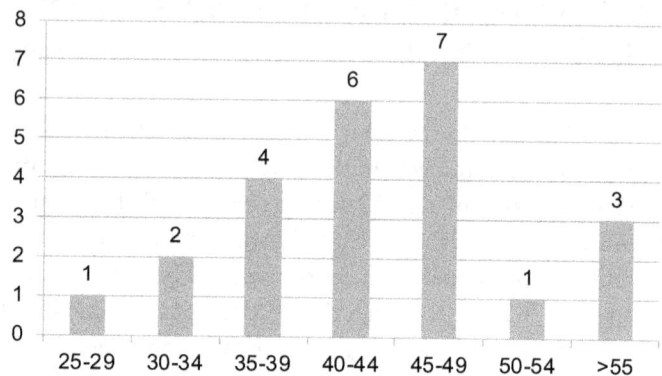

Graph 4.1: Teachers distribution by age group (n=24)

The teacher training course consisted of eight sessions and started on January 4th and ended on February 29th, 2016. In addition to the sessions, the trainer was always available via phone or email and a free website was created, on Edublogs, through which all the resources and links used in the training, as well as the working documents, summaries and other training information were always available.

4.2.1 Work Developed by Teachers, Involving Children, Parents and the Community

Teachers organized themselves into ten groups and developed digital literacy activities with 366 of their students (147 preschoolers and 219 primary school students). The activities were embedded in the work that had been previously planned, and they were to use media (traditional and/or digital) as a resource and/or a study object. Each group established a duly justified topic, its objectives, and the development of the activity. Participants always had the support of the trainer (researcher and journalist) and had access to resources available through a course blog.

The activities (presented in Table 4.1) covered diverse topics and objectives and were related with the operational area of the intervention model they followed, such as organizing a book or creating a collective text from image exploitation. Concerning the critical area, teachers and students discussed the role of newspapers, Internet safety, learning with and through the media, as well as critically analyzing media messages (print and online newspapers, YouTube videos, comics) including advertising. The cultural competency aspect of the program, especially related with social intervention through media, was covered less than the others, as only one group organized an activity aimed at tackling bullying in a school setting.

Table 4.1: Activities developed during the training course (2016)

Group	Participants	Activity core objective
1	Three teachers (2 preschool, 1 Primary); 77 children: 51 aged 4–6; 26 aged 7–8.	Address risks and opportunities on the Internet and use the tablet in an educational context
2	Two preschool teachers; 11 children aged 5/6	Promote the safe and creative use of media for teaching pedagogy and involving the educational caregivers
3	Three preschool teachers; 70 children aged 4–6	Produce a book of illustrated rhymes and develop phonological awareness
4	Two teachers; 20 children aged 9–10	Analyze online newspapers on the government's decision to terminate the national exams in Grade 1
5	Two teachers; 26 children aged 8–9	Increase the interest in the present role of the media in reporting on what is happening in the world
6	Three teachers; 20 children aged 7/8 and 24 aged 9/10	Analyze the issue of the refugee crisis from images of newspapers and online surveys
7	Three teachers; 25 students aged 5/6.	Raise awareness among students of diverse learning contexts, including the media
8	Three teachers; 15 students aged 4/5	Explore the printed newspaper, its role in society, the role of news and images
9	Two teachers; 27 students aged 7/9	Address the concept of bullying through visualization, analysis, and discussion of videos
10	Two teachers; 51 students aged 6/7	Identify advertisements, analyzing their message and purpose

4.2.2 Assessing Teachers' Work

In the developed activities, teachers showed an evident concern to better know the media diet of their students. In one case, amongst 77 students, between ages 4 and 8, 67 had a personal tablet and 15 had a smartphone. In another socioeconomically-disadvantaged school, amongst approximately 51 students, between ages 6 and 7, 39 had a computer at home, 38 had tablet and 24 used a smartphone, although the device wasn't their own.

The use of media raised mainly two types of questions to teachers. Firstly the safe use of the Internet. For example, a primary school teacher previously explored with students the precautions when carrying out online surveys (manual Smartie, the Penguin[1]). Secondly, in many schools, there are usually computers and a projector in the library, but not in the classroom, and no tablets or smartphones. The following was the resulting distribution:

1. Two preschool teachers asked parents to authorize their children to take tablets to school, but most were reticent, fearing that the tablets could be damaged.
2. Two preschool teachers asked parents who used the tablets at home to work together with the children in order to help them to draw, complete word association assignments, and perform numerical assignments. According to the teachers, this activity was very important, as parents and children found that the tablet can be used for more than entertainment purposes.
3. Not having the means to do online research and without the delivery of daily newspapers at school, two teachers created an assignment for students to complete at home, asking them to get news on the decision of the Government to eliminate the 4th grade exams. The students were interested in the task and completed the assignment. This allowed for a richer group discussion at school on the following day.

Students debated current issues by analyzing news stories, in particular news issues that concerned them such as: the government's decision to terminate the tests on the 4th of primary school; the question of Zika virus; domestic violence; the refugee crisis in the Mediterranean Sea; and a bomb threat at Faro Airport. However, when dealing with current issues, many children did not go beyond the headlines to understand the news. This point became clear in an activity developed with 20 students of 2nd Year and 24 students of the 4th Year. The activity began with a look at the body image of Alan Kurdi, a three-year-old Syrian child of three years found on the beach in the Mediterranean in 2015 and immortalized by the media. During the exploration of the image, the students of 2nd year failed to explain what had happened. Only two students of 4th year remembered seeing the image on television and knew that the child had drowned but could not provide an explanation for this occurrence. After researching at home, with parental assistance, family members and/or peers, all the students knew what had happened.

---

1 Available at http://www.childnet.com/resources/smartie-the-penguin

By the same token, there are pupils who demonstrated having a greater knowledge of some news. In an activity with 15 students from kindergarten (five-year-old), the teachers explored an image of a small boat with refugees in the Mediterranean. While some associated the image to a boat ride or the people who were fishing, others mentioned «that boat is going to other worlds», who were «refugees who went to a bigger boat» or «people fleeing war» revealing knowledge that surprised the teachers. In terms of distinguishing advertising from news, the teachers concluded that pupils of 6/7 years of age have a hard time making the separation and were too influenced by ads.

Although the process was more important than the product, we consider that the latter revealed the ease with which teachers have integrated activities in their lesson plans. They were able to integrate the activities in the pedagogical plans organized at the beginning of the school year without changing them. The work of two groups resulted in the production of books: an identification of domestic and wild animals, with a digital component (PowerPoint); a rhyme, in which 70 students (4–6 years old) were asked to write on notecards, two words that rhymed with each other, and draw objects that these words represent.

In the case of the book of rhymes, students participated with the number of productions possibilities. The book was then bound and made available in the library. A digital version (PowerPoint) was also produced. Previously students voted on the title of the book and which drawings /words that should integrate it, thus practicing in democracy at school. In the other groups, the students produced other written materials, such as completing worksheets previously organized by teachers with drawings or collective texts in the classroom. The teachers organized themselves into groups freely. This point was important to note as some teachers belonged to different schools, which limited previous opportunities for working together. Even when it was possible to associate preschool teachers and primary school teachers in the same group, this was not the rule, and in fact, it only occurred in one group.

Even though preschool and primary school teachers recognize great teaching potential to using the media, either in formal or informal contexts, there is a lack of Media Literacy practices in their classrooms, mainly due to two reasons:

1. The lack of teacher training: most teachers point to the lack of training or professional development in the area of media and technology in the classroom, which is consistent with the international literature (De Abreu, 2011; Redecker, Ala-Mukta and Punie, 2010; UNESCO, 2015b).
2. Lack of resources and legal limitations: teachers stated that the use of mobile phones is forbidden to students, as is the use of tablets. That is, the use

of digital equipment most preferred by children is not available in schools (Chaudron, 2016).

Poor use of digital media in the classroom can be attributed to an erroneous perception by teachers (Chaudron, 2015, 2016; Marsh, 2014). This was supported by the teacher training reflections, which stated how surprised they were by the increased use of digital technologies by children. Although the use of digital media in the prescribed activities was not a condition, two teacher groups developed activities using tablets involving children and parents. This inclusion was important because many parents of young children do not know whether their children should use this form of media or not. At the same time, parents believe schools should use these technologies (Palaiologou, 2016).

4.2.3 Assessing the Training

The training course was evaluated using the evaluation form used by the Leonardo Coimbra Training Center. Using a Likert scale (from Low to Very Good), 14 teachers evaluated the action as Very Good and 11 as Good. The usefulness of the knowledge acquired was rated "very useful" by 19, with six stating it was of some use. In their comments, the teachers highlighted four aspects:

1. Improvement of teaching practice: "It has enabled me, with the knowledge acquired, to lead students and to reflect on different resources you can use to learn (T1); "It ended up surprising me, in the sense that I was able to grab the interest of the students and motivate them to critically participate on current issues" (T3); "The action gave much emphasis to issues that seemed irrelevant but, after all, are quite relevant" (T4); "He taught me to further explore some techniques that I was not familiar with, but it was not so aware of the importance that they had" (T11).
2. The working group and the involvement of students "allowed to carry out activities in the classroom for the first time. There was freedom to approaches in the classroom themes/resources according to each class/school" (T13); "Group work allowed new learning/attitudes" (T14); "Conduct activities with students in the classroom was a very positive aspect" (T25).
3. Sharing knowledge: "Very interesting and enriching the shared experience" (T21); "The presentation of the work was very enriching and allowed me to do some learning and put it into practice in my teaching activity" (T23).
4. Knowledge of the use and practice of students with media: "From the work done by the students, we reached the conclusions that we had not even

weighed initially; for example, students from preschool see little television, but use the tablet daily more of an hour" (T24); "I helped to realize the reality with regard to technologies in which my students are inserted" (T8).

Therefore, the teachers did not know the customs and practices of their students in relation to the media, which is understandable because in the questionnaire provided at the beginning of the training it became clear that this was not a subject that was regularly discussed between teachers and students. Although 15 teachers (12/14 in the primary school and 3/10 in preschool) admitted talking to children about the frequency of use and practices in the media, these dialogues took place only occasionally. No teacher admitted to discussing these issues with children many days or every day.

4.3 Media Education through School Newspapers 2017/18: The Training Plans Project

The in-service teacher training course "Media Education through school newspapers and the promotion of language literacy" emerged from a need identified by the teachers participating in the project in June 2017, at the end of the school year (see Chapter 5). The school had started the regular publication of a school newspaper in print format in December 2016, and three editions had been published, but the teachers indicated that they needed more training in school journalism.

The 2016 training course had been accredited since 2008 by the Scientific-Pedagogical Council of Continuous Training course, and its contents were reformulated in 2017. It was a 25-hour course (6 theoretical and 19 practical), conducted through the Leonardo Coimbra Training Center of the National Teachers Association, with the following main objectives:

- Address the evolution of Media Education in Portugal, Europe and worldwide;
- Discuss the goals and need for Media Education;
- Organize activities of critical analysis and reflective production of content for the school newspaper (in print and digital media);
- Include Media Education activities in the planning of the different subject and non-disciplinary curricular areas, in the different levels of education;
- Exercise pedagogical practices related to the production of a school newspaper, to be replicated in a classroom environment, focused on reading and writing text, sound, and images;

- Know technical and didactic procedures for using the school newspaper as an educational resource;
- Use multimedia resources in Media Education activities to be developed in a school environment.

The rules for the course required the enrollment of a minimum of 15 trainees and a maximum of 30, so it was necessary to go beyond the Artur Alves Cardoso School, which had only 11 teachers. Pre-registration was opened in September to teachers from all levels of education in the schools of the micro-local government, the Parish of Ramada and Caneças.

Twenty-seven teachers from various levels of education enrolled in the course: eight from preschool, nine from primary school, seven from the 3rd cycle and secondary school, two of Special Education teachers, and a Librarian. Teachers from 3rd cycle and Secondary level taught Portuguese (4), Geography (1), ICT (1) and Mathematics (1). Eighteen teachers belonged to the Caneças School District[2], where the project is taking place, namely teachers from three of the four primary schools and three kindergartens. The other nine participants belonged to three other school districts.

Seventeen teachers had 20 or more years of service, while nine had between 10 and 20 years, and only one teacher had less than 10 years of teaching experience, which is in line with the ages of the participants in Graph 4.2 (note that data are missing for two teachers who preferred not to reveal their age).

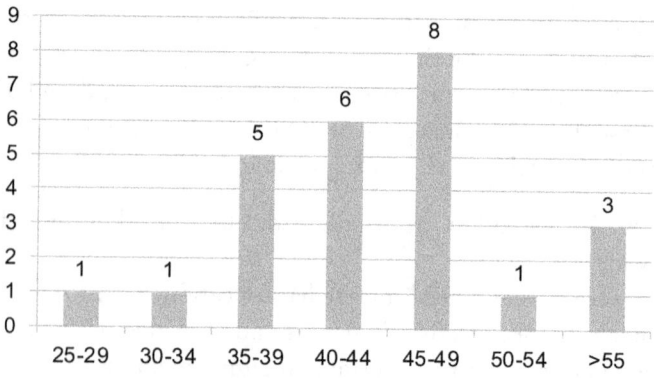

Graph 4.2: Teachers distribution by age group (n=25)

---

2   In Portugal, schools are organized into clusters led by a secondary school and then joined by several schools of other educational levels. In this case, the Caneças School District has a secondary school, a middle and high school (students from 11 to 15 years old), four elementary schools and four kindergartens, totaling about 2000 students.

The opportunity to involve teachers from different levels of education in the training course was an added advantage, but scheduling issues forced us to organize a group with the seven secondary school teachers, whose sessions were held on Mondays, after working hours, while the other group's sessions were held on Wednesday afternoons, starting at 16:30. The course that began on November 13, 2017 and ended on February 5, 2018, was organized into eight sessions of three hours each, except for the first and last, which lasted three and a half hours.

4.3.1 Work Developed by Teachers, Involving Children, Parents and the Community

After the first six hours of theoretical training, teachers were asked to organize themselves into working groups and plan a Media Education activity, focused on content production, which would involve students, families and other members of the school and local community. Media Education, which is a core area of Digital Citizenship Education, should be developed in an integrated, community-based way, which the Council of Europe (2018a) calls a whole-school approach.

As we had already proposed in the training course held in 2016, the activity would not interfere with the general planning that teachers were already implementing. From its implementation, two items would be the end result: a media product and a report with the planning, the description of the production process and the students involved and the analysis of the results according to the objectives set at the beginning. The teachers organized themselves into seven working groups that planned and developed the projects summarized in Table 4.2:

Table 4.2: Activities developed during the in-service training course (2017/18)

Group	Participants	Activity core objective
1	Three teachers (1 preschool, 1 Primary, 1 Special Needs); 42 children: 19 aged 4–6; 23 aged 9–10.	School wall newspaper focused on environment protection, after the application of questionnaires to community members on the same subject. Writing and sending a letter to the City Hall asking for more recycling containers and producing a leaflet to be distributed in the community.
2	Five preschool teachers and 10 children aged 5–6	Creation of a story from three given photos (of forest fires) by a group of 10 preschool children attending three different kindergartens, through a co-creation process during which children drew the story board, presented their ideas on the plot, discussed them with other children and agreed on the story's title.
3	Five teachers (1 pre-school, 4 Primary); 126 children: 25 aged 4–6, 26 aged 7–8, 26 aged 8–9 and 48 aged 9–10.	Series of debates focused on "What do we need to attain happiness?" (4/6 and 7/8) and on "Rights and Responsibilities" (8/9 and 9/10), followed by the production of posters and messages that were disseminated through the brand-new school radio show station.
4	Seven teachers (5 Primary, 1 Librarian, 1 Special needs); 121 children: 50 aged 6–7, 23 aged 7–8, 24 aged 8–9 and 24 aged 9–10.	Production of a school newspaper supplement on bullying, directly involving the children's relatives. Creation and production of a TV News service involving all the Primary school teachers, students and families.
5	Two Secondary school teachers (teaching Portuguese); 28 students aged 13–14	Brainstorming on the pros and cons of the Internet, according to a set of questions previously prepared by the teachers, followed by the production of an opinion article (in large group) on the topic.
6	Three Secondary school teachers (teaching ICT, Portuguese and Mathematics); 90 students aged 13–18 (including vocational students)	"Think before you post," an activity focused on the responsible and safe use of the Internet, improper content and on the production of memes raising awareness about sexting.

Table 4.2: Continued

Group	Participants	Activity core objective
7	Two Secondary school teachers (teaching Geography and Portuguese); 68 students: 24 aged 12/13 and 44 aged 14–15	Production of four sequential wall frames focused on bullying, its causes and consequences and ways of tackling it. The wall frames were exhibited in a busy area of the school and had four different titles and content both produced by the students: Mistery (single words related with bullying), Enigma (emojis chosen by the students to represent the words previously presented on the first wall frame), Problem (photographs chosen by the students to represent the emojis) and Key (sentences written by students aimed to prevent and tackle bullying).

Regarding the activities developed, it should be noted that 14 of the 27 participants (one of the three teachers in Activity 1, four of the five in Activity 2, two of the five in Activity 3, and all seven in Activity 4) in the 2017–18 training course had already participated in the training course held at the beginning of 2016. The 3rd cycle and secondary school teachers could not have participated because enrollment was only open to preschool and primary school teachers.

Of the 14 teachers who participated in both courses, 10 belonged to Escola Básica Artur Alves Cardoso (Primary) or Jardim de Infância Artur Alves Cardoso (Kindergarten). Activities 2 and 4 involved teachers who, in addition to the initial training in 2016, had been involved in the development of the project for about two years, having participated in the creation and development of the school newspaper (in December 2016), as well as in the planning and development of regular activities of Digital Citizenship Education.

4.3.2 Assessing Teachers' Work

The 27 teachers planned and implemented seven Media Education activities, which involved 485 children and students (54 from preschool, 245 from primary and 186 from secondary), but also family members and other community members. All teachers were able to develop the activities without having to change the general planning they had organized at the beginning of the school year, which is a clear indicator of the teachers' ability to include Media Education activities in their regular teaching activities. Moreover, all activities achieved, to a greater or lesser extent, the required results: a media product and a report.

It should be noted here that this training resulted from the identification of training needs by the teachers who had been participating in the project since 2016. Importantly, it attracted teachers from other schools and grades, which points to the existence of similar training needs felt by other teachers in other schools. The results of the work revealed changes in relation to the 2016 training course, not only on the part of the 14 teachers who attended both courses, but also on the part of the other participants. These changes occurred at the following levels:

1. *Collaboration between teachers from different levels of education*—in the first course, teachers formed working groups by level of education, and there was only one group that brought together preschool and primary school teachers, which accentuated the concern of the OECD (2017) with the lack of continuity between the two levels of education. In the second course, although not in a generalized way, this was addressed. For example, Activity 1 was developed by a preschool teacher, a primary school teacher, and a Special Education teacher. Activity 3, the preschool and primary school students participated in a school activity and discussed the same subject as their primary school classmates ("What do we need to attain happiness?"). Also, in Activity 6 ("Think before you post") students from 3rd cycle, secondary and Vocational Education collaborated.
2. *Collaboration between teachers from different schools*—in the first course, teachers formed working groups by school, and did not form groups with teachers from different schools though they all belonged to the same school district. In the 2018 course, the situation changed due to contextual issues. Activity 2 involved teachers from three different kindergartens: three from Alves Cardoso, one from another kindergarten of the Caneças School District and one from a kindergarten in Lisbon who knew her colleagues[3]. Activity 5 was developed by two teachers of Portuguese, working in two different school clusters, both in Odivelas Municipality[4]. Although they had the option of working independently, they preferred to work together.
3. *Cooperation between students from different levels of education and contexts*— The collaboration between teachers from different levels of education and schools allowed students from preschool and primary school to collaborate

---

3 This teacher had worked in 2015/2016 in the kindergarten where the project takes place and, although she changed schools at the end of that school year, to a school in Lisbon, she wanted to attend the training course, as she considered it important for her pedagogical performance.
4 The municipality of Odivelas, north of Lisbon, is organized into four parishes, and the Parish of Ramada and Caneças, in which there are three school clusters, is one of these four.

in joint activities, such as collecting data, producing a wall newspaper and distributing pamphlets in the community (Activity 1), discussing common themes (Activity 3, Activity 5), producing a collective text (Activity 6) or even collaborating in different subjects in 3rd cycle and secondary school (ICT, Portuguese and Mathematics in Activity 6; Portuguese and Geography in Activity 7).

4. *Involvement of the local community in activities*—In the first course, community involvement was restricted to the nuclear family, who participated by allowing children to use their digital equipment in classroom activities, or in the selection of news or advertisements to analyze in class. In the 2017/18 course, this involvement was more extensive, especially in activities in which teachers who participated in both courses were involved. In Activity 1, children collected data from the population, and not just from their relatives, about waste recycling at home and the quality of the waste recycling service provided by the municipality. The wall newspaper produced was shown to the parents and a flyer on the topic was made and distributed in the community, alerting them to the need to recycle. In Activity 4, the children agreed to answer a questionnaire about attitudes they would take in certain situations of bullying and other violence but asked the teachers to adapt the same questionnaire for parents. The results were then analyzed, compared, and they produced a collective text for the school newspaper, which was accompanied by the graphs with the results. Also in Activity 4, children's relatives and other community members helped each child to select the news story that caught his/her attention the most, so that he/she could then participate in the selection of news stories for the TV news service they produced.

5. *Lack of equipment is no longer a central issue and the use of digital resources increased significantly*—The lack of equipment, especially technological equipment, was one of the limitations pointed out by teachers for not carrying out Media Education activities using digital resources. Even so, it was possible to carry out at least one activity, with the support of parents who made their equipment available. In the second course, although there was a lack of equipment in preschools and primary schools, teachers did not consider this a key issue. For example, Activity 4, in which students produced a TV News service, the teachers used their personal cell phones and a school computer. In Activity 3, the school already had radio equipment, which was an important improvement. In 3rd cycle and secondary school (Activities 5, 6 and 7) the necessary technologies existed for students to be able to research, edit, publish and disseminate their productions.

6. *The focus on production instead of just media content analysis*—In the first course one book was produced, using only pens and paper, and the other activities were more focused on content analysis, from media such as news, advertisements, or photographs. In the second course all the activities included actual production of media content, which necessitated analysis of, or reflection on, the way professionals produce media content. This aspect was more noticeable in the activities involving primary and secondary school students, who structured the production and sequential presentation of four murals for an anti-bullying campaign (Activity 7), produced memes drawing attention to sexting (Activity 6) and, after having analyzed in depth the structure of an opinion article, produced a text for the school newspaper with the arguments that resulted from the discussion about the pros and cons of the Internet (Activity 5). The production of content was, however, transversal: a wall newspaper, a letter and a leaflet (Activity 1), a story in drawings that became a PowerPoint story (Activity 2), two radio programs (Activity 3), the supplement of a school newspaper and a video information service (Activity 4). In addition, the production process was monitored and analyzed afterwards, as the product was not more important than the process.

7. *The will to intervene socially through the media became the rule*—In the first course, the activities were especially focused on the students, on their perceptions and opinions about the news, advertisements, and goings-on in the world, but less on participation and social intervention through media. This changed markedly from the beginning of 2016 to the beginning of 2018. The students wrote to the mayor to request more ecopoints for the village of Caneças (Activity 1), wrote a story in which they explained that arsonists should be arrested (Activity 2), shared their opinions about happiness, rights and responsibilities of citizens and the community through the school radio show (Activity 3) and pointed out a set of solutions to prevent and fight bullying situations through the school newspaper (Activity 4). The TV News service they produced allowed them to explain to parents and the community that children had difficulty understanding the news and were scared in many cases, so it was necessary to talk to them about these issues (Activity 4). In the 3rd cycle and secondary school level, students tried to intervene through the media they use most—namely social network sites—especially through the production of memes about sexting (Activity 6). The main focus was on the school community (and not on the extended local community), either by producing

murals in physical support to combat bullying (Activity 7) or alerting to the pros and cons of the Internet in the online school newspaper (Activity 6). The intervention and the will to contribute to change were always underlying each of the productions.

4.3.4 Assessing the Training

As happened with the 2016 course, the training was evaluated by 24 out of 27 participants who filled the evaluation form from the Leonardo Coimbra Training Center of the National Teachers Association. On a scale of four items (from Very Good to Weak), 14 teachers evaluated the action as Very Good, nine as Good and one as Medium. The usefulness of the knowledge acquired (scale of four items from high to very little), 18 considered them very useful, five stated it was of some use and one considered them of little use. In the open-ended questions, the teachers pointed out three main results of the teacher training course:

1. *Improvement of pedagogical practice*—"The course was very interesting, showing us different resources and strategies for student success and for classroom dynamics, using ICT as a key resource in student motivation" (T1); "It allowed us to acquire knowledge and skills in the field of Media Education and in the use of the computer as a support tool for classroom work" (T14).
2. *Sharing knowledge with colleagues from different teaching levels*—"The possibility of sharing experiences with colleagues from different teaching levels was very interesting" (T6); "We contacted with several different levels of education and with different experiences" (T8).
3. *Media as a tool for teachers and students' learning*—"The training was very enriching, focusing on important aspects regarding the use of media to benefit school learning" (T2); "The course allowed us to work in vertical logic, that is, to develop good practices that promote joint learning for students and teachers" (T5).

The participants also mentioned that they were interested in attending more courses and trainings in Media Education, as well as in Environmental Education and Digital Citizenship Education. They also agreed that these training courses should adopt active methodologies, as happened in the 2018 training course, during which they planned and implemented classroom activities involving children, students and other community members.

4.4 Media Literacy, STEAM and Journalism (2020): The Training Plans Project

The training course "Media Literacy and Journalism: pedagogical practices with the media and about the media" (with 40 hours of which 20 were in-person and 20 were asynchronous work) focuses on the intersection of Media Literacy and STEAM. Explores the concepts and the relationship between them in international standards of training citizens and national policies, in which the trainees are based to plan and implement workshops, following the methodology of project work, linking them with the educational project of the school and the curriculum plans.

Accredited in 2018 by the Scientific and Pedagogical Continuous Training Council, for teachers of the 3rd cycle of basic education and Secondary, the training course approaches other content related with elements and principles of journalism, ethics and deontology, misinformation, democratization of information and exercise of active and responsible citizenship through the media. In 2019, it was adapted, by the research team, to be given for the first time, to preschool and primary school teachers.

The course implementation, within the scope of the project, was first scheduled for March 9, 2020, in person, but was canceled due to the measures taken to minimize the effects of the Covid-19 pandemic. The decision also resulted in the cancellation of the creation of a Makerspace on premises provided by the local government (Parish of Ramada and Caneças). This space would have held STEAM and Media Literacy workshops every fortnight, some of them with the presence of the children's relatives and other elements of the community.

The training ended up being delivered at a distance via the Zoom platform, in seven sessions between September and December 2020. The delay in delivery from March to September 2020 was to accommodate the teachers, who were focused on emergency distance learning, with all the resulting adaptations. There was no space to include training. Still, it was necessary to make important adaptations to deliver the training course, with five of the fundamental adaptations, namely:

1. *Format*—changed from face-to-face to online, with each session having a maximum of three hours, which increased the number of sessions from five (four hours each) to seven (six of three hours each and one of two hours);
2. *Cycles covered*—between January and March, data on socioemotional skills (pre-test) had been collected from children attending the 4th year of the primary school, which were carried over to the 5th year and continued at

Caneças School District, so enrollment was open to 2nd cycle teachers[5], with four enrolled;
3. *Number of trainees*—it was only possible to involve 30 applicants (one withdrew later), as the rules of the groups changed, from a minimum of 15 elements to a maximum of 15 participants per class;
4. *Contents*—the workshops would have to be planned and implemented according to the space of the classroom and not a Makerspace, which implied the adaptation of the contents of the training course;
5. *Data collection*—the limitations resulting from the Covid-19 pandemic prevented members of the research team from observing and evaluating the implemented workshops, so, together with the teachers, workshop observation and evaluation sheets were created for teachers and students;

The two editions of the training course started on the 16th of September (Group 1) and on the 23rd of September (Group 2), having ended, respectively, on the 17th of December and 16th of December 2020. 29 teachers participated (27 female and two male), with the following distribution in terms of levels of education: seven teachers of preschool education, 12 teachers of primary school (one librarian), four teachers from the 2nd cycle of basic education (three of Mathematics/Sciences and the other one of Visual Education), and six Special Education teachers.

4.4.1 Work Developed by Teachers, Involving Children, Parents and the Community

Participants were organized into two-element working groups (a group from Group 2 had three elements), each of whom would plan two workshops and implement one of them. The planning framework (Appendix A), which was created by a large group, includes: Title, Target Audience, Keywords, Purpose, Essential Learnings and/or Student Profile at Compulsory School Leaving, Learning Objectives, Description of the Activity, Prerequisites of the Teachers, Materials and Resources Needed, Resources to be Used in the Assessment of Learning, and the Workshop.

Teachers implemented 17 workshops (Table 4.3), totaling 230 hours and involving 410 children (197 females and 213 males). Five workshops focused on preschool education, eight workshops focused on the primary school, involving

---

5 2nd Cycle includes grades 5th and 6th, usually attended by children aged from 11 to 12 years old.

children from all grades of the cycle, and four focused on the 2nd cycle, with students from the 5th and 6th grades. Workshop 8 involved two classes, one 2nd Year and another 4th Year, which performed complementary tasks. Workshop 11 was developed with a class that included 3rd and 4th year students.

Three additional workshops were implemented in addition to the 14 originally planned, for logistical reasons. To implement Workshop 4, teachers needed the musical instruments produced in Workshop 2. The teachers who worked on road safety (Workshops 11 and 12) planned together but developed autonomous projects in different schools. Two teachers from the 2nd cycle (attended by students aged 10–12) advanced with the two planned projects (workshops 16 and 17) in response to the students' requests.

Table 4.3: Workshops implemented, by level, contact hours and number of students

Nº	Workshop title	Level	Duration	Participants
1	Feeling the music	preschool	20	45
2	"Umbrella Stick"—percussion musical instrument	preschool	2	20
3	A Trip to the Solar System	preschool	40	18
4	"Once upon a time …"—Chinese shadow acting	preschool	25	20
5	The Giant Turnip—story illustrated and narrated by the children	preschool	10	21
6	Let's do experiments	preschool / Primary (year 1)	15	20
7	Geometry at Play	Primary (year 1)	21	47
8	Exhibition about the digestive system	Primary (year 2)	10	22
9	Geometric Solids: electronic quiz	Primary (years 2 and 4)	8	40
10	Portugal and its flags: the national and regional flags	Primary (year 3)	4	20
11	For a safe school: better streets!	Primary (years 3 and 4)	12	25
12	Road safety: from Caneças to Islamabad	Primary (year 4)	9	17
13	Number, light and color: making a video with children	Primary (year 4)	12	26
14	Ten fingers, ten secrets: building an articulated hand	2nd cycle (year 5)	4	4

Table 4.3: Continued

Nº	Workshop title	Level	Duration	Participants
15	"4 in a row: mathematical board game	2nd cycle (year 5)	20	7
16	Journalists with a future: news production about Environment	2nd cycle (year 5)	6	29
17	"Knitting ... stories": an interview from wire to wick	2nd cycle (year 6)	12	29
		TOTAL	230	410

	Class 1
	Class 2

Eleven working groups planned new workshops (Table 4.4), to be developed in the second semester (the school year in Caneças School District is organized in semesters) of the 2020/2021 school year. Some of the plans are extensions of those implemented, as is the case with Workshop 20, which consists of the dramatization of the story "The Giant Turnip," which the children recounted, in PowerPoint format, in Workshop 5.

Table 4.4: Planned workshops, by level of education

Nº	Workshop title	Level
18	Painting with magnets: concept of polarity	preschool
19	Puppets: educational characters	preschool
20	The Giant Turnip: role-playing	preschool
21	Dramatic expression through geometry	Primary (year 1)
22	Let's paint the music	Primary (year 1)
23	I know how to be healthy: a TV show	Primary (year 2)
24	From Egypt to the 21st century with SketchUp.com	Primary (years 3 and 4)
25	Geometric Solids: quiz in PowerPoint	Primary (years 3 and 4)
26	Daily TV news using a puppet theater stage	Primary (year 4)
27	"Trace": mathematical board game	2nd cycle (year 5)
28	The Human Body is a House: assembling its parts	2nd cycle (year 5)

	Class 1
	Class 2

In terms of continuity, Workshop 25 involved the inclusion of a game about geometric solids, which was created by two classes of primary (one of 2nd year and one of 4th year), even using electrical circuits from the Workshop 9. Likewise, the work of Workshop 28 focused on measures to support learning according to students' specific conditions, was an extension to the creation of an articulated hand in Workshop 14. Workshop 26 made use of resources expressly created for the implementation of the first workshops, as the "puppet theater stage" used in the Chinese shadow theater (Workshop 4) used in the production of daily TV news, produced together with the children in accordance with their interests. Workshop 27's goal is to reproduce the methodology use to create mathematical games in Workshop 5, as well as the availability of the game at school and the dissemination of news about the process.

Other plans included new experiences for the students, such as painting with magnets (Workshop 18), expressing with geometry (Workshop 21) and with puppets (Workshop 19), exploring emotions through painting and music (Workshop 22). Workshop 23 included the production of a simulation video of a cooking program, but its execution was not possible for technical reasons and due to the pandemic. Workshop 24 marked a foray into architecture through *SketchUp*'s 3D design software.

4.4.2. Constraints and Strategies to Overcome Them

Each teacher participating in the training courses prepared a final report which was organized into five areas: compliance with the planning (dates, hours, constraints and strategies to overcome them); evaluation (strategy and resources used), results (achieved, not achieved); and sustainability of the workshops after the training course and annexes (evidence and resources used). These reports were subject to content analysis, using the software *Atlas.ti*, and the results are presented below.

In the teachers' opinion, all the plans were fulfilled, although some of them required more time than initially foreseen (W3, W4, W11, W13, W16), and the time dedicated to the workshops was not linear but divided over time. As an example, only two workshops (W2 and W10) were started and concluded in the same month, in November. Almost every workshop underwent adaptations, because of constraints mentioned by the teachers, which we organized into five groups:

1. *Physical conditions*—"the extreme luminosity of the room" made it difficult to record the Chinese shadow theater video (W4), as well as "the outside noise at the time of recording" (W5).

2. *Conjuncture*—public health rules to deal with the Covid-19 pandemic meant that "on stipulated days for recordings, some children were absent" and had to be replaced (W5), that some students were prevented from working "at four-seater tables" (W6, W15), or that it was not possible to develop activities for some time ("the classes were in prophylactic isolation, from November 19th to December 9th").
3. *Resources*—the "absence of Internet access, which made research difficult" (W6, W9), the "network failures" (W7), the lack of a "camcorder and a photo and video editing program" (W8), "the reduced number of computer equipment," especially tablets, with which the activity "would have been easier to carry out, due to the possibility of 'dragging' on the *touch* screen" (W7).
4. *Children*—"the lack of autonomy of some elements of the groups" (W1) which "forced a very individualized support for the children" (W2, W4), with some finding it "very difficult to handle the mouse" (W7) and others quickly forgetting the work instructions, which "made it necessary to recall, at the beginning of each 45-minute session, the work objectives, the work done and what was to be done" (W16).
5. *Teachers*—research and selection of information and recording activities "would have been more productive if developed with smaller classes" (W8), as it is difficult to use certain equipment when "there is only one teacher to respond to all requests" (W7), and, at least in some cases, such as "in video editing techniques and even filming (…) the main obstacle was the lack of training in the area (…) so everything was done intuitively" (W13).

In addition to making more time available for activities, providing individual support and betting on the "positive reinforcement" of behaviors (W2), the teachers adopted several strategies, which we organized into seven areas, namely:

1. *Reflection and monitoring*—Strategies such as "the decision to film the rehearsals [Chinese shadow theater], showing the group its performance and [discussing] which aspects to improve" (W4), as well as "some moments of debate and reflection among students" (W8) regarding "knowing how to listen and explain in simple language and with practical examples" (W15). Among teachers, "reflection at each stage of the workshop process was also essential (…) always listening to the children's opinions (…) to show the group which aspects should be improved" (W2).

2. *Chain improvements*—"In order to try to overcome the problems (…) several simulations were carried out, which were evaluated and improved, until a consensus was reached. For example, the voices of several students were recorded, with the presentation of the PowerPoint, and subsequently evaluated, constructively, by everyone, until reaching an approval of what was the final recording" (W13); "We proceeded to read each student's work, making constructive considerations (…) In the end, students were asked to rethink their work and rewrite it" (W16).
3. *Interdisciplinarity*—"this work [the responsibility of two Mathematics teachers who attended the training] was mostly developed during Visual Education and Technological Education classes with the collaboration of Professor Eduardo Abrantes," having also involved "the Workshop Creative and Experimental classes" (W15).
4. *Collaboration between students*—"one way to overcome the constraint felt was to divide the work group, including children with less autonomy in partnership with the more autonomous ones" (W1), encouraging work in pairs who then "presented their observations for the whole class group" (W6).
5. *Use of teacher resources*—"videos (…) were viewed through the teacher's mobile phone" (W6, W8), which was also used to "do research, photographs and videos" (W9).
6. *Work beyond hours*—because the number of students in the class is high, "collaborative work was developed between the teachers, who collaborated outside their hours, in the sense of having one more adult in each class to carry out the task" (W7); "The part related to the report referring to the workshop took place in an afternoon when the students had no teaching activities, with the presence of the teachers (…) , for about 3 hours " (W15).
7. *Families and community support*—"some links were shared with the students, so that they could watch at home with the help and supervision of the Parents" (W6), with the "involvement of families" (W17) being important to support the "Internet research" (W9), and "at home, together with their family, they researched the topic and brought to school what they thought was important" (W8). Other elements of the community supported the workshops, such as "Mr. Saraiva [whose collaboration in creating the model of the solar system] (…) was invaluable in achieving our goal" (W3).

In summary, in spite of the Covid-19 pandemic, in which physical and technological resources were lacking, the teachers implemented strategies to overcome the lack of autonomy of many students, especially younger ones, while also supporting each other when time or even technical knowledge was an obstacle (ex.: video editing).

These strategies consisted, above all, of frequent and joint reflection among the teachers and with the students, creating conditions for gradual improvement of the work carried out. That was done by teachers, with their own resources, and through giving up their personal time and involving families and other members of the community.

4.4.3 Assessing Teachers' Work

The implementation of the aforementioned strategies contributed to the results achieved, which were subject to regular monitoring among teachers, including through the training course sessions. The evaluation carried out throughout the process was also focused on the observation of "situations, attitudes and actions" (W5) of interest, participation and commitment (W10), communication and collaboration, creativity and critical thinking (W14).

The "oral feedback from students" (W15), "through conversations in large/small group meetings and individual conversations" (W5), the completion of evaluation sheets on the covered content (W7), the presentation of papers (W8) "the children's productions (…) and the spirit of observation" (W3) were other elements of evaluation. The final assessment was carried out using self-assessment forms for children in preschool education (Annex III, IV, V and VI), primary school and 2nd cycle of basic education (Annex VII) and for teachers (Annex VIII).

Following the assessment process, teachers identified six types of strengths in the workshops:

1. *Start from the interest of the children*—"it took as its starting point the interest and curiosity of these children in finding out more about the solar system " (W3); "music is popular with children in general, translating into an effective interest" (W1); "the strength of the activity was that it aroused a lot of interest in the children" (W5); "This project is very engaging (…) as it responds to questions that are raised by the students themselves and is built little by little, at the pace of their curiosity" (W17).
2. *Focus on practical and real situations*—"the STEAM approach, with practical resources, allowed (…) the implementation of a practical activity, the construction of an articulated hand" (W14); students were engaged "in the search for pollution situations [in the context of the community] and the appropriate photographic record" as well as the discussion

of topics such as "the pandemic, the importance of environmental protection, the sustainability (…) the importance of being a critical citizen regarding the environment that surrounds them (…) [and the] information that the media delivers" (W16).

3. *Foster interdisciplinarity*—primary school teachers highlighted that the workshop implied "the articulated construction of knowledge in which the different areas were addressed in an integrated and globalizing way" (W3), as they worked "content common to three disciplinary areas, Study of Environment, Portuguese and Education for Citizenship" (W12), in addition to having developed "a set of interdisciplinary activities in the subjects of Mathematics, Art Education and Information and Communication Technologies" (W7); in the 2nd cycle, the "and involvement of various disciplines (Portuguese, Citizenship, Visual Education, Technological Education…)" allowed "the students find solutions to the problems raised" (W17); the workshop also enhanced " the relationship between various areas of knowledge, namely Portuguese and Natural Sciences, in addition to Citizenship and Development" (W16) .

4. *Associate learning with playing*—"the most practical and playful activity motivated the students, making teaching/learning more fun and rewarding," keeping them "constantly motivated to continue learning, inside and outside the classroom" (W14); "The class is unanimous in saying that the students worked, but also had fun," showing "strong desire to create 'products'" (W17)

5. *Involve cooperation and collaboration*—primary school children "were very motivated to create maternities to colleagues from kindergarten" (W6) and "learn very easily when they are searching by themselves and when they hear the explanations from colleagues" (W8), that is, when they have the opportunity to develop "team work (…) because they helped each other in solving problems" (W13); thus, it is understood that, in the workshops "involvement, dynamics, mutual help, resilience, knowing how to listen and respecting the opinion of peers " were considered "strengths " (W15).

6. *Encourage participation and social intervention*—"Proposals for changes and improvements in the streets surrounding the schools" revealed their interest in "immediate intervention" in the sense of changing reality, of intervening socially (W11); "their writings [news] reveal a great concern with environmental issues and the need to alert the community to the protection of the environment and the change in attitudes/behavior" (W16).

Considering the learning objectives set out in the workshop plans, teachers considered the students to have learned content, skills and competences. They mentioned, for example, "the nomenclature of the instruments and their sound" (W1), "the concepts related to the shape of planet Earth, the planets of the solar system and their position in relation to the sun" (W3). They students also acquired "knowledge about geometric solids (…) , how to build and describe an electrical circuit" (W9).

In terms of skills and competences, the teachers pointed out "the structuring of an increasingly elaborate scientific thought" (W3), the "autonomy in their observations (…) and in the organization of records," the ability to identify "and solve problems starting from situations that surround them (…) reflecting on the results" (W6), the use of "computer tools (…) collaborative work and critical thinking regarding the work developed" (W7), for example in the "presentation of works" (W8).

The "development of the aesthetic sense, creativity and leadership" within the working group (W10) were other skills highlighted, along with "resilience" (W15):

> "Despite the limitations that these times raise, the development of this project has been very challenging, as students always have new questions and solutions for the obstacles that arise. The work focuses on the student and is, truly, a construction space." (W17)

Summarizing, evaluations of the workshops took place throughout the process, informally through monitoring and observation, and at the end of the process, through evaluation sheets for teachers and students, which were created during the training courses. In the opinion of the teachers, and in line with the scientific literature, the strengths of the workshops are due to the fact that they are based on the interests of children (Marsh et al., 2019), and that they are focused on practical and real situations (Council of Europe, 2018a; Ministério da Educação, 2017b; UNESCO, 2015a), which refer to problems whose resolution processes are more effective when they assume an interdisciplinary logic.

The practical tasks developed in the STEAM and Media Literacy workshops associate play (Marsh et al., 2019) and creativity to learning not only content, but also cognitive, social and emotional skills and competences. The tasks also encourage cooperation and collaboration between teachers, between students and between teachers and students, fostering resilience and persistence in seeking solutions or improvements to a product (Diego- Mantecón et al., 2021). They can also be seen as key initiatives in terms of participation and social intervention.

4.4.4. Workshops Media Products

Similar to what is common in Media Literacy and STEAM projects, one of the goals of the workshops was to create products (Diego- Mantecón et al., 2021), which happened in all of them. Teachers were provided complete freedom of choice in terms of the type of products, support and methodology followed in their preparation, with some being more associated with the production of multimedia content, and others being associated with science (STEM) and the Arts.

We have organized the multimedia-related products into five categories:

1. Videos about the final product (W2, W4);
2. Videos describing the process (W1, W3, W6, W9, W12, W13, W15, W17);
3. Photo slide show (W8, W10, W14);
4. *PowerPoint* file as final product (W5);
5. *PowerPoint* file describing the process (W7, W11, W16).

The videos about the final product feature the musical instruments constructed by teachers and children from preschool Education (W2) that were used to simulate the sound of rain in the Chinese shadow theater, whose final performance was also recorded (product of W4).

In eight of the 17 workshops, videos were produced that describe the process, such as the exploration of a book ("A Symphony of Animals," by Dan Brown), using digital technologies, the creation of instruments from simple materials (ex: xylophones, using open-end wrenches and cardboard) and the interpretation of "Turkish March" by Mozart, with the students organized in an orchestra formation (W1). Other examples of process videos are:

- The creation of a model of the solar system in 3D, using simple materials (styrofoam balls ...) and electrical circuits (W3);
- The creation of a "kit" for bean growth, by students from the 1st year of primary, who proceeded to record their progress after germination and produced "kits" which they offered to students in preschool education at the same school (W6);
- The creation of geometric solids on cardboard (2nd Year of primary school) and the production of a game with questions about the characteristics of these solids, to which an electrical circuit (4th Year) was associated with a green or red light, depending on the student response to card questions being right or wrong (W9);

- Exploration of the work "Why don't animals drive?," by Pedro Seromenho, and subsequent study of traffic signs, including those around the school, whether in Caneças or Islamabad, Pakistan, where some students of Portuguese Non-Native Language are from (W12);
- Production of objects allusive to the seven days of the week, seven musical notes and seven colors of the Rainbow, using an electrical circuit in one of the cases, followed by choreographed interpretation of the song "7 days, 7 notes, 7 colors," by Maria de Vasconcelos (W13);
- Production of the game "4 in a row," cross-curricularly, with Mathematics, Visual Education and Natural Sciences (W15);
- Preparing a script and organizing an interview with a non-teaching staff member of the school and conducting this interview, followed by writing and preparing for publication (W17).

The slideshows were an option in three workshops, namely the preparation of an exhibition on the digestive system, which included a 3D work (W8), the production of the national flag and the flags of the Madeira and Azores archipelagos (W10) and the production of an articulated hand, involving four students in need of accommodations to support learning due to their specific conditions (W14).

PowerPoint files were used in four cases, the first as a final product, in which preschool students produced drawings for each of the slides and told the story "The Giant Turnip," by Aleksey Tolstoy, allowing the user to choose between listening to the story told by children or by an adult, or listening to both and comparing.

The other three files describe processes such as using the computer to build geometric figures (W7), building a model with proposals to improve road safety around the school, and writing a letter to the micro-local government (Parish of Ramada and Caneças) and another to the Municipality of Odivelas (W11), as well as research on the situation of environmental pollution in the community and production of news on these cases in conjunction with the Sustainable Development Goals (W16).

The products of the workshops were kept in their original versions, without any professional editing, and the teachers produced them without having access to any training or technological equipment other than those they had access to before the beginning of the training course. These authentic products (which only underwent minor changes to protect the data and identity of children) were uploaded to a YouTube channel, created for this purpose, and can be accessed directly from the link: https://bit.ly/3AsnROH

In addition to the multimedia products the workshops allowed the creation of other products, which we have organized here into seven categories:

1. *Musical instruments* created by children to interpret Mozart's Turkish March (W1) and to simulate sound (W2) in Chinese shadow theater;
2. *Models*, namely the solar system (W3), the proposed improvement of road safety around the school (W11), and *3D objects*, such as the puppets of the Chinese shadow theater (W4), materials for the music choreography "7 days, 7 notes, 7 colors," by Maria de Vasconcelos (W13), and the articulated hand (W14);
3. *Drawings* produced to be included in *PowerPoint* with the story "The Giant Turnip" (W5);
4. *Strategies for using software/hardware*, either to produce human or other geometric figures (W7) or the use of robots in educational activities associated with road safety (W12);
5. *Exhibition of products*, namely posters on the digestive system (W8) or the flag of Portugal, the Madeira Archipelago and the Azores Archipelago (W10);
6. *Games and experiments*, such as the creation of the bean maturity "kit" (W6), the game about geometric solids (W9) and the "4 in a row" game, which stayed at school, in the space of mathematical games (W15);
7. *Journalistic text*, like the one of the maids about cases of environmental pollution in the Caneças' community (W16) or about what life was like at one of the non-teaching staff member's grandma's time (W17).

Summarizing, the 17 workshops allowed the creation and availability of two types of products, some in reflective production of media content, and others associated with STEAM, with a clear focus on the arts, but in which science, technology, engineering and mathematics were present. These indicators point, in our opinion, to the fact that STEAM projects gain in relevance when associated with Media Literacy activities, and vice versa.

4.4 5 Evaluation of Workshops from the Perspective of Children

Teachers were free to use, or not, the workshop evaluation forms that were created for the children, though in only three cases, they were not used. Workshop 2 was evaluated by the children together with Workshop 4. Workshops 12 and 14 involved students in need of accommodations for their specific conditions, so the evaluation was carried out through dialogue.

In the other 14 workshops, four of the five sheets created during the training course were applied, identified here on by the annex number that they assume in this book:

- *Appendix C*—A4 form for preschool, in which the children were asked to draw what they liked most about the workshop.
- *Appendix C*—A4 form for children in preschool education, which divided the sheet into two parts. On the left side, children were asked to draw what they liked most about the workshop, while on the right side they would draw what they liked the least;
- *Appendix D*—A4 form, in which the students, on a three-level scale (None, More or less, Much) and painting their emoji, expressed their position in relation to nine statements, such as:
  o I enjoyed participating in the workshop;
  o I enjoyed working in groups with my colleagues;
  o I learned new things;
  o I helped my colleagues to solve problems;
  o I didn't give up in the face of difficulties;
  o I felt that my opinions were important to my colleagues;
  o I worked, but I also had fun;
  o We created something new;
  o I would like to participate in more workshops like this.

They were then asked to draw what they liked best, on the back of the sheet.

- *Appendix E*—Form with a first part similar to Annex VI, followed by a second part with four open questions:

  o How did this Workshop come about?
  o Put the stages of this workshop listed below in chronological order;
  o From everything you learned in the workshop, what was the most important learning for you? Why?
  o Do you have any other ideas for a new work to develop after this workshop?

The forms, referred to in Table 4.5 according to the number they assume as appendixes to this book, were applied unequally.

Table 4.5: Use of workshop evaluation sheets (children)

No	Workshop title	Level	Evaluation form
1	Feeling the music	preschool	Appendix C
2	"Umbrella Stick"—percussion musical instrument	preschool	Appendix D
3	A Trip to the Solar System	preschool	Appendix D
4	"Once upon a time ..."—Chinese shadow acting	preschool	Appendix D
5	The Giant Turnip—story illustrated and narrated by the children	preschool	Appendix D
6	Let's do experiments	preschool / primary (year 1)	Appendix D
7	Geometry at Play	primary (year 1)	Appendix D
8	Exhibition about the digestive system	primary (year 2)	Appendix D
9	Geometric Solids: electronic quiz	primary (years 2 and 4)	Appendix E
10	Portugal and its flags: the national and regional flags	primary (year 3)	Appendix E
11	For a safe school: better streets!	primary (years 3 and 4)	Appendix E
12	Road safety: from Caneças to Islamabad	primary (year 4)	Not applied
13	Number, light and color: making a video with children	primary (year 4)	Appendix E
14	Ten fingers, ten secrets: building an articulated hand	2nd cycle (year 5)	Not applied
15	4 in a row: mathematical board game	2nd cycle (year 5)	Appendix E
16	Journalists with a future: news production about Environment	2nd cycle (year 5)	Appendix E
17	"Knitting ... stories": an interview from wire to wick	2nd cycle (year 6)	Appendix E

	Class 1
	Class 2

The two forms that only involved children's drawing (Appendix C) were applied in the evaluation of a workshop (W1). The form on which children painted emojis to position themselves in relation to statements and drew what they liked the most (Appendix D) was used in the other four workshops at the preschool level (W2, W3, W4 and W5) and in three workshops (W6, W7 and W8) which involved children who attended the 1st and 2nd year of primary.

The 2nd Year of primary school marked a frontier because Workshop 9, which involved children from the 2nd and 4th year, used a single evaluation form, the one in the Appendix E, which would also be used in all other workshops that were evaluated by the children, including those from the 2nd cycle. Also, in the 2nd cycle, it should be noted that the form used in the evaluation of Workshop 17 (Appendix E) was adapted by the teacher, including an image and more questions.

Regarding the results, we carry out a tripartite analysis, depending on the forms used. In the case of Workshop 1 (Photos 4.1 and 4.2) and in the analysis of the teachers, "what most pleased the children was the handling of the mobile phone in the exploration of the book A Symphony of Animals by Dan Brown , which uses augmented reality and allows listening to music by pointing a smartphone camera at pages." From another perspective, "some [children] mentioned that the downside was the time they were seated, as well as the sound of some musical instruments (ex.: xylophone)."

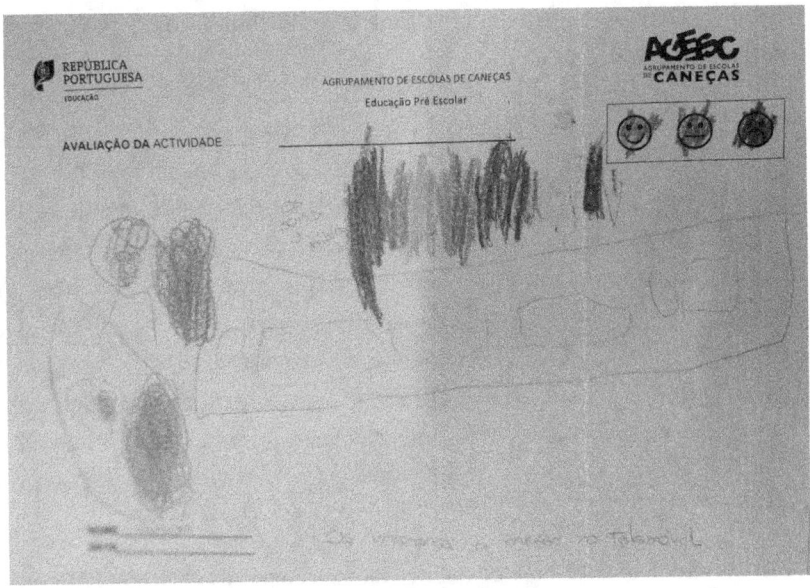

Photo 4.1: Workshop evaluation form for preschool children_ A - Appendix C

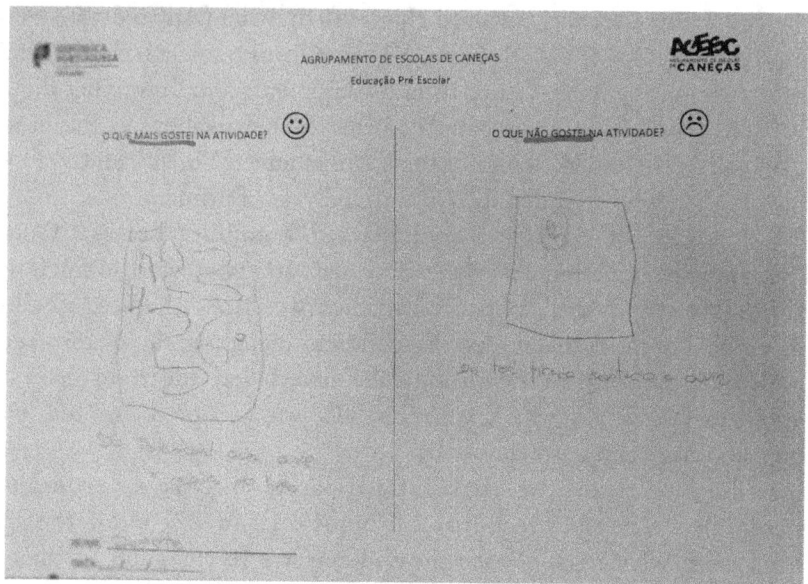

Photo 4.2: Workshop evaluation form for preschool children_ A - Appendix C

For the analysis of the evaluation of Workshops 3 to 8, by the children, we counted all the quantitative data that were made available by the teachers, either in their reports or in the attached documents, having managed to obtain 125 responses, which allow us to conclude that the children enjoyed participating in the activities (Graph 4.3):

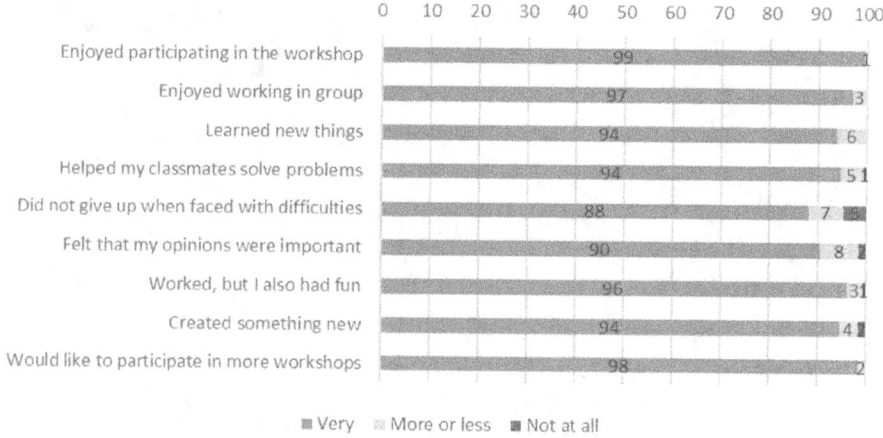

Graph 4.3: Evaluation of workshops by children through Appendix D (%) (n=125)

PREPARING TEACHERS TO WORK WITH THE ENLARGED COMMUNITY | 93

The 125 children considered here enjoyed, more or less, working in groups as they learned new things and are further available to participate in additional workshops. The vast majority felt that they worked, but also had fun (96%), that they helped their colleagues solve problems (94%) and that they created something (94%). It is also important to understand the reasons for there being a fringe of children who responded differently. From the teachers' perspective, the children had difficulty in understanding some statements, which can justify these answers, similarly to what happened with the statement "I didn't give up in the face of difficulties" which, "because I was in the negative, I was not understood" (W3). Finally, 10% of the children felt that their opinions were not important to their peers (2%) or only partially (8%), but the teachers stated that this type of response was more common among children who "are less participatory" (W6).

In the third and last area of the children's workshop evaluation, we focused first on the answers that allowed quantitative analysis, followed by a qualitative analysis (selection of student expressions). We were able to gather responses from 158 children, all of whom enjoyed very much (94%), or more or less (6%), participating in the STEAM and Media Literacy workshops (Graph 4.4).

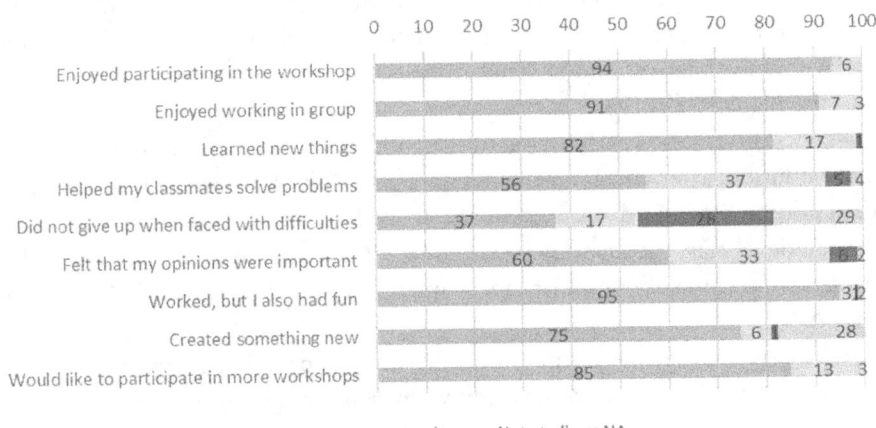

Graph 4.4: Evaluation of workshops by children through Appendix E (%) (n=158)

Similarly, children of the 3rd and the 4th year of the primary school, as well as the 2nd cycle of basic education, considered that they worked, but also had fun, and enjoyed working in groups and would like to participate in future workshops like those in which they had already participated. Their responses align with children of preschool education and the first two years of primary school, although with different percentages of total agreement regarding having learned "new things" and having created something. It is important to mention here that the 28 respondents in this item were all involved in the same workshop.

Students were, however, more critical in relation to the assessment of their performance. In response to the fact that only 56% of children consider that they helped their colleagues to solve problems, teachers did not have an explanation. Further, it is difficult to infer what the students mean by "help colleagues to solve problems" because the answers may even be related to the difficulty in identifying the problems themselves or when they were, in fact, part of the solution. The statement "I didn't give up in the face of difficulties" may not have been understood as explained above, and therefore needs to be reformulated.

After analyzing the answers to the open questions in the form, available in Appendix D, we found that the children always attributed the origin of the workshop to the teachers' ideas, even when this did not happen. For example, Workshop 17 consisted of preparing, conducting and writing an interview with an educational assistant who lent the school a patchwork quilt during an exhibition of traditional objects. The students were interested in the blanket, and they wanted to know the history, and that is where the workshop was born, as explained by the teacher who developed it. However that was not what the students understood, as can be seen from a student's response to the form: "The session came when teacher Natália saw the blanket and showed it to us, and we were curious to hear more about the blanket" (W17).

Workshop 16 also was born out of the children's interest in socially intervening about pollution, after watching the documentary "The Disposable Pandemic," but most children attributed the idea of the workshop to the teacher, which led her to conclude: "From the answers given, some students seemed confused as to how the workshop came about, but there is unanimity on the central theme – pollution" (W16).

With more or less difficulty, the children managed to correctly order the phases of the workshops, having valued various aspects, such as:

1. *Content*—"It was learning that there was more than one flag of Portugal, as I did not know that there were several flags and that they changed over time" (W10); "Traffic signs are very important because we need them" (W11) or "the colors of the rainbow, the lyrics and music of the song" (W13); "It was learning how to live in the old days because, apart from living with people from that time, I had no knowledge of most of the 'ancient history'" (W17).
2. *Technical skills*—"The most important learning was the letter, because we are doing something very important" (W11); "Making

a *PowerPoint*, not making mistakes on the recordings and recognizing our voices on the recordings, though they sound different" (W13).
3. *Social skills*—"From everything I learned in the workshop was friendship, group work and creativity" (W10); "It was working together with my colleagues" (W10); "knowing how to solve problems together" (W13); "I learned to work better in a group" (W16); "The most important thing for me was to learn from mistakes and live with colleagues" (W16); "M. Lurdes said everything sincerely, even when someone asked her about her education background, she replied : '6th grade'" (W17).
4. *Social intervention*—"Union is strength, because all together we can change the streets" (W11, workshop on road safety); "What I learned the most was the topic of the news because we have to alert people to what is happening" (W16); "The most important learning for me was to alert people about pollution" (W16).

In summary, the forms created by the teachers so that children could evaluate the workshops were adapted to the respondents, despite the diversity of ages. They are important on two levels: to give children a voice and to improve, both the following workshops and the evaluation sheets themselves.

It is essential that workshop facilitators be free to use, adapt, or neither, the created evaluation sheets, or even to use other and other workshop evaluation strategies. The responses showed that children in general liked the workshops, wanted to participate in more, liked to work in groups, and liked to have fun and to learn "new things."

However, children did have some difficulty in recognizing situations in which the initiative was theirs, as well as whether they helped their peers in solving problems, or in realizing whether their opinions are listened to and respected. Similarly, they recognized without difficulty that they learn in these workshops not only content, but technical skills, social skills and even ways to intervene socially.

4.4.6 Results Analysis in the Light of the National Policy Educational

The 'Students' Profile by the End of Compulsory Schooling' (Ministério da Educação, 2017b) is a central document of the Portuguese Education Policy, defining the core values, attitudes and skills that students shall develop through their compulsory education (12 years). The document is in line with international models for training citizens, as we explain in the first section of this book ("Empowering citizens shall start in the crib"). It is then a useful document to have in mind during the analysis of work developed during the workshops.

The two training courses that form the basis of this section were carried out with teachers from schools in the Portuguese education system, within the scope of the training center of the Director-General for Education. In this sense, wanting to relate the work developed in the workshops with the competences that a 21st century citizen must develop, we consider the option of crossing the 'Students' Profile by the End of Compulsory Schooling' to be appropriate, as it is the document that explicitly refers to the respective competences by area.

Before an analysis by area of competence, we focus on two cross-cutting issues: transdisciplinary and changing pedagogical practices. In the first case, the interdisciplinary character of the workshops mentioned by the teachers of the 2nd cycle: (i) Mathematic, Visual Education, Technical Education and Creative Workshop and Experimental in W15; (ii) Portuguese, Natural Sciences and Citizenship and Development at W16; (iii) Portuguese, Citizenship, Visual Education, Technological Education at W17). Also in primary: (i) Mathematics, Art Education and Information and Communication Technologies at W7; (ii) Study of the Environment, Portuguese and Education for Citizenship at W12.

In the second case, the change in pedagogical practices was explicitly mentioned by the teachers, who pointed out the need to include the media in learning, "as a way to find common areas of work" (W13) of:

> "developing professional practices that allow teachers to meet the Student Profile when leaving compulsory education implies that teachers take ownership of the document and change the way they operationalize and evaluate the curriculum" (W13).

Teachers also mentioned six types of measures taken to address constraints that emerged during the workshops: (i) reflection (among teachers, and between students and teachers) (W2) and monitoring of workshop activities (W8, W15), including use of autoscopy (W4); (ii) use of simulations (W13) and collective reassessment of work (W16); (iii) formation of heterogeneous groups (W1); (iv) use of technological resources owned by teachers (W6, W8, W9); (v) overtime work, in addition to school hours (W7, W15); (vi) resorting to support from families (W8, W9, W17) and other community members (W3).

These measures allowed the organization of projects focused on global issues (ex.: road safety, W11 and W12; environmental sustainability, W16), adapted to the student's daily life, sociocultural and geographic environment (ex.: traffic changes around the school; soil and water pollution in the community). The search for answers and/or solutions implied the integration of transdisciplinary content (ex.: production of the electronic quiz on geometric solids, W9; production of game "4 in a row." W15) the use of different sources of information (the surveys were transversal) and information and communication technologies (the creation of multimedia products was transversal).

Students also had the opportunity to cooperate, collaborate, debate and participate in monitoring, evaluation and decision-making. Therefore, to a greater or lesser extent, proposals to change the pedagogical practices explained in SPECS were implemented. It remained open how the activities' progress in terms of personal, social and emotional skills, would be reflected in the final semester assessment. However, either observational or oral assessment, as well as the application of workshop assessment sheets to students, under a self-report regime, would have been important contributions. It is important to emphasize that the files were organized by the teachers themselves.

We have now established a relationship between the competences referred to in SPECS, by competence area, and the work carried out in the workshops, also taking into account the products created and the lessons learned, from the perspectives of both teachers and students. We took into account the 17 workshops developed, which we consider as a whole, as we prepared a project document, which had the objective of contributing to reflection and improvement, instead of simply focusing on what could have been done.

Table 4.6: LM/STEAM relation with languages and texts

Competence area: Languages and Texts	LM/ STEAM
Use proficiently different languages and symbols associated with those languages (native and foreign), literature, music, arts, technology, mathematics and science;	X
Apply these languages appropriately to the different contexts of communication, in analogue, digital, formal and non-formal environments;	X
Master nuclear comprehension and production skills within an oral, written, visual or multimodal perspective.	X

The use of languages and symbols (Table 4.6) associated with the mother tongue was transversal to the implemented workshops, involving the exploration of books (W1, W4, W5), music (W1, W2, W4, W13), arts (ex.: Chinese shadow theater from W4), technologies (cross-cutting) mathematics (W7, W9, W13, W14, W15) and science (ex.: the W6 bean maturities, the W8 digestive system exhibition, the W16 photographs and pollution news). The languages were applied in digital and non-digital (ex.: the W8 digestive system exposition) contexts. The comprehension and oral, written, visual and multimodal expression were also transversal.

Table 4.7: LM/STEAM relationship with information and communication

Competence area: information and communication	LM / STEAM
Use and master different tools to research, describe, evaluate, validate and mobilize information in a critical and autonomous way, verifying different documentary sources and their credibility;	X
Turn information into knowledge;	X
Communicate and collaborate appropriately and safely, using different types of tools, following the suitable rules of conduct for each environment.	X

The area of competence referred in Table 4.7 is closely associated with Media Literacy. The development of the workshops involved research and description, but there is still a long way to go in terms of evaluation, validation and training. We believe, however, that the workshops, to a greater or lesser extent, favored the application of knowledge in new situations, including knowledge prior to schooling, which was acquired within the family or in other contexts outside of school (Marsh et al., 2019). Collaboration using different tools was common (W6, W8, W13, W15), as well as the development of technical skills associated with the use of media, such as writing a letter (W11) or creating a *PowerPoint* (W13). Students' progress in the "presentation of work" (W8) was also mentioned.

Table 4.8: LM/STEAM relationship with reasoning and problem solving

Competence area: Reasoning and problem solving	LM / STEAM
Plan and conduct research;	X
Manage projects and make decisions to solve problems;	X
Develop processes, using different resources, that lead to the construction of products and knowledge.	X

Regarding reasoning and problem solving (Table 4.8), the children engaged in conducting research, for example in relation to the solar system (W3) or what life was like in their grandparents' time (W17), participated in the monitoring and management of projects (ex.: monitoring the growth of beans in the W6 maternities) or making decisions to solve real problems (ex.: writing to the local government demanding more road safety around the school, in addition to presenting solutions, in W11). They created products using diversified resources (see subsection "Products from the workshops") and created knowledge, for example, about the flag of Portugal and the flags of the autonomous regions (W10), traffic signs (W11), colors, numbers and musical notes (W13).

Table 4.9: LM/STEAM relation with critical and creative thinking

Competence area: Critical and creative thinking	LM / STEAM
Think broadly and deeply, in a logical way, observing and analyzing information, experiences and ideas, arguing by means of implicit or explicit criteria in order to take a reasoned position;	X
Call for different kinds of knowledge (scientific and humanistic knowledge), using different methodologies and tools to think critically;	X
Foresee and evaluate the impact of their decisions;	X
Develop new ideas and solutions within an imaginative and innovative approach, as a result of the interaction with the others or of personal reflection, applying them to different contexts and learning areas.	

Considering critical and creative thinking (Table 4.9), the teachers considered that the children analyzed certain issues or situations (how the joints of one hand work, in W14; road safety around the school, in W11; what situations of environmental pollution there were in the community, in W16), having thought critically about them, in the sense of finding multidisciplinary solutions, creating models (W11, W14), writing letters (W11) or preparing news (W16) in order to intervene with policy makers. However, these decisions will have implied reflection on their impact. Two teachers also mentioned the students' progress in terms of "critical spirit regarding the work developed" (W7).

Table 4.10: LM/STEAM relationship with interpersonal relations

Competence area: Interpersonal relations	LM / STEAM
Adapt behaviors to contexts of cooperation, sharing, collaboration and competition;	X
Work in teams and use different means and environments, namely computers, to communicate and work in person or in a network;	X
Interact with tolerance, empathy and responsibility as well as argue, negotiate and accept different points of view, developing new ways of being, looking and taking part in society.	X

The children established interprsonal relations (Table 4.9), enjoyed working in groups ("From everything I learned in the Workshop was friendship, group work and creativity," W10) and considered that they also had fun doing it, since they communicated in person, although there is still a way to go here, as teachers are committed to finding solutions for carrying out online activities.

They also had the opportunity to present their opinions, although 10% of the youngest (preschool education and the first two years of primary school) considered that their opinions were not taken into account by their colleagues. The teachers, however, felt that the opinions of the students were respected. Ways of participating in society were also thought out and implemented: "Union is strength, because all together we can change the streets" (W11); "What I learned the most was the topic of the news because we have to alert people to what is happening" (W16).

Table 4.11: LM/STEAM relationship with personal development and autonomy

Competence area: Personal development and autonomy	LM/ STEAM
Relate knowledge, emotions and behavior	X
Identify areas of interest and the need to acquire new competences	X
Consolidate and deepen the competences they already have, within a perspective of lifelong learning	X
Set goals, draw plans and projects and be autonomous and responsible in their implementation	

Having in mind personal development and autonomy (Table 4.11), the teachers considered that the workshops were based on the children's interest ("it took as its starting point the interest and curiosity of these children to find out more about the solar system," W3; "This project (...) responds to questions that are raised by the students themselves," W17). They also consider that the children managed to associate learning and playing, because the practices were structured in this sense (W14, W17), having also shown a willingness to implement projects and "great willingness to create 'products'" (W17).

Even when the children unknowingly chose what they wanted to do, they considered that the decision was made by the teachers, which, in the opinion of the teachers, may result from the fact that they did not understand the ways in which choices were registered on the board (avoiding repetitions on the board, for example, may have implied that not all choices were recorded). Furthermore, the teachers highlighted, as students' progressed, the "autonomy in their observations (...) and in the organization of records," the ability to identify "and solve problems based on situations that surround them (…) reflecting on the results" (W6).

Despite this perception, the vast majority (over 90%) of children who attended preschool education and the first two years of the primary school, and more than half (56%) of the rest, considered having helped their peers to solve problems. or creating something new (94% and 75% respectively). One teacher also highlighted the fact that students "always have new questions and solutions to the obstacles that arise" (W17).

Table 4.12: LM/STEAM relationship with well-being, health and environment

Competence area: Well-being, health and environment	LM/ STEAM
Adopt behaviors that promote health and well-being, especially regarding daily habits, food, physical exercise, sexuality and their relationship with the environment and society	X
Understand the balances and weaknesses of the natural world adopting behaviors that address the major global environmental challenges;	X
Develop environmental and social awareness and responsibility working collaboratively for the common good, aiming to build a sustainable future.	X

Although there are no hierarchies between the areas of competence defined in the Profile of Students upon leaving Compulsory Schooling, we consider the area of well-being, health and environment (Table 4.12) to be fundamental. Although it is directly related to the third of the Sustainable Development Goals ("Health and well-being"), we consider it to be transversal, which we can justify, for example, as the central objective of the learning compass (OECD, 2020).

Two of the workshops were directly related to the skills referred to in this area, one focused on food (W8) and the other on soil and water pollution (W16), thus contributing, albeit modestly, to the development, by children, of the aforementioned skills in this area.

Table 4.13: LM/STEAM relationship with aesthetic and artistic sensitivity/awareness

Competence area: Aesthetic and artistic sensitivity/awareness	LM/STEAM
Recognize the specificities and intentions of different cultural manifestations;	X
Experience processes within the different art forms;	X
Critically appreciate the artistic and technological realities by being exposed to different cultural universes;	
Value the role of various forms of artistic expression, as well as of the material and immaterial heritage in the life and culture of communities.	

Considering aesthetic and artistic sensitivity/awareness competence (Table 4.13), the workshops mainly provided experiences in the areas of music (W1. W13), theater (W4), drawing (W5), photography (W9, W16), video (W6, W12, W15), plastic expression (W1, W2, W3, W8, W10, W11, W13, W14), reading (W1, W4, W5), writing (W11, W16, W17), and expression through the media (W15, W16, W17).

One teacher pointed out, as a result of the workshop, the "development of the aesthetic sense, creativity and leadership" (W10). The children experimented, therefore, with different forms of art, and the diversity in terms of production was greater than that which occurred in terms of exploration. The sharing of these productions with the community was, however, very limited, and eventually it was not enough for children to value the role of these forms of expression in the culture of local, national and global communities.

Table 4.14: LM/STEAM relationship with scientific, technical and technological knowledge

Competence area: Scientific, technical and technological knowledge	LM/STEAM
Understand scientific processes and phenomena that enable decision-making and the participation in citizenship forums	X
Manipulate materials and diverse tools in order to control, use, transform, imagine and create products and systems	
Perform technical operations, following a work methodology, aiming to achieve a goal or to get to a reasoned decision or conclusion, aligning the material and technological resources with the expressed idea or intention	
Adapt the action of products transformation and creation to the different natural, technological and sociocultural contexts, within experimental activities and practical applications in projects developed in physical and digital environments	X

Science-based decision-making took place in the 2nd cycle (production of the mathematical board game "4 in a row," W15; sensitizing the population not to pollute, W16), in primary school (the creation of a bean maternity kit, W6; production of an electronic *quiz* on geometric solids, W9) and even in preschool education (design and production of a model of the Solar System, W3).

However, despite having been pointed out as a result of the workshop "the structuring of an increasingly elaborate scientific thought" (W3), the development of competences in the area of scientific, technical and technological knowledge (Table 4.14) are still be far from the level desired, which are not unrelated to various limitations, such as the lack of technological equipment, Internet access, resources to carry out experimental activities, and the impossibility of some group dynamics, for reasons of public health.

Table 4.15: LM/STEAM relationship with body awareness and mastery

Competence area: Body awareness and mastery	LM / STEAM
Perform motor, locomotor, non-locomotor and manipulative activities, within the different circumstances experienced in the relation of his own body to the space	X
Master the perceptual motor skill (body image, directionality, perceptual fine motor skill and spatial and temporal structuring)	
Be self-aware at emotional, cognitive, psychosocial, aesthetic and moral level so as to keep a healthy and balanced relationship with oneself and others	

The children were mainly involved in manipulative activities (ex.: exploration of an augmented reality book, using a mobile phone, W1; manipulation of Chinese shadow theater characters, W4; production of objects to be used in workshops, W3, W8, W9 and W13; production of models or games, W11, W14), which included the use of technological equipment (W7). It is not to be considered, given the results found, that the two other competences in this area have been sufficiently worked on during the workshops.

Having in mind that aspects such as the fact that the workshops have been held within a workshop training that was suited to online, implemented in a complex environment due to the pandemic and were not accompanied on the ground by the research team, it is our perception that the activities will not have contributed to the development, by the 408 children involved, of all areas of competence referred to in Table 4.15. However, comparing between areas, these contributions would have been uneven.

If, according to the data analyzed and the results obtained, the activities developed contributed to the development of all competences in the five areas (Languages and texts; Information and communication; Reasoning and problem solving; Interpersonal relationships; Well-being, health and environment), the same cannot be said in relation to the other five areas, as, in each of them, there was at least one competence that was not addressed, namely:

- *Critical and creative thinking (1)*—"Develop new ideas and solutions within an imaginative and innovative approach, as a result of the interaction with the others or of personal reflection, applying them to different contexts and learning areas,"
- *Personal development and autonomy (1)*—"Set goals, draw plans and projects and be autonomous and responsible in their implementation."
- *Aesthetic and artistic sensitivity (2)*—"Critically appreciate the artistic and technological realities by being exposed to different cultural universes"; "Value the role of various forms of artistic expression, as well as of the material and immaterial heritage in the life and culture of communities."
- *Scientific, technical and technological knowledge (2)*—"Manipulate materials and diverse tools in order to control, use, transform, imagine and create products and systems"; "Perform technical operations, following a work methodology, aiming to achieve a goal or to get to a reasoned decision or conclusion, aligning the material and technological resources with the expressed idea or intention."
- *Body awareness and mastery (2)*—"Master the perceptual motor skill (body image, directionality, perceptual fine motor skill and spatial and temporal structuring)"; "Be self-aware at emotional, cognitive, psychosocial, aesthetic and moral level so as to keep a healthy and balanced relationship with oneself and others."

In summary, eight of the 34 competences were not addressed in the scope of the 17 workshops developed, which invites a discussion with the teachers in order to understand the reasons why this did not happen, and whether they are related to the level of education (in the case of preschool education), with limitations resulting from the context, the themes of the workshops or others. It is also important to find strategies to contribute to the development of all skills, in a logic of equity, since there are no areas or skills more important than others.

4.5 Assessing the Training

The two sections of the training course took place between September and December, in seven sessions each (one of two hours and six of three hours), on Wednesdays at 4pm. The theoretical contents focused on Media Literacy, STEAM and the relationship between them, having explored articles and other scientific literature, examples of activities and sharing of results. Evaluation sheets, workshop structures and final reports occurred in large groups, with part of the time dedicated to discussion and reflection on the planning and implementation of workshops, to evaluation and the presentation of results.

4.5.1 Trainees' Perspective

The evaluation of the training course, by the teachers, was carried out through an online questionnaire and the final reports produced. The questionnaire consisted of three closed and three open questions. All trainees (n=29) responded by class, although the data are presented together. The first closed question requested the evaluation of seven parameters through a scale with values between 1 (totally disagree) and 5 (totally agree), with the results being available in Graph 4.5:

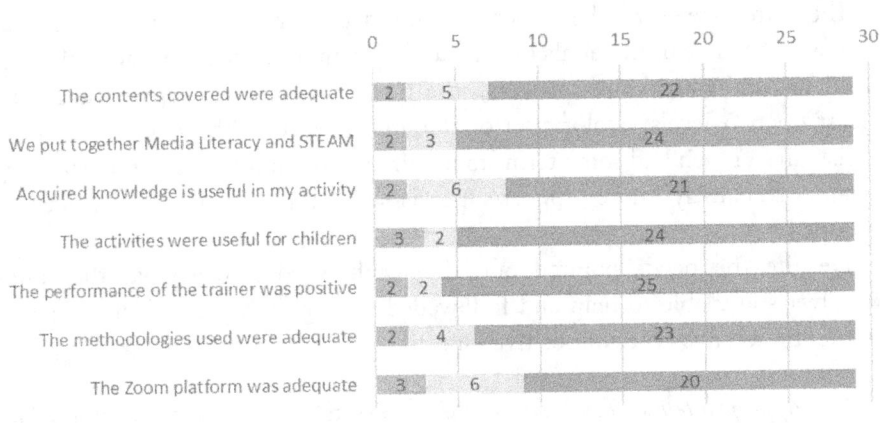

Graph 4.5: Evaluation of the training course by trainees (n=29)

We conclude that the trainees/teachers earned a positive overall assessment regarding the contents, the relationship between the contents and the application of these contents in the teaching activity, although the latter is one of the two in which the total agreement is lower (21). The activities developed in the scope of the workshops were considered useful for the children, although five of the teachers did not fully agree.

In terms of the implementation of the training course, the teachers evaluated the trainer's overall performance positively, but the level of total agreement is lower when evaluating the methodologies used (six teachers selected the value 3 or 4) and even lower when evaluating the platform used (Zoom). In two sessions (1 and 5) there were problems with access, which were, however, solved in good time.

However, the assessment of the suitability of the platform will have been influenced by other reasons, as was clear from the open-ended answers regarding the question "aspects for improvement." Teachers said that it will be "important to have a physical presence in schools," that is, "in-person training," which, in their view, should "be open to a greater number of students." One teacher even stated that this type of training should take place continuously, involving teachers from all education cycles "so as to ensure vertical continuity."

From the teachers' perspective, the constraints arising from the pandemic "may be overcome," so "the dynamics of work in the classroom can improve without these constraints," including practical examples: "I would like to have developed an activity more related to Experimental Sciences. This did not happen due to the constraints we faced caused by the pandemic."

There are, however, other aspects to improve. Although the trainer has provided "a vast source of materials for the development of educational activities" that helped to "understand the contents," the truth is that more support is needed, at least on two levels: exploration of resources, because "the documentation in English and French had some terms more difficult to understand," and technological support, namely "more support/supervision on the IT/digital in the activities developed."

Despite the needs pointed out, the teachers considered that the trainer "was always available to help and followed the work with great interest," having also mentioned five types of positive aspects:

1. *Appropriateness of the workshop theme*: "suitability of the theme and adaptability to the pedagogical practice."
2. *Sharing experiences, ideas and practices*: "sharing" and "exchanging professional experiences" and "pedagogical practices," as well as "ideas of work to be carried out with students," either between trainees or between participants and the trainer. "The sharing strategy between colleagues from different cycles throughout the sessions also proved to be useful and enriching."

3. *Cooperation and interdisciplinarity*: "collaborative work, whether between trainees or between trainer and trainees" and "communication between the different schools in the group and between the different levels of education," along with "interdisciplinarity in project work."
4. *Usefulness of learning*: they were "relevant for classroom practice" and for "day-to-day school," either the "knowledge" about "the importance of Media in the classroom, even in preschool" and the need to "understand the STEAM methodology and cross this knowledge with the Media." The activities allowed the students to "develop skills and learning in a practical and autonomous way," in addition to "going towards the Essential Learnings and being motivating for the subjects involved."
5. *Creation of resources*: "it allowed the creation of useful materials for pedagogical practice."

In addition to these aspects are aspects for improvement, some of which were mentioned in the third open question ("Other comments"). It is important to mention that we collected from the answers to the other closed questions in the questionnaire, unanimous responses: the duration of the training course was "adequate" (and not insufficient or excessive) and all trainees want to continue to collaborate in the "Digital Citizenship Academy" project, even though participation in the training did not imply such a decision.

4.5.2 Evaluation of the Training Course from the Trainer's Perspective

As a trainer and researcher at the 'Digital Citizenship Academy', it was crucial to find a form of assessment that would contribute to reducing the natural evaluative subjectivity of those who are in the midst of a process that has to assess. In this sense, we resorted to a teacher training assessment strategy that we had proposed in 2018, following an assessment of 10 years of continuous teacher training in Media Literacy and Digital Citizenship (Tomé, 2018). We translated into Portuguese the analysis framework developed at that time, which we reproduced below, in three blocks, answering briefly to each question, according to the results mentioned above.

Table 4.16: Analysis of continued teacher training—LEVEL 1—organization

Level 1 – Organization	
Trainees/teachers were able to:	
(a) Organize Media Literacy activities with their students?	Yes
(b) Organize themselves in small working groups?	Yes
(c) Organize groups involving teachers from different educational levels, scientific areas (interdisciplinary/ transdisciplinary)?	No
(d) Ask for the trainer's advice during the activities' development (e.g.: in person or through digital media)?	Yes
The trainer was able to:	
(a) Answer to teachers' requests in due time?	Yes

In terms of organization (Table 4.16), the teachers managed to organize 28 Media Literacy and STEAM workshops with their students, as the aim is for the starting point to be the children's interest. The 29 teachers were organized into 14 working groups, 13 of which had two elements and one with three elements.

The working groups were organized by level of education, with preschool teachers working with colleagues from the same level of education, and so on. The Workshop established a link between primary and preschool education, and Workshop 9 brought together students from the 2nd year and the 4th year of primary school. In addition, there was interdisciplinary collaboration, namely in primary school and in the 2nd cycle, but not between other cycles, at least explicitly.

The trainer was always available, even outside the synchronous training periods, as this was a commitment made right from the start of adapting the training course from face-to-face to online. And the trainees/teachers frequently contacted the trainer, namely via email, mobile phone and WhatsApp.

Table 4.17: Analysis of continued teacher training—LEVEL 2—Development

Level 2—Development	
Trainees/teachers were able to:	
(a) Develop Media Literacy activities with their students?	Yes
(b) Overcome the lack of resources (if it was the case)?	Yes
(c) Integrate those activities in their previous pedagogical plans without major changes?	Yes
(d) Ask for the trainer's advice during the activities' development (e.g.: in person or through digital media)?	Yes
(e) Involve other people in the activities (e.g.: parents, local community …)?	Yes
The trainer was able to:	
(a) Answer to teachers' requests in due time?	Yes

Focusing on development (Table 4.17), it was the aim of the workshop for each working group to implement one of the two planned workshops, but three of the groups decided to implement both for logistical reasons. Therefore, 17 were implemented.

Although the project has its own resources, its implementation has been done gradually, depending on needs, and was limited due to the lack of certain equipment in the market. The teachers used their own resources, supported each other and even worked overtime, in order to overcome the lack of resources.

All activities developed within the scope of the workshops were aligned with Essential Learnings of Basic Education (Ministério da Educação, 2018a). This was, in fact, a condition mentioned at the beginning of the training course, as we did not receive any feedback on any difficulty in integrating the activities into what was already planned.

The teachers regularly requested the trainer's support, usually through digital media, and the trainer responded in good time. They also involved the children's parents in some activities (e.g., online research), as well as other people in the community (e.g., a community member who helped preschool teachers and children in the production of the model of the solar system (W3).

Table 4.18: Analysis of continued teacher training—LEVEL 3—assessment

Level 3—Evaluation	
Trainees/teachers were able to:	
(a) Produce a thorough report on the activity (structure: activity name, time used, objectives, data on students involved, procedure, results and outputs)?	Yes
(b) Critically evaluate the weaknesses and strengths of the procedure, identifying remediation strategies?	Yes
(c) Critically evaluate the in-service teacher training course?	Yes
The trainer was able to:	
(a) Improve the in-service teacher training course having in mind the teachers' evaluation?	Yes
(b) Produce a leaflet or handbook based on the teachers' reports in order to disseminate the practices developed? Are the practices replicable?	Yes
(c) Produce a thorough report on the in-service teacher training course?	Yes

In terms of evaluation (Table 4.18), the trainees/teachers not only prepared the reports, but also actively participated in the creation of the structure of this report, which was approved in a large group, considering the two classes here. All reports followed a structure and presented evidence of the work developed, as well as products of that work, both multimedia and of other means.

As results of the data analysis carried out, the trainees/teachers mentioned the constraints that emerged during the workshops and indicated the strategies implemented to overcome them, in addition to pointing out other possible remediation strategies, as they did in relation to the in-service training course.

The trainer, together with the trainees, and based on the reports produced by them, organized a document to disseminate the implemented practices, as well as the practices still to be implemented, the first being replicable, taking into account the teachers' perception (see 6.3 Sustainability plan). The trainer also produced a report of the training course for the Director-General for Education, for which a reserve was kept.

Based on the three sources referred above, the training course will shortly be improved for future editions. These will be implemented on behalf of the national project "Media Literacy and Journalism," run by professional journalists who were trained and certified as teacher trainers before having started training teachers countrywide, and supporting schools planning and implementing Media Literacy projects. This partnership not only guarantees the continuity of the implementation of more editions of the training course, but also the necessary involvement of journalists in Media Literacy projects (Tomé, 2019).

In summary, the training was positively evaluated by the teachers in terms of content, methodologies, duration and technical support used, although there is a general feeling that the situation resulting from the pandemic prevented the achievement of more significant results. Teachers agreed that this type of training should be more frequent, but with physical presence in schools, reaching more students. This presence may also be useful in terms of supporting the exploration of scientific literature and the use of technological resources. In all, the training course was suitable to pedagogical practices, provided an opportunity for sharing of experiences, practices and ideas, fostered cooperation and interdisciplinarity, and resulted in useful resources.

The trainer concluded that the training courses fulfilled the requirements in terms of organization, development and evaluation. The only criterion that was not met was that the working groups should have included teachers from different levels of education and areas of specialization. Teachers organized and implemented Media Literacy and STEAM activities, overcame a lack of resources, integrated activities into previous planning without having to make significant changes, and involved students' families and other elements of the community in these activities. They used the trainer's support, even outside the synchronous activities, prepared activity reports and evaluated the training through a questionnaire. The trainer produced a report and organized, with the trainees, a manual for the dissemination of best practices, properly framed and evaluated, thus bringing together conditions to improve the training course.

4.6 Data Summarized

The three teacher trainings held throughout the project were attended by a total of 79 teachers (25 in 2016, 25 in 2017/18 and 29 in 2020), with about half (41) belonging to primary school, followed by the group of preschool teachers (25), 3rd and 2nd cycle teachers respectively, as shown in Table 4.19:

Table 4.19: Teachers' distribution by educational level and training course

	Preschool	Primary school	2nd cycle	3rd cycle / Secondary
2016	10	15	0	0
2017/18	8	10	0	7
2020	9	16	4	0
TOTAL	25	41	4	7

The predominance of the teachers of the initial levels of education was a consequence of the project itself, since the first training was only aimed at preschool and primary school teachers. The second training, as it aimed to contribute to fill training gaps in terms of the production of media content, was open all schools of the Municipality of Odivelas and to all levels of education, what explains why teachers from 3rd cycle and high school participated.

The third course was only aimed at preschool and primary school teachers and should have taken place in March 2020. However, due to the closure of schools because of the Covid-19 pandemic, it was postponed until September. This postponement caused a problem, as the 'Digital Citizenship Education Academy' project included the collection of data on social-emotional skills, through pre- and post-test questionnaires for preschool and primary school students.

The pre-test occurred in January and the post-test was scheduled for June, after the STEAM and Media Literacy workshops. Thus, to keep these students involved in the project, it was necessary to invite 2nd cycle teachers in both the training and the project, which allowed these students to participate in the workshops and answer the post-test questionnaire in June 2021. This was the reason why four 2nd cycle teachers participated.

Of the 79 teachers who attended the training sessions, 69 belonged to the Caneças School District's four kindergartens, four elementary schools, and the middle and high school. Nine teachers worked in other schools in the Municipality of Odivelas. One teacher who participated in the 2018 training belonged to a school in Lisbon, but she had worked before at the Caneças School District and took part in the 2016 training.

Among the preschool and primary school teachers, two were librarians (one in 2018 and another in 2017/18) and six were special education teachers (one in 2016, one in 2017/18 and four in 2020). It should also be noted that the 79 participants correspond to 57 people, as some teachers participated in two or even in the three trainings, namely:

- Four participated in the 2016 and in the 2017/18 training courses
- Three participated in the 2016 and in the 2020 training courses

- Five participated in the 2017/18 and in the 2020 training courses
- Five participated in three training courses (2016, 2017/18 and 2020)

This data are key to explain the evolution of the project, as the five teachers who attended the three trainings are all from the Artur Alves Cardoso School, in which the community intervention project was born in 2016, right after the first training course. We consider them the backbone of the project, not only for the activities they have developed and are still developing, but also for their role in recruiting new teachers and other education professionals that arrived at Alves Cardoso School from September 2016 to date.

As an example, Alves Cardoso School has three preschool teachers, and in 2016 all three attended the training. At the end of the school year, two of them changed schools. The two teachers who replaced them attended the 2017/18 and 2020 training courses. The teacher who stayed attended the 2018 training, and is currently a key element of the project. As she stated, the number of places was insufficient for all those interested, which led her to forego signing up for the 2020 training.

A primary school teacher who also joined the school in 2017 attended the 2017/18 and the 2020 trainings. The librarian that arrived after 2018, attended the 2020 training. Thus, at the Alves Cardoso School, which has 10 teachers, only one temporary teacher who nevertheless actively participated in the Digital Citizenship Academy project did not attend the 2020 training. This data clearly helps explain the continuity of the project.

In terms of students involved in the activities carried out in the three training courses, the numbers reported by the teachers point to more than 1261 students, distributed according to Table 4.20:

Table 4.20: Students involved in the activities developed during teacher training courses

	Preschool	Primary school	2nd Cycle	3rd Cycle / Secondary
2016	147	219	0	0
2017/18	54	245	0	186
2020	103	238	69	0
TOTAL	304	702	69	186

Unsurprisingly, five out of six students involved in the training course activities attended preschool or primary school. Of the total number of students, 373 belonged to the Artur Alves Cardoso School, in which the project advanced after the 2016 training, while the remaining 888 attended other schools of the Caneças School District (about 700) or other school districts (about 200). We therefore consider that although the project, in specific terms, is centered on the Artur Alves Cardoso School, it is a project that encompasses all the 10 schools of the Caneças School District's four kindergartens, four elementary schools, a middle school, and a high school.

The Artur Alves Cardoso School, as can be seen in Chapter 6 of this book, is also the engine that ensures the continuity of the project between and beyond the teacher trainings. An evidence of its central role is the fact that a group of seven students who attended the preschool in 2015/2016 participated in the activities carried out during the teacher training held in 2016, 2017/18 and in 2020, during the latter as 2nd cycle students. In addition, since January 2016 and to date, about 200 students from the two levels of education (preschool and primary school) have been involved annually. Estimating that the average annual average of students leaving and new students joining is 50, in six school years about 500 students will have been covered in this school alone.

The training courses were marked by the space dedicated to practical activities, with a total of 68 hours (19 in 2016, 19 in 2017/18 and 60 in 2020) for a total of 130 hours[6]. They aimed to respond to community needs, as is evident from the work developed by the teachers, who organized themselves into small groups and, following the project work methodology, planned, implemented and evaluated practical activities that involved their students, but also, if only in some cases, other members of the community.

In the 2016 course, the focus of the activities was more on media content analysis (e.g. news, advertisements) and children's digital uses and practices (e.g. devices they used most and frequencies) and less on content production (only preschool children produced a rhyming book and another one about wild animals).

In the 2017/18 course, participants were explicitly asked to plan and implement activities that resulted in media products, as well as a report that included the planning, process description, and evaluation of the work developed. The seven groups were able to respond to the request, creating anti-bullying wall frames at school, content for school newspapers (one of them on the wall and another on paper) and a school radio show, creating memes about sexting and a video news service, and they even wrote to the local government to demand more ecopoints for the village of Caneças.

---

6 The total of 130 hours of training results from the sum of 25 hours of the 2016 course, 25 hours of the 2018 course, and the 80 hours of the workshops held in 2020, in two simultaneous editions (of 40 hours each), since each class could not have more than 15 teachers.

The two trainings held in 2020 were completely different from the previous ones, as they had a duration of 40 hours (instead of 25), smaller classes (15 teachers maximum), took place entirely online and required the teachers, themselves, to observe the students during the activities, because the prevention measures taken in the response to the pandemic prevented the research team members from being able to do this observation.

As the training now combined Media Literacy and STEAM, the focus remained on the production of scientific, artistic, technological, but also media content. Photography and video were now required resources to complement the production process. Therefore, media became a resource and a theme (e.g. production of news about environment, interview about community stories), as themes connected school and the world through music, theater, production of models, analog and electronic games, conducting experiments, exhibitions, and application of knowledge to improve the life of the local community (traffic conditions and lighting around the school).

As in previous training sessions, teachers reported that they had no difficulty including the workshops in their annual planning. In terms of the use of technological resources in the activities, an evolution was noted. In 2016, the scarcity of resources was a major issue, so most of the products of the activities were analog, with the exception of photographs and a PowerPoint. The solution, although only used in two cases, was to ask for the collaboration of families through a Bring Your Own Device (BYOD) solution.

In 2018, the lack of equipment continued, namely computers, tablets and Internet access (non-existent in two kindergartens), but teachers were able to overcome these difficulties, mainly using their personal equipment, and most of the activities became digital, including video in one case. By 2020, the lack of technological equipment (and reliable Internet access) was a central issue. Even when it existed, teachers pointed to students' lack of autonomy and difficulties in handling the equipment as major shortcomings. In addition, some teachers lacked ICT training.

The pandemic situation, the infections and the mandatory quarantine periods were another limitation, as they forced students, and also teachers, to alternate between home and school, which created additional difficulties. However, once again, they moved forward through trial and error, with the support of colleagues from other areas and levels of education, using their own resources and those of the students' families, working overtime, and fostering cooperation among students.

Cooperation between teachers grew in 2020 and became a common practice, not because the working groups involved teachers from different teaching cycles, but because the exponential increase in the use of technologies led many teachers to seek help from colleagues. Other reasons were the association of STEAM and Media Literacy, the need to link science and arts, as well as to produce videos of the process, and the collaboration between teachers who attended the training with others who did not.

In 2020, community involvement also increased. The workshops started from the children's interest and, whenever possible, focused on issues that were important to the school community and the local community (e.g. recycling, traffic, news stories …). They encouraged social intervention in order to change situations for the benefit of the community (e.g.: the letters written to the local government to improve recycling, as well as traffic around the school or even garbage collection).

Therefore, the students engaged in the activities and reached out to families and the community by showing what they had done at school, or by raising awareness in the community to work for the improvement of their situation (through word of mouth, and also through the YouTube channel created to disseminate the videos produced), contributing to the improvement of the country and the improvement of the planet. The project has thus reinforced its community character, when in previous training courses, this collaboration had passed through the provision of technological equipment by families (2016), and then evolved into participation in activities by answering a questionnaire or researching media content with the children (2018).

Finally, in relation to the evaluation of the training courses and workshops, the improvement of teaching practices was always highlighted by teachers as an important result, especially in the use of media and technologies in that practice. However, if in 2016 it was the knowledge of children's digital uses and practices that surprised them the most, in 2018 they referred mostly to the advantages of media and technologies in learning and in motivating students for that learning. By 2020, with the connection to STEAM, the use of technologies and media in activities became a necessity.

Knowledge and experience sharing was another result mentioned by the teachers. However, in 2016 it was just a natural byproduct of the process, while in 2018, teachers mentioned their interest in, and intentionality in, actively participating in more training actions on Digital Citizenship and on Media Education. Sharing was also expanded at three levels: (i) to the children, since the workshop themes or the social problems they intended to respond to were selected together with the children and according to their interests; (ii) to other teachers not involved in the training workshops, since the implementation of STEAM activities led the teachers to work cross-curricular; (iii) to the sharing of resources created within the workshops, such as the puppet stage, the electronic game about geometric solids, and the story of the Giant Turnip in PowerPoint, among others.

References

De Abreu, B. (2011). *Media literacy, social networking and the Web 2.0 environment for the K-12 educator*. New York: Peter Lang Publishing.

Chaudron, S. (2015). *Young children & digital technology: A qualitative exploratory study across seven countries*. Luxembourg: Publications Office of the European Union.

Chaudron, S. (2016). *Young children, parents and digital technology in the home context across Europe: The findings of the extension of the young children (0–8) and digital technology pilot study to 17 European countries*. DigiLitEY Project Meeting, 3., Lordos Hotel, Larnaca, Chipre, 17–18 May.

Council of Europe. (2018a). *Reference framework of competences for democratic culture*. Accessed from: https://www.coe.int/en/web/reference-framework-of-competences-for-democratic-culture/

Council of the European Union. (2012, 19 December). Council conclusions of 26 November 2012 on literacy. Official Journal of the European Union http://eur-lex.europa.eu/legal-content/EN/TXT/PDF/?uri=OJ:C:2012:393:FULL&from=EN

Cunningham, S., Dezzuani, M., Goldsmith, B., Burns, M., Miles, P, Henkel, C., Ryan, M., & Murphy, K. (2016). *Screen content in Australian education: Digital promise and pitfalls*. Brisbane: Digital Media Research Centre.

Diego-Mantecón, J., Blanco, T., Ortiz-Laso, Z., e Lavicza, Z, (2021). Proyectos STEAM con formato KIKS para el desarrollo de competencias clave. *Comunicar, 66*(XXIX), 33–43. Accessed from: DOI https://doi.org/10.3916/C66-2021-03

Frau-Meigs, D., & Torrent, J. (2009). *Mapping media education policies worldwide: Visions, programmes and challenges*. New York: UN Aoc.

Marsh, J. (2014). *Young children's online practices: Past, present and future*. Literacy Research Association Conference, Marco Island, USA. Accessed from: https://www.academia.edu/9799081/Young_Childrens_Online_Practices_Past_Present_and_Future

Marsh, J., Wood, E., Chesworth, L., Nisha, B., Nutbrown, B., & Olney, B. (2019). Makerspaces in early childhood education: Principles of pedagogy and practice. *Mind, Culture, and Activity, 26*(3), 221–233, DOI: 10.1080/10749039.2019.1655651

Ministério da Educação. (2017b). *Perfil dos Alunos à Saída da Escolaridade Obrigatória*. Lisboa: Editorial do Ministério da Educação e Ciência. Accessed from: https://www.dge.mec.pt/sites/default/files/Curriculo/Projeto_Autonomia_e_Flexibilidade/perfil_dos_alunos.pdf

OECD. (2017). Starting Strong V: Transitions from Early Childhood Education and Care to Primary Education. OECD Publishing, Paris. Available at: http://dx.doi.org/10.1787/9789264276253-en.

OECD. (2020). *PISA 2018 results (Volume VI): Are students ready to thrive in an interconnected world?*. PISA. Paris: OECD Publishing. Accessed from: https://doi.org/10.1787/d5f68679-en.

Palaiologou, I. (2016). Children under five and digital technologies: Implications for early years pedagogy. *European Early Childhood Education Research Journal, 24*(1), 5–24.

Pinto, M., Pereira, S., Pereira, L. e Ferreira, T. (2011). *Educação para os Media em Portugal: experiências, actores e contextos*. Lisboa: ERC.

Redecker, C., Ala-Mukta, K., & Punie, Y. (2010). *Learning 2.0 – The impact of social media on learning in Europe*. Luxembourg: Office for the Official Publications of the European Communities.

Rivoltella, P. (2007). Realidad y desafíos de la educación en medios en Italia. *Comunicar, 28,* 17–24.

Tomé, V. (2008). *CD-Rom "Vamos fazer jornais escolares": um contributo para o desenvolvimento da Educação para os Média em Portugal*. Unpublished PhD Thesis, Faculdade de Psicologia e de Ciências da Educação da Universidade de Lisboa, Portugal.

Tomé, V. (2018). Assessing media literacy in teacher education. In Melda N. Yildiz, Steven S. Funk, & Belinha S. De Abreu (Eds.), *Promoting global competencies through media literacy* (pp. 1–18). Hershey (PA): IGI Global.

Tomé, V. (2019). O papel dos jornalistas na criação de projetos de escola em Cidadania Digital. In Paula Lopes e Bruno Reis (Orgs.), *Comunicação digital: media, práticas e consumos* (pp. 183–215). Lisboa: NIPCOM. DOI: 10.26619/978-989-8191-87-8.9

UNESCO. (2007). *Paris Agenda or 12 recommendations for media education*. Accessed from: http://www.diplomatie.gouv.fr/fr/IMG/pdf/Parisagendafin_en.pdf.

UNESCO. (2015a). *Global citizenship education: Topics and learning objectives*. Paris: UNESCO. Accessed from: http://unesdoc.unesco.org/images/0023/002329/232993e.pdf

UNESCO. (2015b). *Keystones to foster inclusive knowledge societies – Access to information and knowledge, freedom of expression, privacy, and ethics on a global Internet*. Paris: UNESCO. Accessed from: http://www.unesco.org/new/fileadmin/MULTIMEDIA/HQ/CI/CI/pdf/Internet_draft_study.pdf.

CHAPTER 5

The Community in Action – From Printed School Newspaper to Video News Services

This chapter explains the project's evolution since the end of teacher training in February 2016 and the end of the 2020–2021 school year, which ended in July. We first mention how the intervention strategy came to follow a model developed by Sefton-Green et al. (2016) and the implications that such a decision had on the process. The chapter then presents the results of the data analysis collected in 2016, which justified the first phase of the intervention plan (September-December 2016), focused on the creation of a school newspaper that would be a vehicle for the promotion and implementation of Digital Citizenship activities in the Caneças community. After creating the newspaper and publishing the first issue, the teachers and researcher developed the second phase of the plan (January-June 2017), which consisted of organizing Digital Citizenship activities involving all students and teachers of the Artur Alves Cardoso School, as well as parents and other community members. The chapter continues to explain how the intervention plan was implemented in the field, how it was monitored, and it concludes with the results of the implementation, both from the teachers' and the researcher's perspective.

5.1 Refining the Community-Based Action Research Approach

Recognizing the need to develop children's digital literacy through the implementation of multidimensional projects that aim to create 'digital citizens' who can fully exert their "digital participation in society" (Ribble, 2011), we decided to design a participatory research project involving children aged 3–9, their families and teachers, as well as community organizations and decision makers, putting the focus on schools following a "whole-school approach" (Huber and Reynolds, 2014; Raulin-Serrier, Soriani, Styslavska and Tomé, 2020).

According to this approach, the school culture considers diversity and mutual understanding between cultures at the heart of all aspects of school life, from leadership, to management, to relationships between people involved. In fact, the EU Kids Online (2011) recommendations showed that school "should take a major responsibility for supporting children and their parents in gaining digital literacy and safety skills" (p. 58), which raises intergenerational questions that are also pointed as key-questions by Shamrova and Cummings (2017).

At the "action level" (Burns et al., 2011), our starting problem was: How can preschool and primary school children be empowered as digital citizens able to actively participate in communities (local, national, global), whether online or offline, in a responsible and safe way? The resources available were a certified teacher training course on Digital Citizenship Education for Democratic Participation, a trainer/researcher, some funding (an individual research grant from the Science and Technology Portuguese Foundation), and the availability of the local government to contact the school boards.

The proposed solution was training of preschool and primary school teachers, and progressive involvement of their pupils, families and the community. Our plan consisted of:

1. Presenting the training course and the project to the school boards of the municipality (Oct–Nov 2015)
2. Inviting teachers to enroll in the course (Oct–Dec 2015)
3. Implementing the course and asking the trainees to draw and develop Digital Citizenship activities with their pupils and their pupils' families (Jan–Feb 2016)
4. Assessing the trainees, the course itself, the trainer's performance, and the training process (Mar 2016)
5. Co-designing an intervention plan, based on the results and on collected data analysis (Apr 2016)

6. Inviting teachers to volunteer to continue working with us to plan and implement activities with children and families (Apr–May 2016)
7. Monitoring the activities and the intervention plan, on a regular basis, in order to improve it gradually, based on the feedback from the school and the community (including partners and stakeholders).

According to our plan, the project aimed to contribute to identify best practices in formal, non-formal and informal learning contexts, to influence public policies, to integrate Digital Citizenship education in the school curricula, and to be replicable elsewhere in Portugal and abroad.

At the "research level" (Burns et al., 2011), our starting query was: To what extent a community-based project can empower preschool and primary school age children in order to become active and effective citizens in the digital era? Our sub-questions were:

- How can in-service teacher training on Digital Citizenship education improve teachers' digital literacy practices in classrooms?
- What are the digital literacy practices of young children in school, family and community contexts?
- How do formal and informal learning contexts shape children's digital literacy practices?

Our hypotheses were:

- A concerted approach within the family, school and out-of-school contexts empowers preschool and primary school children to exercise an active and effective citizenship in the digital era.
- Teachers of preschool and primary school, provided they have access to training and support, can develop pedagogical practices and activities aimed at empowering children to be active and effective citizens in the digital era.
- Families can develop strategies to empower their children to exercise an active and effective citizenship in the digital era.
- Local community entities can develop strategies aimed to empower preschool and primary school children to exercise an active and effective citizenship in the digital era.

As was referenced earlier, the research methodology focused on a mixed-method approach (Creswell and Clark, 2013), relying on questionnaires (applied to teachers when the training course began, and from families, after the course, in order to characterize them), interviews (with children, after the training course, and with teachers who would be available to continue participating in the project after the training), field notes (during and after the training) and report analyses (produced by the teachers after the training).

The study has undergone frequent improvements as the authors followed a research model proposed by Sefton-Green et al. (2016), and inspired by authors such as Carrington (2013), Colvert (2015), and Green (1988). According to the model (Figure 5.1), there are three interrelated areas that form the basis of how the individual produces and receives media messages, whether in formal settings or in an informal context:

1. Operational – capacities and skills needed to read, write, and interpret messages from different media and its various platforms;
2. Critical – interaction with texts and digital products, seeking to answer questions related to power and agency, representation and voice, authenticity and veracity;
3. Cultural – concerns interpretations and actions that develop according to its involvement in digital literacy practices in specific social and cultural contexts.

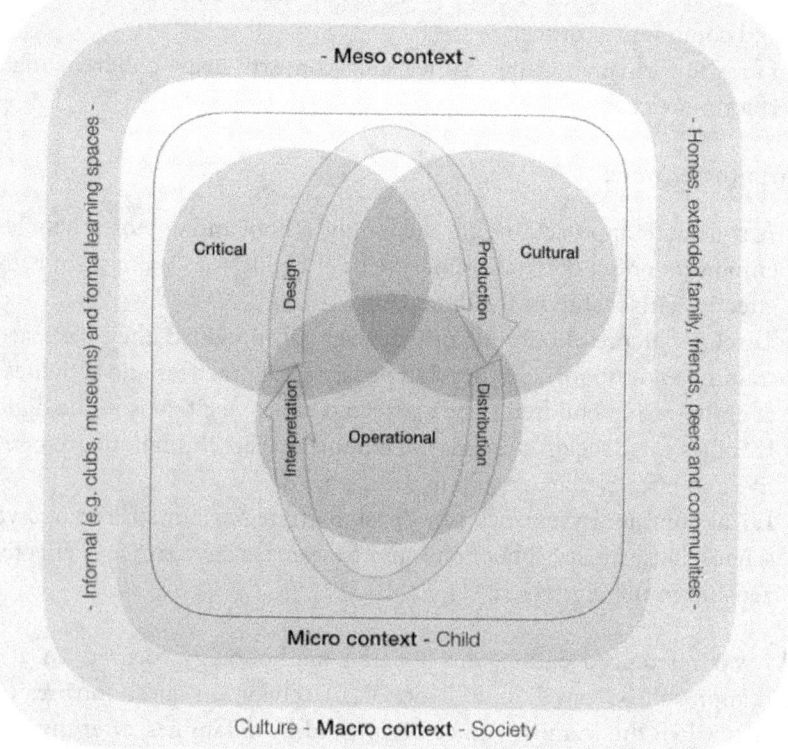

Figure 5.1: The processes of and contexts for children's digital literacy practices (in Sefton-Green et al., 2016, adapted from Colvert, 2015).

When a citizen wants, for example, to communicate a message, he/she draws on these three areas and makes decisions within the context of the following four levels: design (whether the message is multimodal or not); production (creation of the text); distribution (choosing the appropriate channels); and implementation (imagining how the receivers will interpret the message). All these processes take place within the frameworks that influence the digital literacy practices of children, including: micro (with the child), meso (formal and informal learning contexts with family, friends, and the local community), and macro (the nation state).

Similarly to the predicted model, our project design went from the micro to the macro framework. It aimed to intervene in micro and meso frameworks with children, teachers, families and the local community, focusing on the empowerment of children concerning digital literacy skills. As a whole, and given its characteristic replicable nature, our long-term aim is to have an impact on the macro framework.

Following a model keeps balance and consistency, but the use of technology results in fluidity, as it is multidimensional and changing rapidly (Carrington, 2013, quoted by Sefton-Green et al., 2016). Without disregarding balance and consistency, the research design was tailored to the local context, i.e., the project was very dynamic and subject to frequent rebalancing and reconfigurations in order to overcome tensions, incompatibilities, and to maintain the participants' active involvement.

5.2 Results Informing the Intervention Plan

Between April and June 2016, we worked with eight teachers, three from preschool, three from primary school, one library teacher and one teacher of Special Needs, all who worked at Artur Alves Cardoso School. One was 29 years old while six were between 39 and 49. The other teacher was 58 years old and was the only one who held a master's degree.

Those eight teachers developed Digital Citizenship activities with children between April and June. Preschool children, organized in groups of two, wrote words and explored these concepts in an activity called "Construction of Writing in an Interactive Situation." The primary school children were involved in two activities, one focused on deconstructing objects in order to analyze the raw materials used in their production, and the other organized in small working groups, focused on the analysis of news selected by the students and then retelling the news in a way that the classmates could easily understand.

It was the crucial to collect data from parents and children, in order to characterize the groups. After obtaining authorization from the administration of the Caneças School District, we went to the Artur Alves Cardoso School, to approach the guardians in their regular meetings held in April, when the 3rd term began. Our presence there had been agreed to by the teachers but not yet the parents.

Following guidelines from the Caneças School Board, the teachers asked parents whether we could talk to them for 10 minutes. All parents agreed and thus we explained the project and asked for their collaboration. While only a few had agreed to further participate in the project, it was already an important step, because following international studies, such as a study developed by Chaudron (2015), it was crucial to have a minimum of 10 families agreeing to participate.

The eight teachers also played another key role after the meetings, contacting parents directly, motivating them to agree to be interviewed and to allow us to interview their children. Even the other two teachers working at the Artur Alves Cardoso School, who had participated in the training course but chose not to continue in the project at this stage, contacted parents to facilitate trust between the families and us.

Between April and June 2016, we were able to collect data from 42 parents and 45 children, which far exceeded our expectations. However, since data had to be collected for the child and at least one guardian, we moved forward with only 38 children / parents. We interviewed 38 children (20 females and 18 males), of whom 22 were aged between four and six years old (preschool) and 16 were aged between seven and 10 (primary school). Six children had no siblings and lived in a single-parent household (with their mother). Eight children lived with both parents and no siblings, while the rest lived with both parents and at least one sibling.

The 38 parents who were interviewed (of whom, four were males) ranged in age from 27 to 46 years old, with the largest group being 36 to 40 years old (15 individuals). Only 12 parents had higher education qualifications. In terms of the household's average monthly net income, there were strong inequalities. Four families had an income of less than 600 euros, eight had an income of up to a thousand euros, 10 had an income of between a thousand and 1500 euros, and seven had an income of between 1501 and 2000. Only six had incomes of 2001 or more euros. Three preferred not to answer.

5.2.1 Media Use and Media Perceptions of Teachers, Children and Parents

Regarding media use, most teachers (22 of 24) and parents (30 of 38) used the Internet daily, while all children consumed the same amount of television (36 of

38, every day) and YouTube (although with varying frequency). However, this was not the case with digital games (3 of the 38 children did not play them) even though only five of them did not have access to the Internet at home. These reported practices were in line with the observation by Edwards, Nolan, Henderson, Mantilla, Plowman, and Skouteris (2016) that children consider three categories related to their everyday life and the Internet: "1. Family: Use of the Internet by and for family members/ 2. Information: To access and/or produce information/ 3. Entertainment: Enjoy movies/games for fun and/or relaxation" (p. 6).

The research also revealed that parents used the Internet via their smartphone the most (28 out of 38), followed by the children (18 of the 38) and the teachers (8 of the 24). Among the adults, the most used means to access the Internet was through their personal laptops. Among the children, tablet devices were the most popular (33 of the 38), with 17 also using the Internet through console devices. There was also clear evidence that the time children spent using digital equipment increased during the weekend. If, from Monday to Friday, three children did not use any digital device and 19 only used them up to an hour per day, they all used them on the weekend, with 12 using them up to one hour, 10 (instead of four during the week) using them for two to four hours and seven (instead of one during the week) for more than four hours.

According to the guardians, children had learned to use and access digital media from their mother (26 of the 38) and/or father (20), with other family members (12), or friends (2). Only one parent stated that his son had learned how to use the computer at school and nine stated that the child had learned on his/her own, which is consistent with learning through imitating adult practices, through trial and error, or learning through the games' interactive tutorials (Edwards et al., 2016). All guardians stated they watched television with their children and 34 stated that they went with them to the cinema (30 on the weekend). However, only 16 read books with their children and only 15 read newspapers or magazines with them. Parent mediation was lower when it came to the children's use of mobile digital media. While 31 stated they researched online with the children (26 solely on the weekend), only 14 played video games with them (13 solely on the weekend). When considering the parent's perception, parent mediation practices included restrictive (implying usage restraints) and active (implying debate with children) and joint use mediation (implying the use of both parents and children). Even so, it is important to exclude no mediation in some cases or distance mediation (use of media as a baby-sitter). However, there is no clear evidence of mediation through participatory learning, in which parents and children debate use, learn together, and define use strategies (Zaman, Nouwen, Vanattenhoven, de Ferrerre, and Van Looy, 2016).

All the teachers considered that digital media has pedagogical value, yet it was in these teachers' classrooms that media content was used sporadically. Around three out of four of the teacher respondents stated that they used media content in their teaching practices, especially printed newspapers (79%), magazines (83%), and films (83%), while two out of three stated that they used videos (67%), and one out of two used digital games (50%). Other media formats such as televisions, smartphones, or tablets were absent from their classrooms. Furthermore, if and when media content was used, the children's direct interaction with digital technology in the classroom was either weak or entirely absent. In this respect, the digital materials that are most preferred by European children under eight years of age is not made largely available in schools (Chaudron, 2016). The reasons for this infrequent use were explained by the teacher respondents as being due to the lack of time available for children to be able to use media and technology in the classroom (22 out of 24) (92%), the pressure to prepare students for exams, the lack of resources available to be used by students, and the lack of technical support in schools (22 out of 24 for all issues identified) (92%), the latter being the reason why most teachers said they totally agree (11 out of 24) (46%). Most parents agreed that children learn school content (30 of the 38) and non-school content (35 of the 38) through media, highlighting the importance of digital technologies in helping their children do their homework (especially parents of children attending primary school).

Nevertheless, while 33 out of the 38 parent respondents admitted to talking with their children about digital media, the conversations generally focused on limiting usage time and risk and focused less on encouraging informational usage, including for homework, and the advantages of online gaming. In brief, "even when holding negative attitudes towards digital media penetrating the home environment, parents seem to acknowledge beneficial uses" (Zaman et al., 2016, p. 15). This suggests that the "'digital generation' keep on being recalibrated" and the familiar context is "now entering a period where the parents of children born today might themselves very much come from a generation that itself had been labelled, digital" (Sefton-Green et al., 2016, p. 3). Even if parents are moving from beyond "the debate whether their children should or not use digital devices.......there are still some concerns on the use of digital devices that parents are finding themselves being 'confused' and 'without clear guidance'" (Palaiologou, 2017).

Finally, the results showed a lack of dialogue between teachers and parents regarding children's digital media use and practices (16 teachers admitted to having these conversations, while only seven parents answered similarly). When they communicated with each other, digital media was always negatively referred to (that it was used for too long, the potential for video game addiction, and the dangers of the Internet). Even the dialogue between teachers and students (referred to by 15 teachers but not confirmed by the children) allegedly occurred occasionally ('some days'), with teachers admitting to discussing these issues with children 'many days' or 'everyday'. This lack of dialogue may explain why teachers' perceptions of media practices and uses by children clearly differed from the perspectives of the parents.

5.3 Co-designing the Intervention Plan

The intervention plan was discussed and approved in September 2016. It was decidedly an exploratory plan, which followed a work in progress logic. Its main goals were to develop digital literacy activities involving the children's teachers, families, and their broader community, focusing on the operational, critical, and cultural areas when designing, producing, distributing, and implementing media messages. It was also decided to organize monthly formal meetings at school, apart from informal contacts when needed, as well as to start the publication of a printed school newspaper with four main objectives:

1. To reinforce the link between the school, the families, and the community
2. To ensure that the children have the opportunity to express their opinion through the media.
3. To reinforce children's critical thinking on the media and on social issues through the production of media messages.
4. To promote democracy at school and in the community, to advocate for human rights in general and children's rights in particular.

Although aware of the contradiction of having a project on Digital Citizenship based on traditional printed media, the team decided to start this way as a means of overcoming limitations, namely the lack of technological and trained human resources at the school, and the fact that some families (around 10% of the inquired ones) had no Internet access at home. The Parents' Association was formally informed of the draft plan during a meeting held on 7 October, during which all parents were invited to participate directly and/or support their children in participating.

A decision was made that the school newspaper would include diverse news stories from both the school and community, all selected by students and teachers, and each edition would have a central theme from which teachers would organize activities involving all students and, whenever possible, families and other community members. As the school year was organized in three terms (Sep-Dec, Jan-Mar, Apr-Jun), it was decided to produce three issues of the newspaper, one per term, and the following themes were provisionally defined: Being a digital citizen (1st edition), Bullying at school (2nd edition) and Advertising (3rd edition).

Further, as part of this piece, a school-wide contest would be held in which students would submit proposals for the newspaper's title and logo. The graphic design and layout would be the responsibility of the researcher (who is also a journalist), while the newspaper's direction would be the responsibility of the coordinator of the Artur Alves Cardoso School. The activities to be developed in each edition should be co-organized with the children, according to their interests. The contents to be published in the school newspaper should be intentionally designed for this purpose, instead of publishing schoolworks produced by students and selected for publication by teachers.

As planned, the newspaper's name ("O Cusco," "The Busybody" in English) and logo were chosen through a contest open to all the pupils. The design was completed free-of-charge by a company in collaboration with the research team, and the printing of the newspaper (250 copies per edition) was sponsored by the Odivelas Municipality. The edition was designed at the beginning of the term in collaboration with the eight teachers (three from preschool and five from primary school). The school coordinator collected all the stories and information and co-ordinated the layout of the newspaper. The draft layout was analyzed by the team, who suggested alterations, after which it was printed. The newspaper was first distributed within the school and among the families.

5.4 Applying, Monitoring and Assessing the Intervention Plan

In this sub-chapter we present the work developed after the approval of the intervention plan from September 2016 until the end of the post-doctoral individual research grant project funded by the Science and Technology Portuguese Foundation (FCT), on the 28th of February, 2018. We focus on the progress of the project, as well as the teachers and parents' assessments. Finally, we discuss the reasons for which the project did not end as expected in February 2018, especially because of the action of the teachers, who continued to develop activities and took over the organization of the school newspaper. These discussions motivated us to continue, even after the end of the grant that had allowed the development of the project.

5.4.1 "The Busybody": The Printed Newspaper That Turned the Project Visible

The headline of the first edition was "Being a digital citizen" (December 2016) and involved preschool children interviewing their parents and grandparents about what toys they had when they were little and what they played with. Children with special needs organized an interview guide and went out of the school to interview community members on what they viewed a digital citizen to be. The activity was developed with the support and equipment of the Special Needs teacher.

First and second year pupils asked their parents and grandparents what the media was like when they were children, while third- and fourth-year pupils organized debates on the development of the media. One of these debates was marked by a pupil's question: "teacher, what was the Internet like when you were a child?." The intergenerational activity contributed to the pupils' better understanding of how the media, toys, and games have developed over the years. It also allowed for dialogue and reflection at school, within the families, and in the community.

The images used in the newspaper were mainly photographs taken by students and teachers, but also drawings produced by the students of the preschool and Primary school. Other news included the newspaper title contest, a fieldtrip to Lisbon, a brief history of the school's patron, the painter Artur Alves Cardoso, and the Book Fair, which had taken place at the school's library. Children produced media messages, participated and intervened socially and, in this respect, the intervention model was being applied.

The publication of the school newspaper was a success, especially among students and teachers, but also among parents. The greatest advantage of the newspaper was the way it contributed to the visibility of the project with the board of Caneças School District. Days after its publication, in December 2016, the principal invited us to present the project and the work developed thus far at a meeting where the members of the board, the Artur Alves Cardoso teachers and the coordinators of the other three primary schools were present. Secondarily, the meeting aimed to consider the possibility of extending the project to all preschools and primary schools in the District. The challenge was approved for gradual implementation, in the medium term.

The school newspaper also increased the project's visibility at Odivelas Municipality, to whom we regularly reported the progress of the activities[1]. On

---

[1] In addition to these contacts, we met regularly with the Councilor of Education of the Municipality of Odivelas, not only to give her an account of our progress, but also to involve the entire Education team. Beyond the meetings held in 2015, we met on 19 February, 17 June and 3 October 2016. From that date on, we had weekly informal briefings until November 2017.

January 18, 2017, we presented the project at the Municipal Council of Education, where the main policy makers were present, as well as representatives of all entities that could play a role in a larger Education for Citizenship project. We then proposed the organization of a municipal project on Digital Citizenship Education, which would be replicable at national and international levels. To make our proposal sustainable, we highlighted the following developments between January 2016 and January 2017:

1. The training of 25 teachers, who had developed Digital Citizenship activities with 366 preschool and primary school children.
2. The longitudinal project that was taking place at Artur Alves Cardoso School, with eight teachers, under which the school newspaper had been produced.
3. The interest of the Odivelas Municipality in the project, as proved by the fact that we were presenting it at that meeting.
4. The interest of Caneças School District in the project and the will to involve all preschools and primary schools.
5. The fact that on January 9, 2017, we started a teacher training course[2] on Digital Citizenship at the Pedro Alexandrino School District (Odivelas), which was being attended by 25 teachers.
6. The fact that we are collaborating, as researchers, in international reference projects in the area, namely the "Digital Citizenship Education" (Council of Europe, 47 countries—since March 2016), the COST Action "The Digital Literacy And Multimodal Practices Of Young Children" (University of Sheffield, funded by the European Union, involving 36 European countries + Brazil and Australia—since March 2016), and "Competences for Democratic Culture" (Council of Europe, 47 countries—since October 2016).
7. The fact that we have published three articles[3] in international journals in the United States of America, Italy and Brazil and have presented the

---

2 This teacher training course is not mentioned in detail in this book, as it was part of a possible larger project, which would be the municipal project. This book focuses on the Artur Alves Cardoso School project.

3 Tomé, V. & De Abreu, B. (2016). Developing digital citizenship in children aged from 3 to 9: a pilot project in the Portuguese region of Odivelas. Special Issue of the *Journal Media Education: Studi, Ricerche, Buone Pratiche*, V. 7, n. 2, pp. 215–233. / Tomé, V. (2016). Cidadania na era digital: um projeto-piloto de formação de crianças dos 3 aos 9 anos em contexto formal e informal de aprendizagem. *Revista Educação e Cultura Contemporânea*, 13, 31, 372–403. / Tomé, V. (2016). Media education in Portuguese curricula. *The Journal of Media Literacy*, 63, 1–2, 42–49.

project at an international scientific meeting[4], while other publications were in progress and other presentations planned.

The proposal of creating a municipal project was well received by the Education sector of Odivelas Municipality and, as we will discuss later, it progressed. Meanwhile, in January 2017, it was necessary to prepare the second edition of the school newspaper, to be published in March and the teachers wanted to organize a new plan focused on bullying and on the Rights of the Child.

In discussions with the teachers, it became clear that it was necessary to take a broad perspective in the organization of the plan, framing the activities within the framework of Human Rights Education and Democratic Citizenship Education. Therefore, we adopted as a note a phrase we wrote on a blank sheet of paper: "Children are the center. Listen to them. Let them express themselves freely. Do not limit them with adult 'truths'. Learn with them because that is the only way we can learn together. Only in this way will you be able to contribute so that they can be active and participatory citizens in the 21st century."

We analyzed several publications which we considered key, such as the Universal Convention of Human Rights (United Nations, 1948) and the Convention of the Rights of the Child (United Nations, 1989), focusing on the four general principles, namely non-discrimination which must be guaranteed by the States (Article 2), the interest of the child over the interest of adults (Article 3), the right to life, survival and development (Article 6) and the respect for the opinions of the child, who has the right to express his or her opinion and that this opinion be taken into consideration in any matter that affects him or her (Article 12).

We then explored the book Compasito (Flowers, 2007), which defines Human Rights Education as "a process that aims to establish a culture of human rights. The educational process builds on children's active participation by which they learn about human rights and understand human rights issues, acquire skills and abilities to be able to defend human rights and develop attitudes of respect of equality and dignity" (p. 9). The book posits a holistic approach that includes learning—about human rights, with human rights, and through human rights.

The spectrum view was precisely what we were looking for, so we explored the practical activity proposals that Compasito suggests for educators to adapt

---

4 Tomé, V. Digital Citizenship Education: acting with children (3–9), their teachers, parents and out-of-school entities. ECREA 2016 preconference - Research of Children, Youth and Media. Department of Media Studies and Journalism, Masaryk University, Brno& Institute for Research on Children, Youth and Families, Masaryk University & ECREA TWG: Children, Youth and Media & COST Action IS1410, The Digital Literacy and Multimodal Practices of Young Children (November, 8). Prague. Czech Republic, 2016.

according to the context. The proposals were aimed at children aged 6–13 years, though the group felt it was perfectly possible to adapt them for use in preschool education. We explored the aims of Human Rights Education, the objectives for children and the strategies proposed in the book and came to three main conclusions, which were considered in all the decisions taken:

1. Children need values, skills, attitudes, knowledge and critical understanding of reality. They should develop these in formal, non-formal and informal learning environments, and there should be continuity between contexts.
2. At the end of each activity, it is essential to reflect on what has been done, because omitting this phase can be harmful, can reinforce stereotypes and devalue the emotions that the activity has stimulated in children.
3. No child can learn about human rights in an environment that does not respect it, or which does not promote the culture of human rights. The best contribution a teacher can make to children's understanding of human rights is to create such an environment.

According to the teachers, the children were interested in developing an activity about bullying, as it was a relevant and current theme in the daily life of the school and families. In late 2016, we had developed a small collaboration with the European Network Against Bullying in Learning and Leisure Environments (ENABLE) project, led by the European Schoolnet and involving partners from five European countries. This project had then created a body of literature, supported by research findings, which were internationally recognized. We therefore followed the logic of the project, which had adopted as definition of bullying that proposed by the Antibullying Alliance (n.d.): "Bullying is the repetitive, intentional hurting of one person or group by another person or group, where the relationship involves an imbalance of power. It can happen face to face or online."

The project had also published an in-depth review of scientific literature in the area of bullying, and concluded that although there were variations between the definitions found, there was some consensus on five identifying characteristics of bullying (ENABLE, 2015), namely:

1. The bully intends to inflict harm or fear upon the victim.
2. Aggression toward the victim occurs repeatedly.
3. The victim does not provoke bullying behavior by using verbal or physical aggression.
4. Bullying occurs in familiar social groups.
5. The bully is more powerful (either actual or perceived power) than the victim (pp. 8–9).

We analyzed different forms of bullying (e.g. discrimination against minorities, homophobia, bullying of children with special educational needs, bullying of vulnerable children), its main causes and consequences (e.g.: emotional, psychological and academic problems, effects on aggressors, aggressor-victims and even among bystanders, such as low self-esteem, anxiety, depression or suicidal ideas) and some strategies to combat bullying, such as parent and teacher training, increased supervision of children, multidisciplinary teamwork, intervening at the behavioral level or even an integrated anti-bullying policy at school (Downes and Cefai, 2016).

We concluded that it was necessary to directly involve families as well as professionals, such as the psychologist and the nurse who provided support to the school. In short, both in relation to the Human Rights approach and in the approach to bullying, the strategy would have to be community-based. The teachers then select four activities from Compasito: (i) "Human Rights Calendar" (p. 60); (ii) "Rabbit's Rights" (p. 138); (iii) "Bullying Scenes" (p. 85) and (iv) "From Bystander to Helper" (p. 108).

Two of these activities would be developed at school: "Rabbit's Rights," with preschool children, and "Bullying Scenes," for primary school students in the 3rd and 4th years. First, we translated it into Portuguese, a task in which we had the support of the coordinator of Artur Alves Cardoso School who is an English teacher. Then teachers and pupils adapted the activities to the context and, together, developed a plan what each group would do.

One of the preschool teachers brought a rabbit to school inside a wooden box and asked children to think about the animal's needs, imagining that it was alone in the world. The children named the rabbit "Pantufa" (translated to Slipper, which was the most-voted-for name) and listed all its necessities, including its need for a home, family, and food. Next, they were asked to imagine that, instead of a rabbit, they were considering a child. Although many children confused rights and duties, the activity allowed, through drawing, to stress that the interests of children come before those of adults (Article 3), that their right to life is inalienable (Article 6), as is the right to express their opinions, and, furthermore, that their opinions should be considered regarding any matter that concerns them (Article 12). These ideas were reinforced in the school newspaper for the adults to read.

The activity "Bullying Scenes" consisted of a questionnaire with nine scenarios of different types of violence, each of which the students could answer by choosing one of four possible answers. The teacher read out the question and answers while the students stood in the classroom. The students listened to the questions and chose to go to a corner, each corner corresponding to one of the answers. Following, the teacher would go around the room and ask them to justify their choice. The activity was discussed with the children, who proposed a structural change to the activity: each of them would answer the questionnaire on a printed sheet of paper, as would the parents.

To meet the request of the 3rd and 4th year students we created a version of the questionnaire for parents (adapted from the children's version) and sent it home. Comparative graphs were created based on the results, and the graphs were analyzed in class. After the debate (in Year 3 and 4 classes), the children wrote a collective text, which was published in the school newspaper, as were the graphs and their interpretations. The results were further analyzed with the school psychologist, who also wrote an article for the school newspaper.

The community thus reflected on a social problem: violence at school in its various forms. Some children (and some parents too) clearly indicated that they would respond to violence with more violence. Seven children admitted not reacting to situations of psychological violence because they imagined that if it happened, it would be because of something they had done wrong, which led the teachers to analyze the specific situation of each child.

Most of the children were willing to implement more appropriate strategies to combat violence at school (e.g.: dialogue, helping each other, preparing children and even adults to deal with bullying). The children were also beginning to take a more critical look at reality: "In the meantime, we have seen two boys playing and then hitting another one. We have also seen two girls who wouldn't let another play with them. They don't seem to have learned anything!" (Rita, 3rd grade).

The activities developed within the plan were covered in the March edition of the school newspaper. The contents were more diversified, and some of the activities started to be organized in a different way than usual, due to the influence of the ongoing project. One example was an activity consisting in an exhibition of a set of 3D models of the castles of Portugal, which Year 4 students had built using recycled materials, with the support of their families. The goal was to display the castles in the school library, where parents could then visit the exhibition.

After a discussion with teachers about this activity, students were asked to produce a poster of the exhibition and to display it in the community, to produce printed and digital invitations and to send them to all their families and friends. An exhibition book was created, in which visitors could leave comments, and a ballot box was created, where each visitor had the right to vote for the castle that they considered the most interesting. Finally, a space was created so that the preschool children visiting the exhibition could draw the castle they liked the most.

The exhibition was very dynamic and the fact that visitors could vote for the castle they liked the most led the children to write a short story about each castle, which they added to the model. They also maintained the appearance of the castle and stood by its construction to explain how they had developed the work, so that their work would be recognized. The results of the election revealed which had been the three most voted castles, and the result of the election was accepted by the children, who thus understood the importance of voting.

The second edition of the school newspaper was distributed in March, not only to students and parents, but also to the other schools and the community of Caneças. The schoolteachers left copies in public places, such as hairdressers, shops and coffee shops. At the same time as the newspaper was reaching a wider network, it was also gaining status in Odivelas Municipality. The education services were preparing an application for European funds, a process in which we were actively involved. The application focused on social support for students from schools in the municipality and included several initiatives, one of them being support for the Artur Alves Cardoso School project, ensuring the continuity of the edition of the school newspaper 'O Cusco' until June 2020. It was approved in July 2017, and was an incentive for the continuity of the project, which had been scheduled to end in February 2018.

Even before the application was approved, in April, preparation had begun for the next edition of the school newspaper to be published in June. In the first preparation meeting, the teachers considered that it was not necessary to make a plan, as had happened with the previous newspaper, because the third term of the school year was only two months old, and they had already discussed work proposals for the school newspaper. In compliance with new legislation which decreed outdoor recess was pedagogical time, if under teacher supervision, pupils were invited to submit proposals to improve their school yard (which consisted of a football field and areas surrounding the primary school, where there was no equipment at all). Given the opportunity to express their opinions and wishes through the school newspaper, either through text or drawing, the preschoolers drew a yard with wooden houses in trees, swings, and slides, whereas the primary-school children expressed their desire for a swimming pool, a disco, and even a circus.

Second-year pupils wrote to the local authorities and concluded their letter saying: "we would just like to be heard and that our requests are taken into consideration when you consider and are able to renovate the school, which belongs to everyone but mostly to the children's." Both the drawings and the letters were published in the school newspaper, which included several other stories such as a play that teachers and students prepared based on the book "The Boy Who Used to Have Zero at Maths," a book by the Portuguese writer Luísa Ducla Soares, who visited the school, watched the play and was interviewed by the students. "They were real actors and writers. I would like to highlight them all."

Children also developed a set of 14 scientific experiences, such as building dunes, mixing vinegar with baking soda and observing the water cycle using a lamp. They have also learned new concepts such as carbon dioxide, acetic acid (vinegar), density, calcium carbonate, oxidant, fuel, PH and fermentation. These experiments, as well as other happenings, such as field trips, were part of the school newspaper that was published in June, on the last day of school, when parents came to school to see their children's assessment. There were then eight months to go before the end of the project, and it was necessary to evaluate the developed activities.

5.4.2 Assessing the Intervention with Teachers (July 2017)

The teachers' assessment of the intervention plan took place on July 13, 2017, through a focus group attended by nine of the 11 teachers of the Artur Alves Cardoso School (the Special Education teacher and librarian teacher only managed to arrive at the end of the interview). The data analysis resulted in a set of seven key findings, which are presented below, listed from A to F.

A Impact of the Training

The theoretical and practical organization of the training, as well as its contents, met the teachers' needs in the field and, in fact, supported the activities developed afterwards. "It made perfect sense for the training to take place at the beginning" (T3). "This theoretical basis was essential," because "the work we did [in the training], the criticism we received, the corrections that were pointed out to us, were useful for this year … any idea that emerged or any work we started … we already had an idea of what was more concrete (…) to do" (T4). "There was a certain harmony between what was proposed in the training session and then the practice" (T1), i.e. "a good interconnection between the training and the work developed afterwards" (T2).

B Evaluation of the Activities Developed

The teachers had a clear notion that the Digital Citizenship Education activities were based on a traditional type of media, the printed school newspaper, but they highlighted that this cautious advance in terms of media content production had allowed other gains, such as the "smooth" adaptation of the project to the curriculum, taking into account the context and the characteristics of the teachers, students and families. They were also aware that it was possible to go much further, but they praised the logic of social intervention through the school newspaper.

In terms of activities, teachers stated, more to citizenship in general [colleagues agree]. Even this paper [the 3rd term school newspaper edition] is just that" (T5).

"Yes. Even bullying [theme of 2nd term school newspaper edition], it is something more general" (T6). This is better understood at the preschool than in primary school, because "our little ones, when we talk about digital age, for them we are talking about games" (T5), i.e., "computer equals games. Period" (T1). A question we should keep in mind is: "Looking at what we do in the project, how is this different from what others do?" (R), not least because the project is very focused on paper and so are the activities (R). Some positive social interventions can already be seen: "In an election year, from an adult point of view, this newspaper, made by children, is in the right timing, politically speaking" (T5). "Yes. It is political" (T8).

C Cooperation Established at Five Levels

The intervention plan had enabled collaborations to be established at five levels: between teachers, between levels of education, between the school and the family, between Artur Alves Cardoso School and the other schools in the Caneças School District and between the school and the community.

C.1 *Between Teachers* The role played by the Artur Alves Cardoso School coordinator was key. She organized and coordinated the Digital Citizenship activities, as well as the editions of the school newspaper, in conjunction with the researcher. The teachers highlighted the fact that the activities were designed according to the students' interests (but also their age and school level) and were organized in order to have products for the school newspaper, taking into account the need to produce a diverse set of journalistic genres (reportage, news, interviews ...). Instead of asking the same activities from each of the teachers, more laborious and time-consuming activities were organized, but they were feasible because the tasks were divided between the teachers and the students, which was intentional for the quality of the newspaper as a final product. "There is interdisciplinarity because, we are in single teaching, but there are other teachers, such as ICT and English and, despite everything, we teach more than one subject" (T7). "And there is Special [Needs] Education" (T2). The organization was done so that the teachers and classes were doing different things: "I suggested several activities and then I would say: 'Maybe you do this more because it is more appropriate'. And I tried not to have repetition because, if all classes were repeating the same thing, the activity would end up not making sense. Or each group, for example, in the case of primary school, each classroom should do something different, so as not to repeat" (T8).

C.2 *Between Cycles* The greater relationship between cycles and/or educational levels, advocated by various entities such as OECD (2017) and the Ministry of

Education in Portugal, began to be a reality, with collaboration between preschool and primary school children (e.g.: they participated in common activities in the area of Human Rights, but also in the History of Portugal, namely in the organization of an exhibition of the castles of Portugal, whose models were built by the students of Year 4). The collaboration between primary school and second cycle (5th and 6th grades) was already a reality, with success in terms of Science, ICT and English, but it started to be reflected in the school newspaper. The teachers believed that Digital Citizenship could be a common area, which would enhance collaboration between cycles, in order to respond to community problems.

The teachers highlight the "relationship between Kindergarten and Primary School" (T8), which they consider sustainable, in addition to paying attention to the continuity of the students who moved to the 1st Year of Primary, for example in terms of continuing to address Human Rights, because "Human Rights end up being a theme that is addressed in all years" (T4). Those who "arrive at Primary 1 with another awareness and are already able to separate rights from duties. Because ours [preschool children], for them, everything is the same" (T5). In addition to the collaboration of 5th and 6th grade teachers in the area of ICT (coding, online information search) and English, a teacher came to school for "coadjuvant work with the Sciences" (T7), whose work, together with students and teachers, was referenced in the school newspaper, and "the colleague [Science teacher] was enthusiastic and wanted to take a copy with her" (T7).

C.3 *With the Students' Families* The school newspaper played a key role at several levels, namely the participation and collaboration of parents, the interest of parents in their children's work at school, and as a means of information within the educational community. Some parents talked among themselves and came to believe in the project, asking fewer questions. However, the teachers admitted that they talked little with parents and needed to be more proactive, informing them about what was being done within the project and asking their opinions about this work, as well as the perception in terms of any progress of their children. The newspaper was also important as a motivational element for the children, because with each issue published, their interest in participating grew.

"Parents talked more about the project last year than this year" (T7), mainly "because they were already more aware of the subject. This year they already participated because they already knew what it was about" (T8). They may also have talked less about the project because "we didn't ask them" (T7), since the teachers considered that parents "were more relaxed than uninterested" (T8) in the project. The proof is that "they were very cooperative, for example when we sent them asking what kind of games they preferred in their childhood time" (T1). Moreover, when the teachers asked the students if they read the newspaper at home "there is always good feedback" (T7, T2, T5) and "they said that the parents were very proud to see their children's work there" (T1). Also, the children are motivated: "When we said 'let's do this for the newspaper', they were very motivated" (T2).

C.4 *With the Other Three Schools in the Project* It was necessary to strengthen the exchange with the other three primary schools (Cesário Verde, Fontes de Caneças, Maria Costa) and kindergartens (Cesário Verde, Maria Costa, Vieira Caldas) of the Caneças School District. This could be done by enhancing more, if possible, the work of the librarian [who worked in two of the four primary schools] but also of the researcher, as they were the ones who circulated more between the schools. "The exchange occurred mainly through the librarian [who also works at Cesário Verde] and Vitor Tomé, who went to all primary schools and kindergartens more than once" (T2).

C.5 *With the Community, Beyond the Family* The teachers agreed unanimously about the need to raise community awareness and take steps to make the project more community-based. "Although we try to involve everyone in the community, our society is increasingly individualistic. And I think, at the level of institutions, the same thing happens. They see the school as 'that's a school problem' and I think that, at the very beginning of the project, we talked about this problem in the library …" (P7).

There was a connection with Odivelas Municipality, which printed the school newspaper for free, provided logistical support to the project (e.g.: photocopies, transport of students) and had a psychological and social support service for the school students. There was a close relationship with Health Services, as a nurse developed Health Education activities with students. Also, after-school activities became part of the project. And all these collaborations resulted in products for the school newspaper. It was clearly necessary, although gradually, to involve the community more.

D Project Perceptions (from April 2016 to June 2017)

Teachers saw the project as an added value, both for preschool and primary school, but considered that it was easier to implement it in preschool, because it fit better into the objectives and because there would be more time, as the curriculum was more adaptable. "The fact that we can integrate the project into what we do on a daily basis (…) is good" (P3). For the Preschool it is an added value because "it has a lot to do with our objectives and our specifications" (P1) and "enriches a lot" the pedagogical practice (P5) for "the 1st cycle[primary school] as well" (P2).

E Limitations on Project Development

The limitations pointed out focused on the lack of technological resources, the lack of Internet access in kindergarten rooms and the difficulty in raising the families' awareness so that children could use the digital resources they had at home for school activities. The lack of time and space was another major limitation.

E.1 *Lack of Digital Resources and Internet* The school lacked equipment, namely computers that worked well (there was a new laptop, an old computer and a projector in the school library, plus one computer per primary school room, but they were very old and processed very slowly). The same was true for the only computer available for the three kindergarten classrooms. Internet access needed to be improved, as it did not exist in the kindergarten, so teachers had to use their personal equipment to access the Internet.

> "I find it difficult to talk about digital in this school, when there is no well-functioning computer" (T7).

> "In classroom context, a doubt appears. They, sometimes, even say 'go to the computer to see'. But let's see where? Sometimes I try with my mobile phone, but the signal is not working [the school Internet does not reach the JI building]" (T5). "And in my room ... there are days. The better rooms are the ones on the ... [1st floor of the primary school building] (T4).

> "If we had a room where we could do, for example, search on the Internet, it would already create a need (…) from the moment it existed and we could work on it, they would also feel the need to handle and work and, from there, we could develop other works and alerts for which they are not remotely awake" (T7).

There was a lack of interactive whiteboards and fixed multimedia stations (because the portable station took time to set up) in each room. "What I feel is that, every time I want to use the projector, you have to set up the screen, you have to turn on the projector, you have to connect the projector to the computer, whereas if it were already on …." (P3). "It's just that a lot of time is lost right away. While we're doing this, the kids are already completely distracted, under the table …" (T2).

E.2 *The Regression of Students in Terms of Internet Use* Teachers regretted the effects of the suspension of the e-school program[5], as students who received

---

5 The e-escolinha program was integrated in the National Technological Plan and aimed to provide a personal computer to each primary school student. It was active between 2007 and 2011, but was discontinued when Portugal defaulted and had to resort to an international loan from the International Monetary Fund and the European Union.

computers (whose brand was 'Magalhães' the name of an important navigator from the XVI Century) developed *online* research habits, which was not the case now.

> "They don't research. They copy information. I'm talking about Year 4. They know how to research, but then they have a lot of difficulty in selecting what interests them, in selecting what is important" (T2).

> "I can make a little comparison here with the time of Magalhães ... we managed to do that. And we reached a point where we had presentations of work in PowerPoint, in Word ... work that they did in which great care could be seen. Why was that? Because there had been a journey there. Because they all had access to a computer (...). This was worked on in the classroom and, little by little, they would go home with a research project, with a homework assignment ... and we would say 'I don't want a copy, I don't want things from Wikipedia, pay attention to this, this and this'. And then, yeah. At this point there was this breakdown, because they stopped having the computer" (T8). "At the time, I had a 3rd or 4th Year and it was very good, because they had Magalhães and when we entered that classroom it seemed that we were entering the classroom of the future" (T8).

E.3 *The Difficulty of Using Family Digital Media at the Service of the School* The problem of lack of means could be transformed into an opportunity, for example by involving families and betting on the bring your own device (BYOD) approach, which was not easy, but it should be tried. "At home they can even have computers, but parents want them to be quiet, playing. Not researching or doing research work" (T8).

E.4 *The Lack of Space to Divide the Classes into Groups* Class size (27 students) was another problem that the teachers would like to overcome, which did not necessarily imply a reduction in the number of students per class, but an adaptation, such as a division of the class into two groups, when carrying out certain activities. However, this division was not possible because there were no classrooms or other free spaces in which the groups could work. Added to this limitation of space was the lack of time to comply with extensive curricular programs, particularly at the primary school. However, they considered that the school's human resources were sufficient. In ICT assistantships, activities did not always work because it was "a very big class" [27 students], which was not unique to the school (T9).

> "It's 27 students working for only one computer. Even if there are two adults in the room, it's very complicated" (T3). The division of the class could be a solution, but "we don't have spaces to divide the class and half do one thing and half do another. We don't even have physical space for that. Where do we put the other half if there is no space?" (T3). "I still think that time is always too short to do everything we would like

to do, or to develop ... sometimes we have to cut, to stop there, because then we have the material to give, too, don't we?" (T3).

F Proposals for Improving the Project

The teachers also presented a set of proposals to improve the project, which included a more frequent and effective connection with families and the community, namely in the activities to be developed in the promotion of the school newspaper, as well as an adaptation of the project to the curricular flexibility in progress.

F.1 *Connecting with Families through the Newspaper* The school newspaper can play a key role in improving relationships with students' families:

- Send them the newspaper in digital format—"Send [the school newspaper] in digital format to parents" (T7).
- Make a PDF of the newspaper available on the District's website (view/download)—"We even managed to make a PDF version available on the District's website for download, or to view on the website itself" (E).
- Distribute the school newspaper before the last day of classes of each school term— "Don't distribute the last newspaper even on the last day of classes. Next year, the distribution in the last period has to be earlier, because parents don't take the newspaper home" (P7).
- Ask parents for suggestions for content during the first meeting of the year—"It would not be bad to have a page of family suggestions, for example" (T4), not only from the Parents' Association, because (…) there are only three or four (T6), "but ask families to send suggestions, even to the school" (T4). "Or involve families and ask them: 'what would you like to see covered in the newspaper?' For example, the theme of the dossier or other issues they would like to see covered" (T7). "At the very first meeting, we can give parents the space to suggest themes" (T8).
- Create a section written by people other than teachers on everyday issues related to these children (e.g., present problem and give three pieces of advice in 20 lines) —"A short article for each issue on issues very specific to these ages of preschool and 1st grade [of primary school] that could be covered in the paper. That's three 20–line articles per year. It doesn't seem like much to me. For example, food issues, at a time when you were working on food. Personal hygiene issues, clothing issues, how we relate to others" (E). "Maybe if it was a parent talking, it would be more interesting and the other parents would call more" (T8). "We can talk to Cláudia [school psychologist] and nurse Alexandra, and have a little page of questions and answers

here, in which one of them or nurse Sandra, can have an important participation" (T8).
- Highlight in the newspaper the project that the preschool develops with parents and guardians, who regularly come to school to tell stories and/or cook with the students—"We have a project (...) that appears every year in our planning, which is parents in action. They are always invited to come to the classroom (...) to tell a story or do some cooking. And, in our wall newspapers, we have a column for parents, where they leave their opinion on how it went, what was the impact (...) of the activity. (...) So we can use that column to highlight some activities that had more impact. (...) At the beginning of the year we will already draw the parents' attention to that fact" (T1).

F.2 *Connecting with the Community through the Newspaper* The school newspaper could improve the relationship with the community and broaden it, which was sorely needed, and could be done in the following ways:

- Improve the dissemination of the newspaper by sending it to libraries, Kidzania, other schools and all entities mentioned in each issue (digital sending and, if financially possible, by mail)—"Maybe we also lack a little of this dissemination on our part ..." (P5). (P5). "Our newspaper can reach the Caneças [Library] pole ..." (P5), "it can reach, for example, Kidzania" (P7) and Why not also send the newspaper up there, to the Castanheiros [2nd and 3rd cycles school of Caneças School District]" (P7). "And to all the entities involved in the newspaper" (P9). "We went to the Centro de Ciência Viva, in Sintra. We could send one, yes" (P2), "And with a sheet to everyone [to accompany the newspaper], explaining what is intended with this" (P7). The distribution can be both digital and physical, if there is the possibility and are financial means (E).
- Create workshops at schools inviting other stakeholders and community entities (e.g. Rural police, Health services) and eventually report on these entities from the Caneças community, sports, culture, leisure ...—"And maybe, for example, on Children's Day, instead of us, we can try to do a workshop with the PSP [urban police], although it is a difficult day for them. Or with the nurse ... do a workshop" (T4).

F.3 *Newspaper Content* Improving the contents of the newspaper was possible. For example, two drawings of the same student appeared in the same issue, thus ruining the chance of publication to others. "We have to be careful because in this newspaper [3rd edition] two drawings of the same boy appeared" (T5). "But look, you can also choose the drawings. In my case it was me who selected them. Then I no longer choose two drawings of the same child" (T4).

F.4 *Link with Curricular Flexibility and New Methodologies* Teachers looked favorably on the possibility of integrating the project into the curriculum as part of the continual adaptation of the curriculum[6]:

- They clearly supported the logic advocated by the OECD (2017) in the *Starting Strong* study and were willing to work towards a better integration between preschool and primary school, continuing the activities already developed by the two levels of education (e.g.: activity on Human Rights)—"We need to help them to think for themselves, to be creative and that's what doesn't happen very often, even in Preschool. It is important in that it gives them tools and challenges to make them autonomous from the point of view of their thinking" (T1). "It is important to praise our educators, who try to do it and do it" (T8). "If we can explore emotional intelligence, that would be interesting, at the level of activities that we can promote" (E). "That activity of the Human Rights calendar, we can go there, one, two or three days, and we can celebrate one day for each school period, at school" (E).
- They clearly embraced the implementation of a *Guided Inquiry* activity, at 3rd and 4th year level, with parental support (BYOD—*Bring Your Own Device*), focusing on an *online* and *offline* research, in order to point solutions to a social problem identified by students and to which they wanted to respond—"Students identify an existing social problem and we will motivate them to find the solution. We can ask students to, in their search for solutions, do some guided online research and when they find solutions, they can produce something on paper and/or online to present the solution or solutions they point to solve that problem" (E). "And we can even insert this activity in the lessons of the 3rd and 4th years, once a week ... an activity in this scope" (T2). "This implies making a proposal at the beginning of the year, talking to the parents because, in the 3rd and 4th years, the time allotted for environmental studies is very short. But if

---

6 The Portuguese educational system was at this time undergoing transformation, in the sense of abandoning the logic of a single school curriculum, defined by the central government for compulsory schooling, giving schools the possibility to make a local management of up to 25% of the curriculum.

the parents were available, either with a tablet or with something else, although we will continue with ICT. But this is a little different. Maybe, in an hour when they bring a tablet, we can work much more on the content of Environmental and social studies and some other content that is part of the program ... ." (T8).
- Citizenship Education should be a concern in school playground activities and those associated with dramatic expression and physical-motor expression—"There will be a break in which targeted activities will take place and one of them may be citizenship. We had thought about physical-motor expression and dramatic expression and we can think about it" (T8).

G Teacher Training and Resources

Following the interview, a second in-service teacher training course was agreed upon, between October and December 2017, focused on the school newspaper, which should take place at the Artur Alves Cardoso School. This would be an end-of-project training session, in order to create conditions for teachers to continue the project after the end of February 2018, when the researcher's individual grant ended. They also requested that every effort should be made to obtain 28 *tablets*, five interactive whiteboards and better Internet access at the Artur Alves Cardoso School.

5.4.3 The End of the Project Turned into a Restart

We met with the Artur Alves Cardoso School teachers on September 11th, at the beginning of the school year 2017-2018, having analyzed the results of the focus group we had conducted in July. The teachers analyzed the results and agreed with the conclusions, and the intervention plan had to undergo changes at the following levels:

- Further evolve the activities developed, going beyond the printed school newspaper, betting on digital technologies to intervene socially.
- Continue the collaboration initiated among teachers (coordinating Digital Citizenship activities), between cycles and levels of education (reinforcing the connection with 2nd cycle teachers in Science and English), with the children's families (involving them in the activities), with other schools in the Caneças School District (developing joint activities) and with the various institutions in the community (e.g., inviting students to produce articles about these entities for the school newspaper).

- Request more digital resources, namely Internet access in preschool rooms, but also computers, tablets (teachers requested at least 28), interactive whiteboards (teachers requested at least five) and multimedia stations.
- Create a digital edition of the school newspaper and make the various editions available in PDF format, and the printed newspaper should be distributed before the last day of school, so that parents receive it at home and not at the end-of-term party.
- Involve parents in the production of content for the newspaper, also asking them for suggestions of topics to cover and promoting projects in which they were already involved, such as one in the preschool, through which they came to school to tell stories and cook with the children.
- Plan citizenship activities for the playground space, namely associated with dramatic expression and physical-motor expression, since the then-new legislation now considers playground time as academic time.
- Organize a new in-service teacher training course, focused on print and digital school newspapers, between October and December 2017.

The acquisition of digital equipment could only had beeen done by Odivelas Municipality, but it did not depend directly on the Councilor for Education, nor could it be done under the application for European funds that had been approved, so the teachers' wishes were not met. The scarcity of equipment made it difficult to plan and implement digital activities. However, it was possible to move forward at three levels, namely improving the contents of the school newspaper, involving family and community, discussing with students what the school of their dreams would be like, and organizing a second in-service teacher training course focused on the school newspaper and digital media.

In September 2017, the Caneças School District, of which the project school is a part, was selected by the Ministry of Education for a visit by the Minister of Education and the Secretary of State for Education, as part of 'The World's Largest Lesson', a United Nations initiative to promote the achievement of the Sustainable Development Goals 2030. The school children presented an activity and had the opportunity to speak with the minister, who told them that if they needed anything, to write to him. In October 2017, they wrote a letter to the Minister of Education (headline of the fourth edition, published in December 2017). Among their several requests, children focused on the renovation of the school yard and the changes to course contents: "we have analyzed course contents and consider them too long. We do not have time to practice what we are taught! We suggest that the contents are revised and improved and take us, six to ten-year-old pupils, into consideration."

In the same edition of the school newspaper, the 4th Grade students were very concerned about the big fires that had destroyed thousands of hectares of forest in Portugal between July and September, so they decided to appeal to the community to offer them trees that they would take care of until they could be planted. The 3rd grade students organized a survey with their parents, in order to know what subjects they would like to see covered in the school newspaper. 54 parents answered. The most popular topics were professions (14 votes), Caneças Fire Brigade (12 votes), sport (10 votes), cooking (6 votes), fashion (5 votes), traditional games (4 votes) and dancing (3 votes).

The teachers had not discussed with the pupils how they imagined their dream school, nor had they involved the children in more digital activities. The opportunity to do so would be during the second teacher training course, which started on November 13, 2017 and lasted until February 5, 2018. And it was during this course that the Artur Alves Cardoso School teachers expressed their clear intention to continue the project beyond the end of February, having organized an edition of the school newspaper, to be published in March 2018, on their own initiative, after which they requested our collaboration.

"The Busybody is on TV" ['O Cusco já está na TV'] was the headline of the edition of the school newspaper published in March 2018. Children expressed their interest in creating audio-visual content, so the teachers designed a proposal that linked the pupils' interests in terms of current affairs and critical analysis of the news through the production of a news broadcast, hosted by the children and videorecorded. On a Friday, all the children were asked to choose a news story that interested them, a task they could carry out with the help of their family or someone within the broader community. On Monday, the topics of the news were listed on the board of all the classrooms and the pupils voted on the news they considered most relevant. The 16 most-voted-for pieces of news were selected for Cusco TV's first news broadcast, which they called "Telecusco." The images were recorded with a mobile phone and edited using Movie Maker. The pupils debated current affairs and involved their families and members of their community. The video was watched and discussed with the children as well as with the parents (on the last day of the second term, in March 2018), to whom the need to talk about current affairs with their children was reiterated, as many of the pupils found it difficult to understand what was being said, as adults are the intended audience of the TV news services.

The results showed that the children were interested in news (only three said they were not) and consumed news in multiple formats. TV dominated, but radio, Internet, printed newspaper and even family members were also mentioned as news sources. Thirteen of the 16 chosen news items had a negative theme: a plane crash in Iran, two fires and a bus accident in Portugal, the murder of a child in Brazil, some American parents who kept their children at home for years, a lady who disappeared in Caneças, two cases of aggression in sport and in court, one in Portugal and the other in the United States of America, a bomb that exploded in Ukraine, a collapse of a rubbish dump in Mozambique that caused 17 deaths, the floods in Paris or a case of corruption in sport in Portugal. Among the positive news items were a lunar eclipse in South America, the birth of a giraffe in Lisbon Zoo and a machine that purifies water. In conclusion, the news globalized the children's worldview. It does not matter if the event took place in the USA, in Ukraine or in Paris. Only seven of the selected news items refer to facts that occurred in Portugal. The rule seems to be that 'if it impresses, it is chosen'.

This edition of the school newspaper was the first in which the children wrote reports about entities in the community of Caneças. Three children reported on the Ginásio Clube de Odivelas (GCO), a club that involves young people in the practice of soccer, hip-hop, acrobatic gymnastics, handball, chess, handball, roller field hockey and figure skating, a sport in which some students from the school participated. A group of three other children went to visit the 'MCDance' Dance Academy, a private entity dedicated to teaching creative dance, ballet, hip-hop, contemporary dance, and acrobatic dance, among others. At the time it was attended by 150 people aged three years old and up, and it organized three shows a year.

The community was becoming more prominent in the school newspaper, which was a goal of the intervention plan. Teachers started by helping children produce news stories, including planning them and also writing interview guides as well as thinking about the necessary visual images to coincide with the news items. Parents also helped children, which assisted with boosting new learning. During a journalistic assignment at the Ginásio Clube de Odivelas, when a couple tried to take photos of their children for the school newspaper, children asked them to take only pictures of them with their backs to the camera. In fact, at school we had started discussing with the children the General Data Protection Regulation (GDPR), the then new European data protection law that would come into effect in May 2018.

The Year 4 children wrote and published an open letter to the Caneças community, requesting more support for their 'Let's reforest Portugal' program, which they had started in September 2017, following the large fires that had destroyed thousands of hectares of forest. They were appealing for more trees, as they had only received 73 since the December edition of the school newspaper had been published. Also in this edition of the newspaper the 2nd and 4th grade children debated and wrote about rights and duties, while the 1st grade children talked about emotions and empathy. As in previous editions, news about field trips, dance activities, music, and poetry, among others, were also published.

After Easter vacation, teachers continued to plan and develop Digital Citizenship activities, in order to respond to the intervention plan that had been approved at the beginning of the school year. The three preschool teachers developed a common activity, which started by rethinking, with the children, the activities that could be developed in the playground. The activity started with a discussion about the best way to make the kindergarten a richer, more interesting and appealing space. The children imagined and designed a kindergarten that had animals, fruit trees, a swimming pool with slide, a soccer field, inflatables, hot air balloons, swings, a climbing wall, bicycles and even an Indian tent.

In one of the meetings with the teachers, the idea arose to link this interest of the children to STEAM, which could be done through a project in which the children's drawings could be turned into a 3D scale model. The model would no longer be solely centered on the playground, but the challenge lay in creating the model of the school the children dreamed of. First, the students drew the school of their dreams on scenery paper. Then, with the support of the husband of one of the teachers (who is an electrical engineer) and the mother of one of the children (who is an architect) they built a model, including the three preschool rooms, the cafeteria, the swimming pool, the slide, the climbing wall, the playground, the soccer field, the animal corner, trees, a hot air balloon and even a road to learn traffic rules. On the road were placed traffic lights whose lights actually came on.

The children actively participated in a social intervention activity focused on school, by creating a STEAM project showing adults how they would re-imagine the school they attend. They expressed their willingness to talk to policy makers so that the school they dreamed of could become a reality. And they expressed themselves, through drawing, through the model, and through words, as each child made statements to the newspaper about the model, as was the case with Gabriel: "I really wish our school was like this, because there are many things we can do: play ball, swim in the pool, climb the ladder ... ."

The headline of the June 2018 issue would then be 'The school we always dreamed of', in an issue that highlighted an initiative of the Parents' Association, which joined Blue Day with the US-based Make-a-Wish Foundation, offering children the opportunity to participate in the recording of a video entitled 'A world full of wishes'. The children also created the following message for Make-a-Wish: "We really enjoyed celebrating Blue Day. It was a lot of fun. Thank you for making the wishes come true for the kids who are sick, so they can get better and happier. We really enjoyed dancing to the Make-a-Wish anthem, being superheroes, pretending to fly between the clouds, and running between the balloons that were in the air. It was really cute!"

The children went on to do reports in the community. One report focused on the school "Arte e Dança," located at Póvoa de Santo Adrião, where it was possible to learn hip-hop, salsa, ballet and oriental dances. The second report was about the Bombeiros Voluntários de Caneças (Caneças Voluntary Fire Brigade), with a focus on their Philharmonic Band, of which one of the children from the Artur Alves Cardoso School was a member. The activities developed on the World Children's Day also deserved a report. Other news focused on environmental sustainability, so the children discussed the need to recycle and reforest, and even participated in the creation of pages of the 'Sustainability Book', a project promoted by the European Blue Flag, of the European Environment Agency.

This edition also included news about activities the children had developed in the area of expressions (physical-motor, plastic, dramatic and musical), which they had rehearsed throughout the school year, because the Ministry of Education organized national activities to test the performance of 4th grade students in these areas. These activities had taken place in May and the children wanted to highlight their performance. An interview with Portuguese writer Paula Ruivo, who had been in the School Library in April to talk about the books she writes for children, was also published.

The 2017/2018 school year was coming to an end, and the teachers and researcher agreed that they had exceeded the goals of the initial project, since it was supposed to end in February and did not. On the other hand, the work done up to June 2018 had met the community intervention plan that had been approved in September 2017. The teacher training was carried out, which helped to further develop activities that went beyond the printed newspaper, namely the production of videos and activities involving science, technology, engineering, arts and mathematics. Collaboration was strengthened between teachers, across grade levels, as well as with the children's families, and with community members. Playground activities were planned and implemented, and parents were more involved in the production of the school newspaper, which, after all, did not yet have a digital version. And it was still necessary to strengthen collaboration with the other schools in the Caneças School District. It was also essential to listen to the children's parents, which we did in July, as we will see below.

5.4.4 Assessing the Intervention Plan with Parents (July 2018)

The initial plan was to collect data from parents in February 2018. However, because teachers continued the project, we postponed data collection until the end of the school year in July. We sent a printed questionnaire to each family, which was to be answered by a parent and returned to the school in a sealed envelope. The first part of the questionnaire characterized the respondent (age, gender, education, profession) and the household (number of members and age of each). The second part aimed to assess the knowledge the parent had about the project (one question, six items), the knowledge he had about the school newspaper (one question, six items), whether the school newspaper was an asset to the household (one question, six items), as well as for the child's learning and for the dialogue with the children's teachers and other parents (one question, four items). Part 3, an open-ended response, asked for suggestions to improve the project.

Of the 190 questionnaires sent out, 85 responded, but some questionnaires were incomplete so we only accepted 72 (38% response rate). 21 of those 72 had been interviewed in 2016. The respondents were aged between 24 and 51, with the following distribution (Table 5.1):

Table 5.1: Parents who participated in the intervention plan assessment (N = 72)

Age range	N
Until 30	11
31–35	21
36–40	24
41–45	13
46–50	2
>50	1

Eight out of 10 parents were between the ages of 31 and 45, with only 11 being under 30 and only 3 aged 46 or above. The majority (66, or 91.7%) were female and only 22 (30.6%) had a college degree or higher. One in four had completed high school, and all the others had lower levels of education. About three-quarters of the households had between three (25, or 35.7%) and four people (27, or 37.5%). Only eight households (11.1%) were single parent, while 12 (16.7%) had five or more members.

The results revealed that almost two thirds of the parents (63.9%) knew about the project 'Digital Citizenship Education for Democratic Participation' in progress at Artur Alves Cardoso School and regularly talked to the schoolteachers about the activities in progress. The percentage of parents who said they talked with their children about the project activities grew to 72.3% (52 parents). The participation of parents in concrete project activities was lower, as only 31 (43%) admitted to having been invited to participate in project activities, and only 22 (30.6%) reported that they had actually participated in at least one activity.

The interpretation of the results revealed that the project and its activities needed to be better promoted, either through the school newspaper or through initiatives to be developed in the community. The school newspaper seemed to be an appropriate vehicle, since 67 (94.4%) of the 72 parents agreed with the item 'The school newspaper allows me to know better the work that is developed at school', and 36 (50%) said that the school newspaper was a subject of conversation with the teachers of the school. The newspaper was, therefore, a means of taking the school, and the work developed at the school, to the family and the community. It was also a topic of conversation between parents and children (55 parents, or 76.4% admitted to it) and even between parents of different children (mentioned by 27 parents, or 37.5%). The truth is that the number of parents who reported having directly participated in school newspaper activities was low (only 14 parents, or 19.5%). It was therefore essential to enhance the participation of parents in the activities of the project and the newspaper.

In terms of content, the newspaper was valued by parents, as it had contributed to parents being more informed about the risks of Internet and digital media use by their children (57, or 79.2% admitted it), and kept them apprised of the opportunities that children had access to via Internet and digital media (58, or 80.5% admitted it). It had also contributed to increasing conversations between parents and children about Internet and digital media use (according to 57 parents, i.e. 77.8%) and that parents developed online activities together with their children, from doing homework to playing video games together (55 parents, i.e. 76.4%).

The school newspaper influenced parents to set clear rules for their children's use of the Internet and digital media (58 parents, or 80.6%, admitted this) or to install parental control systems on the digital equipment they had at home (50 parents, or 69.5% admitted this). This greater attention to their children's uses and practices on the Internet and digital media allowed parents to have a clearer view of the importance of these devices for children in terms of learning. Parents mentioned that their children were learning non-school contents of great importance there (50 parents, or 69.4%), but also school contents (54 parents, or 75%). Despite this, few talked about this learning with their children's teachers (only 18, or 25% admitted to doing so), although conversations were more common with other children's parents (32 parents, or 44.4% admitted to doing so).

The vast majority of parents (53) did not make any proposals for improvement or make any observations about the project, which can be justified with the words of the 19 parents who wrote observations and comments, who requested "greater dissemination of the project to parents" (P7), via "email or school website" (P9) or "through written information for parents" (P15), "that it is not reduced to paper" (P20), because "teachers do not inform us much about the project" (P10), despite being "an important project in the relationship between students, school, parents and use of Internet and digital media" (P13). Parents even justified the importance of the project by highlighting a set of four aspects that we organized into four areas which we related with the 10 digital domains (referred in the sub-section 2.2.1 of this book) as they were organized by the Council of Europe (2018b):

- *Access and inclusion*: the project should be continued because it "improves the students' education" (P24) and is also "an important project to understand and fit the new technologies into the students' daily lives, both at a playful level and to research school topics" (P22).
- *Rights and responsibilities / Health and Wellbeing / Privacy and Security*: it is "very important to continue to inform/alert students and parents (through the newspaper) about the dangers of the Internet, as well as the harm caused by excessive use of new technologies" (P1) and "the advantages of using the Internet" (P4), because it is a project that is "helping children, parents, and teachers to use the media in the digital age in a healthy way" (P18)
- *Media and Information Literacy / Learning and creativity*: "for children to have some formative knowledge about the news" (P2); "it improves the learning of my student and the other students" (P5); "children's cognitive abilities and the increasingly necessary computer training/practical training in technologies" (P6)
- *Active participation*: "it would be important for students to explore more the subjects to be published; during a period, for example, they could interview people outside the school on a topic, so that they could also actively participate in the newspaper" (P11), and parents were also available for "the development of activities with students" (P15), contributing this way to prepare them to exercise "a more active citizenship" (P16).

Parents were less concerned with the other three domains: Ethics and Empathy, ePresence and Communications and Consumer Awareness. But they reinforced a key aspect, the lack of resources at the school: "It was important for the school to have more computers available for the preschool" (P14). One of the demands was precisely the desire to know more about the project, because "there is little information about the project 'Digital Citizenship Education for Democratic Participation'" (P15), but "I don't know the project very well and don't have a fixed opinion" (P17), although there were some who recognized a lack of initiative: "I take part of the responsibility for not trying to be more up-to-date, but the school also does not promote the project much" (P20).

It was necessary to invest in the dissemination of the project and the newspaper itself, because as one parent stated: "I only saw the newspaper once. Nobody informed me about anything, and I never talked about it with the other parents" (P25). However, difficult times were approaching, as the project had no funding since February 2018, except for the printing of the newspaper, which was done by Odivelas Municipality. The page layout, for example, was done by a company, for free, which had no availability in June 2018, so the newspaper was paginated at the Centro Protocolar de Formação Profissional para Jornalistas (CENJOR), the national training center for journalists, in Lisbon, which lent the facilities and equipment, but we had to do a job that was new to us.

In 2019, the situation was going to be even more difficult, as there were elections for local government in October 2017 and the Odivelas Municipality's education sector team had been completely changed by July 2018, so even the printing of the school newspaper was at risk. It was necessary to find a source of funding to continue the project, as the goodwill of the community could not be enough to proceed.

5.5 From a Goodwill-Based Project to a Funded Project

In the 2018/2019 school year, which started in September, our support to the school teachers was provided remotely, mainly due to our own work issues, as we were involved in other funded projects to which we had to dedicate our time. However, the teachers did not stop organizing Digital Citizenship activities and continued producing articles for the school newspaper, even though the newspaper was now without any funding and there would be no means to print it. We immediately made the decision to publish only two editions of the newspaper, because until then the school year was organized in three school periods (Sep-Dec, Jan-Mar, Apr-Jun), but the Ministry of Education changed the legislation, so the school year could be organized in two periods (Sep-Feb, Mar-Jun), and Caneças School District was one of the first Portuguese school districts to adopt this change. Between January and February 2019 we did not get the means to produce the newspaper, but it was then that the opportunity arose for us to apply for a funded program.

In March 2019, we submitted a pre-application for the project "Digital Citizenship Education for Democratic Participation" to a call for projects opened by the Calouste Gulbenkian Foundation, under the Gulbenkian Academies of Knowledge Program, to which projects already underway could apply. Although the application was submitted by the Autonoma University of Lisbon, where we are teaching staff, it was developed in conjunction with the teachers of the Artur Alves Cardoso School.

The proposal to create an Academy was based on the ongoing project at Artur Alves Cardoso School, with children aged 3–10, which was centered on a printed school newspaper since 2016. It consisted of enhancing the project, contributing to the development of Digital Citizenship skills at school and in the community through three core activities, which were innovative in terms of the project:

1. Production and analysis of digital content by children—television (e.g. community news), podcast and image, with online broadcasting.
2. Science, technology, engineering, arts and mathematics (STEAM) activities, in a makerspace to be created in Caneças, the "Caneças Makers."
3. Teacher training in the areas of Digital Citizenship, STEAM and audiovisuals, in which teachers would organize and implement STEAM and Media Literacy activities with children, their families and community stakeholders.

The pre-application was approved, so we were invited to submit the final application in April, which was approved in May, ensuring the project's funding for three years (the maximum period allowed by the call), between November 2019 and August 2022. The team decided to change the project name to "Digital Citizenship Academy," though the name change was not imposed by the call.

Its target audience was about 200 preschool and primary school children, attending the Artur Alves Cardoso School, who would be involved in STEAM activities, analysis and production of digital media content, adapted to their interests, their micro, meso and macro contexts, as well as the Sustainable Development Goals, involving critical thinking, creative thinking, problem solving and communication. It aimed to achieve three goals:

1. Developing Digital Citizenship skills (active social, personal and professional participation) from the early years involves adapting activities to children and the context (to be characterized), preparing teachers (workshops), providing appropriate spaces (at school, in the Caneças Makerspace and in UALMedia, the TV studios of Autonoma University of Lisbon) and the involvement of families and the community.
2. Ensuring existing media products (school newspaper) and their evolution to online digital, creating content (e.g.: TV News services in video, STEAM activities products), enhancing critical and creative thinking, problem solving and communication skills through media.

3. To become a sustainable project through the infusion of the intervention methodology into the daily life of the school, the creation and continuity of the Caneças Makers and the knowledge and skills of teachers (through debate with researchers, training, and possible workshops with specialists). This knowledge would be fundamental for the eventual replication of the project in other contexts, along with a manual of sense-making practices to be created.

The Digital Citizenship Academy was anchored on a participatory methodology (action research), based on an integrated intervention strategy (formal, non-formal and informal contexts), which implied the promotion of two types of continuity: (i) curricular and pedagogical continuity between preschool and primary school; (ii) continuity of intervention between school, family and community. The implementation of the project, as well as its monitoring and evaluation was guaranteed by three partners, namely:

1. The Parish of Ramada and Caneças created the Caneças Makerspace for STEAM activities, provided space for three conferences to present the results to the community, and supported the costs of the layout and publication of the school newspaper 'O Cusco'/The Busybody, in the printed version.
2. The Caneças School District (Artur Alves Cardoso School) provided facilities and human resources, organized and developed the activities for the school newspaper and STEAM activities, and prepared and monitored the production of TV News Services (UALMedia studios). It also participated in the characterization of the field, monitoring and evaluation of activities.
3. Autonoma University of Lisbon (UAL) assumed the management of the project, monitoring and following up the activities, as well as providing its television studios and human resources.

The funding awarded by the Calouste Gulbenkian Foundation would be used for human resources, goods and equipment (for the "Caneças Makers") and their maintenance, travel for monitoring and follow-up of the project and the children's travel to UAL to record the TV News services on video.

The preparation work for the application to the Calouste Gulbenkian Foundation's Knowledge Program motivated the whole project team, which gained confidence and committed itself to producing another edition of the school newspaper to be published in June. We immediately mobilized the project partners, asking the Parish of Ramada and Caneças to support the costs of printing the newspaper, a proposal that was accepted. The project team also decided to produce a second edition of the TV news service "Telecusco," but this time in the studios of the Autonoma University of Lisbon. This production required renting a bus to transport the children to the center of Lisbon. The parents mobilized, the company lowered the price and the school was able to pay the rental.

On February 9, a group of children from the 3rd and 4th grades went to the university's radio and television studios, accompanied by two teachers. They had previously selected the news items that interested them most and prepared the texts, but there was still a learning process to go through with the studio director, who explained how news is produced and presented on television. Among the various pieces of advice given to the children, the director mentioned the need to read slowly, to look at the camera naturally, and to apply techniques to hide some nervousness, such as avoiding turning the chair while presenting the news.

After a short training session, the test recording was made. First, the presenters recorded the opening and ending of 'Telecusco', as well as the entrance to each of the news items. Then it was each team's turn to record their news, according to the previously defined model: the news was presented by two children and commented by a third one, in order to involve all the children. This was followed by editing work in which many aspects to be improved were identified, which will be worked on at school, so that the next edition of 'Telecusco' will be better than the previous one and so on. The teachers highlighted, above all, the learning achieved and the experience of getting to know a television studio.

This activity would be one of the headlines of the newspaper edition published in June 2019, the other headline being a race of homemade go-karts, built by the children's families. The initiative was held in front of Artur Alves Cardoso School to celebrate World Children's Day and was supported by the Parents' Association. The edition of the school newspaper also included two news items about scientific experiments developed with all the primary school students, which focused on the production of lighting candles, and the study of the reasons why these candles go out. The experiments were carried out with the collaboration of a Nature Science teacher who worked at the Caneças School District 2nd cycle school.

The teachers also developed an activity about video games, during which the 4th grade children discussed what they learned from the games, and six out of 10 responded that the games developed thinking, creativity and imagination, as well as attention span and concentration. The student reports focused on Pajama Day, where teachers and students brought their pajamas to school, and an earthquake drill where 2nd grade children learned what to do if the situation was real. The third report focused on the planting of trees that the children had created at school as part of the "Let's Reforest Portugal" initiative. The trees were planted on April

6th, in a forest area in the Parish of Casal de Cambra, which also belongs to the Odivelas Municipality.

Preschool children were involved in an activity aimed at learning to recognize differences between fiction and news, namely in terms of the format used for each type of text (e.g.: newspaper is usually used to publish news, while books are more often used to publish stories), but also the type of content. In the end, the children produced drawings about news and about stories, and the teachers considered the activity to be productive. The children also produced news about the 'magusto' (a popular feast to celebrate the chestnut, held in many parts of Portugal and Spain), about reading activities in the school library and about the importance of recycling. And so ended the school year.

5.5.1 A New Quantitative Study within the Project

In July 2019, even before we started implementing the plan, scheduled for September 2019, the Calouste Gulbenkian Foundation proposed that we conduct a study, integrated into the Academy and focused on the development of social and emotional skills. It consisted of applying metrics created by the Organisation for Economic Co-operation and Development (OECD) to measure the impact that the activities of the Digital Citizenship Academy would have on the development of social and emotional skills of the children involved in the project.

The set of metrics was designed to measure six competencies (adaptability, self-regulation, communication, creative thinking, resilience, problem solving) and was adapted for children ages 8 and up, but it was possible to use only a subset of metrics in the case of children under 8 years old. In addition, we could choose to measure only two of the six competencies, as it would be a time-consuming process, involving informed consent from the children's parents, followed by the completion of metrics by each child, a parent of that child, and the child's teacher. In addition, the process would be based on a pre-test and post-test.

The Calouste Gulbenkian Foundation's monitoring and evaluation team also suggested that the metrics should be applied in a quasi-experimental setting, with an experimental group and a control group. If there were difficulties in randomly selecting research subjects, the option would be to choose a sample, composed of an intervention group and a comparison group. Children in both groups would answer the pre- and post-test questionnaires, but children in the comparison group would not be involved in the activities of the Digital Citizenship Academy, at least until the application of the post-test.

The possibility of developing a study with an intervention group and a comparison group at the Artur Alves Cardoso School was not feasible, because the activities to be developed involved all students and teachers. Creating two groups, with one not developing any activities, would go against the logic of the work developed until then. The solution was to involve another school from the Caneças School District, whose teachers agreed to join the Digital Citizenship Academy.

In mid-September 2019, at the beginning of the school year, we contacted Fontes de Caneças School, as it was about one kilometer from Artur Alves Cardoso School, had roughly the same number of students (200) and teachers (10), and some of its teachers had attended at least one of the training courses we had delivered in 2016 and 2017/18.

The proposal was to integrate Fontes de Caneças School in the Digital Citizenship Academy, apply the pre- and post-test questionnaires during the 2019/2020 school year and, in the following school year (2020/2021), after the study measuring social and emotional competencies, implement the planned Media Literacy and STEAM activities. The teacher training could take place at the same time as the Artur Alves Cardoso School teacher training or at a later time, depending on teacher availability.

The school coordinator and the teachers accepted the proposal, but the social and emotional competencies to be measured remained to be defined. Together with the teachers of the Artur Alves Cardoso School, it was decided to apply the metrics related to communication and problem-solving competencies, because although they were of equal importance, these two were more associated with Media Literacy and STEAM, respectively. The decision was made in October, so we requested the metrics and formal authorization to apply them from the Calouste Gulbenkian Foundation, which approved the process in November.

In November, we prepared the informed consent documents, which would be approved by the monitoring and evaluation team of the Calouste Gulbenkian Foundation. Following this approval, we sent the informed consent documents to all parents or caregivers at both schools, totaling approximately 400 students, at a rate of 200 per school. The minimum goal was to obtain 75 positive responses among parents at Artur Alves Cardoso School (intervention group) and 25 at Fontes de Caneças School (comparison group). By mid-December we received 94 and 91 positive responses, respectively. The conditions for developing the study were met.

5.5.2 Towards the Implementation of the Intervention Plan

The intervention plan of the Digital Citizenship Academy was to start with the teacher training, which differed from the training courses held in 2016 and 2017/

18, as it was a workshop (see section 4.4.) that immediately required student involvement in STEAM and Media Literacy tasks planned and implemented by the teachers who were part of the trainee group. As the pre-test questionnaires had to be answered before the start of the training, the start was postponed to the beginning of March 2020, with the consent of the teachers. This would prove to be a key decision in terms of the project's success.

In January 2020, we started to apply the questionnaires, with the social and emotional competencies metrics, to children aged 8 and up who had been previously authorized by their parents. In the case of children younger than 8, the study used only the perceptions of the teachers and parents of these children as data. We also started to apply questionnaires to teachers, who had to complete one per child, in a total of 185 between the two schools.

We also sent two questionnaires to each of the 185 parents, one concerning demographic data (characterization of the family context) and uses and practices in digital environments, and another aimed at collecting their perceptions regarding their children's social and emotional skills (pre-test). The questionnaires were returned slowly, as priorities were being dominated by Covid-19 and by the strong possibility of school closures to contain the spread of the pandemic.

At the beginning of March, we had received 127 answers to the questionnaires for characterization of the family context and 117 pre-test questionnaires, some of which were incomplete. After checking the answers received, we found that only data from 100 individuals should be considered, 54 from Artur Alves Cardoso School (intervention group) and 46 from Fontes de Caneças School (comparison group). This response rate (54%) made the comparative study unfeasible, as the intervention group should have a minimum of 75 individuals.

Returning to the end of January 2020 and because the funded project was already underway, the eighth edition of the school newspaper was published, which had as its headline an interview with the Director of Caneças School District, Fernando Costa, whose title was "Students are the most important part of our school." In the four-page interview, conducted by 4th grade students, the principal talked about his personal life, his background, his preference for shared governance over individual management, and stressed the importance of respecting others. Another prominent issue in the newspaper was that the Artur Alves Cardoso School project had achieved international[7] and

---

[7] Tomé, V., Lopes, P. Reis, B., & Dias, C.P. (2019). Active citizenship and participation through the media: a community project focused on preschoolpreschool and primary school

national[8] publicity, being recognized as a replicable good practice (Richardson and Milovidov, 2017) and even contributing to the Caneças School District being selected for the Democratic Schools Network. This network was created by the Council of Europe which officially began in November 2019, in Florence, during a meeting attended by a teacher of Artur Alves Cardoso School, representing the Caneças School District. The last page of the school newspaper was dedicated to this presence in Florence.

This edition of the school newspaper also highlighted the presence of the Police at the Artur Alves Cardoso School, who came to talk to the children about bullying and ways to prevent and combat it. In the preschool, animal rights were discussed and a model of an aquarium was built to represent a real aquarium they wanted to have in the classroom. The children also questioned their families about what these adults expected from them when they grow up. The results were processed and analyzed in class, and the children concluded that adults had the following expectations:

> Adults wish there were more family moments where everyone can talk and be heard. They trust that we will be good people, that is, that we will respect others, that we will be responsible and able to face challenges without giving up at the first difficulty. To this perseverance they want us to be self-confident and humble. / They expect us to have healthier habits and lifestyles, practicing sports, eating carefully and in a balanced way, as well as being defenders of the environment and the planet's sustainability. / They want us to be proactive and more entrepreneurial than they were, that is, to want to create new things, including our own jobs, because their generation was not as good as we would like it to be in this area.

The January 2020 issue also devoted part of the final page to explaining what the Digital Citizenship Academy, which had been started in November 2019. At that point data was being collected from families, followed by teacher training focused on Media Literacy and STEAM. The data to be collected from families and during the training would be essential to adapt all the activities to be developed to the

children. *Comunicação e Sociedade 36*, 101–120. Available at: http://dx.doi.org/10.17231/comsoc.36(2019).2347 / Tomé, V. (2019). Usos de tecnologias analógicas e digitais na formação de cidadãos ativos: um percurso com crianças dos 3 aos 9 anos, seus professores, pais e comunidade local. *Revista Educação e Cultura Contemporânea, 42*, 432–469. Available at: http://periodicos.estacio.br/index.php/reeduc/article/viewArticle/5895 / Tomé, V. (2018). Assessing media literacy in teacher education. In Melda N. Yildiz, Steven S. Funk & Belinha S. De Abreu (Eds.), *Promoting global competencies through media literacy* (pp. 1–18). Hershey (PA): IGI Global.

8 Tomé, Vitor. Preparar cidadãos ativos e capazes de ler o(s) mundo(s) hoje: desafios e constrangimentos (key note speaker). VII Encontro de Bibliotecas Escolas do Alentejo (1 julho). Auditório da DGEstE-DSRA, Évora, 2019. / Tomé, Vitor. Para uma escola cidadã: o modelo 'whole school approach'. Encontro de Educação 'A par e passo, todos juntos vamos construir o futuro' (8 de junho). Figueira de Castelo Rodrigo, 2019.

context, as four years had passed since the last characterization of the families, so it was essential to make a new characterization, which we present below, based on the essential data.

5.5.2.1 Characterizing the New Family Context

Between January and March 2020, we collected data from 127 parents, 56 from Fontes de Caneças School and 71 from Artur Alves Cardoso School. The 71 parents (7 males) were between 25 and 49 years old, with one-third in the age range 36–40. More than one-third (29) had higher education qualifications while 23 had graduated from secondary school.

Like in 2016, there were strong inequalities in terms of the household's average monthly net income. Three families had an income of less than 600 euros, 25 had an income of up to a thousand euros, 15 had an income of between a thousand and 1500 euros, and nine had an income of between 1501 and 2000. Only 11 had incomes of 2001 or more euros. Eight preferred not to answer.

Out of the 71 children (36 females), 30 were aged between four and six years old (22 attended preschool and eight primary school) and 41 between seven and 10 (41 attended primary school). Five children had no siblings and lived in a single-parent household (with their mother). Twenty-five single children lived with both parents, while 29 lived with both parents and one sibling, two siblings or other relatives (10 cases).

Regarding media use, most parents (63 of the 71) watched TV and used the Internet daily, especially via smartphone (63 of the 71) and to surf social networks like Facebook (56), YouTube (37), and Instagram (33). Other social networks usage was minimal and 15 parents did not have a social network profile. Regarding children, 53 watched TV everyday (12 from 2 to 5 days a week, and only two did not watch), which was a higher consumption than Internet (24 everyday, 31 from 2 to 5 days per week and 6 did not use), and that Internet use was mostly synonymous of YouTube (61 users, but only 15 everyday and 6 did not use) and video games (58 users but only 12 everyday, and 10 did not play at all).

Among the adults, the most common means to access the Internet was no longer via a personal laptop (like it was in 2016), but the mobile phone. Among the children, the tablet devices remained the most popular device (46 of the 71), followed by the smartphone (38 of the 71) and console devices (30 of the 71). As was true in 2016, it was clear that the time children spent using digital equipment increased on the weekend, since 38 of the 71 used more than two hours a day, while during working days only seven parents reported similar usage.

According to the guardians, children had learned to use and access digital media from their mother and/or father (52 of the 71), from other family members

(27), or from friends (13). Only three parents stated that their child had learned how to use the computer at school and another three stated that the child had learned on his/her own.

Sixty-three parents stated they watched television with their children and 53 stated that they went with them to the cinema (51 on the weekend). Reading books was another important activity (58 of the 71 parents), followed by outdoor activities (48), but only 27 read newspapers or magazines with them. Parent mediation was lower when it came to the children's use of mobile digital media. While 43 stated they researched online with the children (27 solely on the weekend), only 25 played video games with them (18 solely on the weekend). Like in 2016, there was no clear evidence of mediation through participatory learning, in which parents and children debate use, learn together, and define use strategies (Zaman, Nouwen, Vanattenhoven, de Ferrerre, and Van Looy, 2016).

Even if 56 out of the 71 parent respondents admitted to talk with their children about digital media, the conversations focused more on limiting usage time (55 of the 71) and risk (50 of the 71), and less on encouraging research practices, including homework, or the advantages of online gaming (39 of the 71). In general, the results were similar to 2016's, which we did not read as a failure of the project, since the students and the parents surveyed were not the same as in 2016, and therefore it was not possible to establish a comparison.

Even when teachers mentioned that they talked more with the children's parents about the Internet and the children's use of digital equipment, the truth is that only 12 out of 71 parents admitted to having these conversations. This characterization, four years after the first round, again pointed to the need to establish more dialogue between teachers and parents. However, if we analyze the data collected from parents in 2018, two years after we started the project, we could see some progress, for example in parental mediation and children's perception of learning (formal and informal) in digital environments.

Therefore, a greater investment in the dissemination of students' formal and informal learning, a better dissemination of activities, not only through the printed newspaper, but also through the online newspaper and other means (e.g.: YouTube Channel), could contribute to a closer relationship between parents, children and teachers, in terms of digital practices and learning, which could be an added value to the community project.

5.5.3 How the Covid-19 Changed the Intervention Plan

The household characterization data did not change the intervention plan previously established with the teachers. The fact that it was organized by a team that already knew the community well and had been working together for more than three years was an added value. Everything was ready to move forward with the teacher training in March 2020, but Covid-19 required changing all the plans. Teacher training was supposed to start on March 11, but the Ministry of Education canceled all training on March 9 and decided to close the schools five days later. The project stopped!

With schools closed and teachers trying to adapt to emergency distance learning, we started to make adaptations to the project, as all activities had to be rescheduled. Between March and July, in coordination with the Ministry of Education, the teacher training workshop was redesigned and adapted to the on-line environment and accredited as e-learning training. In July we managed to set new dates and times for the training. A problem persisted, as the students who attended the 4th Grade and transitioned to the 5th Grade, changed school and it would no longer be possible to complete the post-test questionnaires. We then contacted the teachers at 'Escola dos Castanheiros' (translated as Chestnut Trees School), which is the school of the Caneças School District for 5th to 9th graders. Four of the teachers, three from Mathematics and Nature Sciences and one from Arts agreed to participate in the training and accompany the students, involving them in STEAM and Media Literacy activities.

The two teacher training workshops took place between September and December (see Section 4.4), with the teachers organized in two classes, one with 15 and the other with 14. From the beginning of the training until the beginning of January we developed the following activities:

1. Production of templates, one for planning STEAM and Media Literacy activities, and another for the final evaluation report to be produced by teachers.
2. Planning, implementation and evaluation of 17 STEAM and Media Literacy workshops and planned another 11, using the template created, which would allow organizing the manual of best practices. The activities were developed in the classroom, as the creation of a Makerspace in the facilities of the Parish of Ramada and Caneças was made impossible by the pandemic.
3. Creation of activity evaluation/observation sheets to be filled in by teachers, but also by children, since health rules did not allow the observation of STEAM and Media Literacy activities in the classroom, as initially planned.
4. Production of an edition of the school newspaper 'O Cusco' in January 2020.

At the end of the training workshops, the 29 teachers expressed their willingness to continue collaborating in the project, so they were involved in the process of reorganizing the intervention plan, which included the following activities:

- January 2021 – December 2022:
    - Planning, implementation and evaluation of STEAM and Media Literacy activities, by the 29 teachers, organized in teams and using resources provided by the project;
    - Production of two TV news services (one per year), by children and teachers, and possibly involving the community;
    - Possible short term trainings in robotics and other areas suggested by the teachers involved;
    - Frequent monitoring of and support to teachers (via Zoom, on Wednesdays from 17 to 19, and via phone or WhatsApp on an ongoing basis);
    - Possible interviews with teachers, children and parents, if circumstances permit;
- February 2021: publication of the newspaper 'O Cusco', which will have three more editions through the end of 2022;
- March 2021: publication and dissemination of a good practice manual;
- May/June 2021: application of the post-test questionnaires to children, parents and teachers;
- July 2021:
    - Presentation of the results to the community (in a format to be defined);
    - Analysis of results (teachers, students, parents, researchers …)
- Sept 2021: redefinition of the community intervention plan with the group of teachers and project partners, which will run until July 2022.
- July 2022:
    - Presentation of results to the community (in a format to be defined);
    - Analysis of results (teachers, students, parents, researchers …)
- September 2022: ensure continuity of the project through organization and implementation of a sustainability plan.

The plan was approved, together with the teachers, on January 15, 2021, but by then the evolution of the Covid-19 pandemic was worrying, which led the Government to decide to close the schools a week later, on January 22. Initially, the general closure of schools was to last two weeks, but it was extended, so that preschool and primary school children did not return to school until March 15, while students in the following school levels would only return to school in April, after the Easter vacation period.

With the schools closed again, the production of the school newspaper edition scheduled for February was canceled, as was the TV news service 'Telecusco'. The teachers had restarted emergency distance learning at the beginning of February, so they had no room for any short-term actions. So, we opted to keep the monitoring meetings on Wednesdays and spent the time producing the best practices manual in digital form. Although the teachers produced the evaluation reports and the plans, as well as the final products, the process required a lot of coordination, so meetings were essential for the completion of this task.

The manual is entitled "Doing the Whole World - STEAM and Media Literacy Activities from Preschool to 2nd Cycle." The first part of the title is a quote from a 2nd grade child, who answered the question "What other activities would you like to do as part of the Digital Citizenship Academy" this way. The second part of the title was what had been initially defined by us. Although we had advanced with the written part of the manual, we had not yet defined who would be the editor. This issue was resolved quickly, as the Director of Special Projects of the Ministry of Education, upon learning that we were writing the book, informed us of his interest in editing, publishing and presenting the book.

As for the structure, the manual is organized in four parts. The first part presents the framework of the teacher training workshop based on international models and Portuguese educational policy[9]. The second part describes the process of the teacher training, presents the results and the evaluation of the training, by the teachers and the trainer, with reference to the objectives of the Portuguese education policy. The third part includes the 28 activity plans created by teachers, and the 17 implemented plans refer to the videos created by teachers within these activities.

The fourth part of the manual presents the project's sustainability plan as of March 2021. Finally, the manual also includes short texts from four people connected to the Digital Citizenship Academy: the Director-General of Education (who directs the entity that supervised the teacher training), the Director of the Gulbenkian Knowledge Program (which finances the project), the Director of Caneças School District (whose support has been fundamental to maintaining the project) and the president of the Friends of Caneças Association, the main cultural association in the community.

The text was completed on March 1st and editing began at the offices of the Ministry of Education. Because classes had not restarted yet, we decided to move forward with the creation of the online version of the school newspaper, through a site created on the free platform Wix, developed by a student who was finishing

---

9 The member states of the European Union have complete autonomy in terms of educational policies, and there is no European policy that overrides national policies.

her degree in Communication Sciences and started collaborating on the project. At the same time, and because the teachers had produced multimedia content related to the STEAM and Media Literacy activities they had developed, we decided to go ahead with the creation of a YouTube channel, which would be linked to the manual. Each activity plan has a QR Code that allows you to link to the corresponding video on the YouTube Channel 'O Cusco'.

With classes restarted on March 15, the teachers had planned new STEAM and Media Literacy activities, but their implementation was complicated, because situations of precautionary quarantine of students, teachers and other school staff were frequent. There was even one teacher who was quarantined at home for 14 days, and after a day at school in which he had contact with an infected student, he went home for another 14 days. In spite of situations like this, it was necessary to continue teaching and learning—both of which had become very complex.

At Caneças School, the teachers were unable to implement STEAM and Media Literacy activities between March and June. At Caneças' Kindergarten, the teachers were able to plan and implement the activity "Talking Chicken," which consisted of exploring the story "Os ovos Misteriosos" (The Mysterious Eggs), by Luísa Ducla Soares, followed by the creation of a board game, in which the children, following instructions on cards created by the teachers, should give instructions to a robot (shaped like a chicken) to make a certain route on the board, stopping at a house defined on the card.

The four teachers at Castanheiros School created a one-minute video festival, which the students joined and produced about 30 videos, followed by a vote to choose the three videos they liked best. The authors of the videos with the most votes received books that the teachers bought with funds provided by the Digital Citizenship Academy. At Maria Costa School (one of the four primary schools in the Caneças School District), three teachers were able to explore the story "The Princess and the Pea" with 4th grade children using Plickers cards. Faced with a question about the text, the students could choose among several possible answers, and each of the answers corresponded to a Plickers card. To check if the students had gotten it right, the teacher used a cell phone, which read the Plickers cards and returned the results.

In Vieira Caldas Kindergarten, since there was no space to create a traditional vegetable garden, teachers and students created a vertical vegetable patch, in which they produced sunflowers and lettuces that were then used to make salad at school. Also at Artur Alves Cardoso Kindergarten a vegetable garden was created by teachers and children, in which lettuces, cabbages and strawberries were grown and then eaten by the children in the school cafeteria. This activity would be the headline of the ninth edition of the school newspaper, which would be published in June 2021. The second headline of this edition highlighted the activity in which the children created a model that proposed changes to the traffic around the school, to increase road safety, and then wrote to the president of the Odivelas Municipality and the president of the Parish of Ramada and Caneças, requesting the implementation of the proposed changes.

The June 2021 newspaper edition also showed that the Caneças community project had gained dimension and recognition. Pages 12 and 13 contained the news of the presentation of the ebook "Doing the Whole World - STEAM and Media Literacy Activities from Preschool to 2nd Cycle," which took place online on May 3, at the 5th National Meeting on Media Education, organized by the Director-General for Education. Five of the 30 authors, four teachers and the trainer participated in this presentation, but also the Director of the Gulbenkian Knowledge Program and the Director-General of Education, who showed their availability to continue supporting the project. On the same day 'O Cusco' would also be presented online and the YouTube channel 'O Cusco', in which are all the videos produced by the teachers and even the video of the ebook presentation.

The channel 'O Cusco' also included a broadcast by RTP, the Portuguese Public TV Broadcaster, in which the 3rd grade students and the teacher participated and addressed the issue of misinformation in the media and the negative effects of this information. The report was recorded and broadcast on the same day, June 15, 2021, as part of the debate program 'Is It or Isn't It?', which focused on human rights in the digital age and Media Literacy. The children from Artur Alves Cardoso School were on national television, in a report in which some of them took on the role of journalists and interviewed their peers about misinformation. The main interviewer, the primary school student Debora Costa, was very natural in the performance, as happens with those who have had this role for years, asked questions like, "Where do you look for the real and fake news?," "What do you think about the older kids learning the same as us?," "How do you see that a news story is fake?." She received several valid answers, as the RTP news report shows, such as "a fake news is a news that doesn't make sense," "it is easier to find a fake news on the Internet," and "we can see real news on RTP news."

The intervention plan was being carried out, despite some deviations. Even in such a non-ideal situation, more STEAM and Media Literacy activities were planned and implemented in schools, and regular monitoring was maintained. The best practices manual was organized and published, the online school newspaper and a YouTube channel were created, and results were publicly presented with the book's presentation in May 2021. However, the TV News Service was not recorded, nor was the February edition of the school newspaper published.

At the end of the school year, it was not possible to collect data to evaluate the project with children, parents and teachers, because in June we applied the post-test questionnaires on social and emotional competencies, which was a very complex process due to public health concerns. Even so, we were able to collect data for 77 of the 87 children who had answered the pre-test in early 2020. At the time of this publication, the data is now being processed by the Calouste Gulbenkian Foundation's monitoring services. At this point in our writing, we will pause as this book comes to an end. However, not to worry, other books will follow since the project seems to be one of those that has no end!

References

Burns, J., Cooke, D., & Schweidler, C. (2011). *A short guide to community based participatory action research*. Los Angeles: Advancement Project.

Carrington, V. (2013). An argument for assemblage theory: Integrated spaces, mobility and polycentricity. In A. Burke & J. Marsh (Eds.), *Children's virtual play worlds: Culture, learning and participation* (pp. 200–216). New York: Peter Lang.

Chaudron, S. (2015). *Young children & digital technology: A qualitative exploratory study across seven countries*. Luxembourg: Publications Office of the European Union.

Chaudron, S. (2016). *Young children, parents and digital technology in the home context across Europe: The findings of the extension of the young children (0–8) and digital technology pilot study to 17 European countries*. DigiLitEY Project Meeting, 3., Lordos Hotel, Larnaca, Chipre, 17–18 May.

Colvert, A. (2015). *Ludic authorship: Reframing literacies through peer-to-peer alternate reality game design in the primary classroom*. Unpublished PhD, Institute of Education, University College of London.

Council of Europe. (2018b). *Digital Citizenship Education (DCE) - 10 domains*. Available at: https://rm.coe.int/10-domains-dce/168077668e

Creswell, J. & Clark, V (2013). *Designing and conducting mixed methods research*. Thousand Oaks (CA): Sage.

Downes, P., & Cefai, C. (2016). *How to prevent and tackle bullying and school violence: Evidence and practices for strategies for inclusive and safe schools, NESET II report*. Luxembourg: Publications Office of the European Union. doi: 10.2766/0799.

Edwards, S., Nolan, A., Henderson, M., Mantilla, A., Plowman, L., & Skouteris, H. (2016). Young children's everyday concepts of the Internet: A platform for cyber-safety education in the early years. *British Journal of Educational Technology*. doi:10.1111/bjet.12529.

ENABLE. (2015). *The enable research review – A scientific review of the school bullying phenomenon and anti-bullying programmes for adolescent health*. Available at: http://files.eun.org/enable/assets/downloads/D1_1%20Review%20of%20bullying%20and%20cyber%20bullying.pdf

Flowers, N. (Ed.) (2007). *Compasito – manual on human rights education for children*. Strasbourg: Council of Europe.

Green, B. (1988). Subject-specific literacy and school learning: A focus on writing. *Australian Journal of Education, 32*(2), 156–179.

Huber, J., & Reynolds, C. (2014). *Developing intercultural competence through education.* Strasbourg: Council of Europe. Accessed from: https://rm.coe.int/developing-intercultural-enfr/16808ce258

OECD. (2017). *Starting strong V: Transitions from early childhood education and care to primary education.* OECD Publishing, Paris. Accessed from: http://dx.doi.org/10.1787/9789264276253-en.

Palaiologou, I. (2017). Digital violence and children under five: The phantom menace within digital homes of the 21st century?. *Education Sciences & Society, 1,* 123–136.

Raulin-Serrier, P., Soriani, A., Styslavska, O., & Tomé, V. (2020). *Digital citizenship education – Trainers' pack.* Strasbourg: Council of Europe. Accessed from: https://book.coe.int/en/human-rights-democratic-citizenship-and-interculturalism/8161-digital-citizenship-education-trainers-pack.html

Ribble, M. (2011). *Digital citizenship in schools* (2nd ed.). Eugen, OR: International Society for Technology in Education (ISTE).

Richardson, J., & Milovidov, E. (2017). *Digital citizenship education: Multi-stakeholder consultation report.* Strasbourg: Council of Europe.

Sefton-Green, J., Marsh, J., Erstad, O., & Flewitt, R. (2016). Establishing a research agenda for the digital literacy practices of young children: A White Paper for COST Action IS1410. Accessed from: http://digilitey.eu

Shamrova, D., & Cummings, C. (2017). Participatory action research (PAR) with children and youth: An integrative review of methodology and PAR outcomes for participants, organizations, and communities. *Children and Youth Services Review, 81,* 400–412. Accessed from: https://www.sciencedirect.com/science/article/pii/S0190740917302086?via%3Dihub

Tomé, V. Digital Citizenship Education: acting with children (3–9), their teachers, parents and out-of-school entities. ECREA 2016 preconference – Research of Children, Youth and Media. Department of Media Studies and Journalism, Masaryk University, Brno & Institute for Research on Children, Youth and Families, Masaryk University & ECREA TWG: Children, Youth and Media & COST Action IS1410, The Digital Literacy and Multimodal Practices of Young Children (November, 8). Prague: Czech Republic, 2016.

United Nations. (1948). *Universal Convention of Human Rights.* Accessed from: https://www.un.org/en/about-us/universal-declaration-of-human-rights

United Nations. (1989). *Convention of the Rights of the Child.* Accessed from: https://www.ohchr.org/en/professionalinterest/pages/crc.aspx

Zaman, B., Nouwen, M., Vanattenhoven, J., De Ferrerre, E., & Van Looy, J. (2016). A qualitative inquiry into the contextualized parental mediation practices of young children's digital media use at home. *Journal of Broadcasting & Electronic Media, 60*(1), 1–22.

CHAPTER 6

A Never Ending Project

This chapter points out the main results of the project, answering the starting questions. It also makes an evaluation of the project as a sense-making practice on Digital Citizenship Education. It then points out the five reasons why the project withstood all setbacks and did not fail, and ends with a portrait of plans for the replication of the project in the countryside of Portugal, which will move forward in the near future.

6.1 Evaluation: Results 2015–2020

Broadly speaking, the 'Digital Citizenship Academy' project, in its six years of existence, has managed to implement four teacher trainings, benefiting a total of 79 teachers. It has published a book of best practices in STEAM and Media Literacy, produced nine editions of the school newspaper 'O Cusco', the online version of the school newspaper and the YouTube channel 'O Cusco'. It has been the focus of 10 international and national scientific publications and 20 papers in scientific conferences, continues to gain international visibility, which would not be expected for a local project which was developed in a small country. In national terms it has contributed, at least in part, to the inclusion of Media Education and Digital

Citizenship in curricula, creating and disseminating activities that can be used in formal, non-formal and informal learning contexts. It is a project that has created conditions for its replication and having influenced public policies.

Going now straight to our starting problem, at the research level—the extent to which a community-based project can empower preschool and primary school age children in order to become active and effective citizens in the digital era. The project and its results showed that the methodological model followed is suitable to develop a community-based action research project aimed to develop very young children's citizenship and digital literacy competences.

They also show that the children's voice, the social intervention through the school newspaper, clearly grew throughout the project. Children went from having a more subdued and sometimes almost decorative role in the activities, to being able to decide what they wanted to do, how they wanted to do it, and how they wanted to communicate these decisions to the community. The course of the project clearly shows that children were gaining space and climbing Hart's Ladder (Hart, 1992).

The research problem had three further sub-questions, with the first being: "How can in-service teacher training on Digital Citizenship education improve teachers' digital literacy practices in classrooms?." Starting with an in-service teacher training program (and continuing to support teachers through planning and assessment meetings), to then characterizing the community context, and adapting the model on a regular basis, it became possible to continuously develop adequate digital literacy activities involving teachers, children, parents, and other community members.

The teachers organized educational activities aimed at encouraging students to analyze and produce media content and develop skills of critical analysis that were reflective and creative. They analyzed media content focused on current themes, and in some cases, themes were chosen and researched by students, thus linking popular culture and school culture. Students reflected on communication in different media and the media's function in society. Therefore, teachers did not use only the media to teach, but also used media to teach about media.

K-12 teachers are able to develop Media Literacy activities with their pupils, using traditional and/or digital technologies, especially during in-service teacher training courses that last for a period of two to four months. It is also important to offer them certified in-service teacher training, not only because it attracts them (because they need to attend training courses do progress in their professional careers), but also because pre-service teacher training in Media Literacy is lacking.

Teachers also lack specific training on the technical use of media in classrooms, and especially on digital media. These technologies must be used in teacher training courses in order to help them find new ways to incorporate available resources in an educational context. Moreover, during training courses, teachers should be invited to present activities they have developed with students, because this is an effective way to share knowledge and practices.

Teachers are able to overcome the lack of technologies in their classrooms by using their own devices and/or pupils' devices. However, the technology does not change pedagogy by itself. Media Literacy activities become richer and more effective if they are developed by small groups of teachers, preferably from several school levels and disciplines.

As for the second question—What are the digital literacies practices of young children in school, family and community contexts?—we might say that children are "digitally fluent from a very young age," suggesting the need for "a re-conceptualization of young children's learning in early years pedagogy" as well as a re-examination of "the way children learn and the way in which the early years workforce organize their learning environments" (Palaiologou, 2016). As the project shows, children limited to traditional printed media are slowly adopting digital media, as exemplified by the production of the news broadcast. The situation should evolve rapidly to bridge the gap between high digital use at home versus low digital use at school. The continual improvement of the intervention plan boosted the technology usage and the complexity of the digital practices. In the first teacher training (2016), the activities were very school-based and almost entirely analog. In the third training (2020), all groups created digital products with the children.

Question number three was "How do both formal and informal learning contexts shape children's digital literacy practices?." The school's voluntary adoption of the project enabled its continued sustainability, with the school's newspaper progressively becoming the community's newspaper. According to the teachers' perceptions, the activities have helped children to hone their operational, critical, and cultural skills, as well as increasing the children's social participation both in and outside the school and shaping their practices as citizens.

After an analysis focused on the results from the field, we now analyze the project itself, using a "tool for analysis of best practices in Digital Citizenship education" (Frau-Meigs, O'Neill, Soriani and Tomé, 2017, p. 77) provided by the Council of Europe and organized into 12 fields:

1. *Sense-making rationale/vision*: the project has a community focus and intends to be a vehicle for change, mobilizing the community to solve problems that affect it.

2. *Project type*: ACD is a research project focused on practices and end-user engagement, also involving resource production.
3. *Actors/stakeholders*: from this point of view the project involves civil society, academia, public and private sectors, and others, such as journalist associations.
4. *Public aimed/target*: the project targets children, professionals, parents and other community members, such as the elderly.
5. *Funding*: the funding is mixed.
6. *Evaluation/performance*: the types of evaluations used are summative, formative, transformative, iterative/agile external and internal.
7. *Resources*: the project focused on teacher training, since four training courses were developed since 2016, but also on skill-building, informing (the school newspaper) and networking ('O Cusco' website and YouTube channel), and reporting through scientific publication and oral presentations.
8. *Digital Citizenship competences*: it assumes transversality, focusing on values, attitudes, skills, knowledge and critical understanding, while also engaging community members and policymakers.
9. *Setting*: it started within a school but was progressively extended to their schools and to the community, involving digital media companies and platforms, as well as the local government.
10. *Duration*: the project started in March 2015 and arrived to the field in January 2016.
11. *Governance level*: it is local or regional, but it will soon be replicated in the countryside of Portugal.
12. *Digital specificities*: the project is based on participatory pedagogies (through the training courses and activities developed by children and teachers), through a consistently dynamic model that allows the regular adaptation of the intervention plan. It generates products and outcomes delivered in print and online, including organic, bottom-up input.

The project answers to the 12 areas of Digital Citizenship Education. It is however limited by a set of factors. Firstly, it has been developed in a local context and its results cannot be extrapolated. Secondly, the results are also based on teachers' and parents' perceptions, and on data collected by the researchers through tools adapted or designed by them and not validated for the Portuguese population. Thirdly, study participants were those who voluntarily accepted and/or those authorized to participate, which means that the results may have been different even if they involved individuals in the same context.

6.3 Sustainability Plan

The community intervention project will continue at least until December 2022, when the financial support from the Calouste Gulbenkian Foundation ceases. At that time, the project will have been in the field for seven years, which goes far beyond the initial planned duration, which was two years, between the beginning of 2016 and the beginning of 2018. At this point, it is important to mention a set of five factors that prevented the project ending in February 2018, as was initially planned, but that has also caused it to move forward until now.

1 - *Support from institutions*: the project started with an individual post-doctoral fellowship (March 2015 - February 2018) that was granted to us by the Science and Technology Foundation, the Portuguese public agency that supports science, technology and innovation, in all scientific domains, under responsibility of the Ministry for Science, Technology and Higher Education. We obtained logistical support from Odivelas Municipality in 2015, which granted contact with schools in the municipality, among them the Caneças School District, whose support was fundamental. It was the administration of Caneças School District that provided facilities for teacher training and requested the expansion of the project to all preschool and primary schools in the group in December 2016. We also had the support of the Leonardo Coimbra Training Center of the National Association of Teachers, which supervised the first two teacher trainings. The project also has, since the end of 2019, the support of the Parish of Ramada and Caneças, which has supported the printing costs of the newspaper, but which could be a much more significant partner if the creation of a makerspace on their premises becomes a reality (as was planned, but made unfeasible by the pandemic). And we had the collaboration of the Ministry of Education in publishing news from the school newspaper 'O Cusco' right from 2016. Further, in 2020, it supervised the teacher trainings, as well as edited and published the project's book of best practices. And we have the support of Portugal's largest cultural foundation, the Calouste Gulbenkian Foundation, which funded the project at a time when the team's commitment was starting to wane. The Foundation also monitors, follows up, and contributes decisively to the project's visibility. In 2018, we started to count on the support of the Autonoma University of Lisbon, which allowed us to continue the project, providing financial and human resources.

2 - *The engagement of the community*: the support of the institutions is fundamental but is not enough, as a community intervention project must assume a double format, which is top-down and bottom-up at the same time. It must be desired by the community and must create conditions for the engagement of all

stakeholders in a "whole-school approach" (Huber and Reynolds, 2014). The project did not end right after the training in early 2016 because a group of eight teachers agreed to work with us on a voluntary basis until February 2018. And it was these teachers who paved the way for us to present the project to parents, for parents to agree to be interviewed and to agree to have their children interviewed as well. These parents talked to other parents and supported the students' interaction with the community and collaboration on the newspaper activities (e.g., supporting their children in writing reports in the community; answering questionnaires). The teaching staff at Artur Alves Cardoso School has taken us in and treated us as equals. The school coordinator has done a remarkable job since the beginning, coordinating the production of the school newspaper from the design of the activities to the production of the contents, being one of five teachers who have been in the project since January 2016 and who attended the three training courses. It was also the teachers who started to distribute the school newspaper in the Caneças community, which allowed the establishment of a communication that contributes to the engagement of the community in the project. It was also the teachers who brought in husbands and fathers to develop common projects (e.g.: model of the school the students dreamed of, model of the solar system). And then the students started intervening through the school newspaper, writing to local politicians to ask for improvements to the common spaces and traffic, writing to the Minister of Education to improve the school's resources, asking the community to offer them trees for their reforestation project after the 2017 fires. The students involved their family members and other community members, interviewing them, for example, about bullying, what they liked to see covered in the newspaper, and how they played when they were kids. It is also all this mutual support and collaboration between community members that keeps the project going.

3 - *The balanced and dynamic intervention model*: the project was structured from the beginning assuming a double approach in the field, balancing action and research, in line with what is proposed by Burns, Coke and Schweidler (2011, p. 8), which we systematize in Table 6.1, illustrating with the work developed:

Table 6.1: Project structure at the "Action level" and the "Research level"

Action level	Research level
Choose a problem: How can preschool and primary school children be empowered as digital citizens able to actively participate in communities (local, national, global) either online and offline, in a responsible and safe way?	**Identifying a research question**: To what extent a community-based project can empower preschool and primary school age children in order to become active and effective citizens in the digital era?
Identify resources ... a certified training course on Digital Citizenship, a trainer, funding (individual grant), the availability of the local government to contact schools; **and solutions** ... training preschool and primary school teachers, and involve their pupils, families and the community	**Choosing a research methodology**: the research methodology focused on mixed-methods approach relying on questionnaires, interviews, field notes and report analysis. In 2016, it starts following the research model with very young children designed by Sefton-Green et al. (2016)
Develop a plan: invite teachers and implement the training, co-designing an intervention plan based on data collected from the community and motivate teachers to collaborate on its implementation until February 2018	**Implementing the methodology**: data were collected from teachers, children and parents in 2016, in order to inform the codesign of the intervention plan. Other data were collected regularly, through reports, field notes, and observation
Implement the plan: the plan was implemented in due time, and the codesigned intervention plan in the community started in September 2016	**Analyzing the results**: The collected data were analyzed regularly, either for produce scientific articles or to inform the renewal of the intervention plans
Evaluate, and perhaps return to step 1: the intervention plan was regularly monitored and evaluated in deep in July 2017, July 2018, March 2019, and March 2020. After data analyzes, the intervention plans were renewed (codesigning)	**Reporting on the results**: three book chapters, four scientific articles, and three other publications were focused on the project. It was also presented in 20 scientific conferences in Portugal, US, Brazil, Georgia, Latvia, Spain, and Czech Republic

The project has been sustained by constant evaluation, informed by data collected from the community, in order to adapt the action to the needs, without neglecting the research level. Therefore, like the research model structured by Sefton-Green et al. (2016), which we decided to follow in 2016, we seek balance and consistency, but we seek to implement a dynamic project, adapted and further adaptable, so it is subject to frequent rebalancing and reconfigurations, in order to overcome tensions or incompatibilities and keep the level of involvement of community participants as high as possible.

4 - *Internal and external monitoring*: regular internal monitoring often took place in lunchtime meetings with most of the teachers, who ate lunch at school in a room next to the children's cafeteria. These meetings were fundamental to creating commitment among people. An agenda was organized for each meeting, starting with the presentation of the progress made in the project (e.g. number of interviews held, preliminary results), the dissemination of the project (e.g. collaboration from Odivelas Municipality, participation in conferences or scientific publications), followed by the discussion of proposals, some of which were milestones in the project and did not let it end, such as

- The creation of a school newspaper (September 2016).
- The a second teacher training (July 2017).
- The continuation of the school newspaper, and therefore of the project, even without funding (February 2018).
- The application to the Knowledge Program of the Calouste Gulbenkian Foundation (March 2019).
- The implementation of the teacher training workshops in e-learning format (July 2020).
- The anticipated publication of the book of best practices, which was planned for the end of the project (January 2021).
- The creation of the online version of the school newspaper and of the YouTube channel (February 2021).

The monitoring was also external, as we worked with experts in the area at the stage of project execution as was the case of Belinha de Abreu (Sacred Heart University, US), who is a co-author of this book. In 2016 we began to work with Altina Ramos (University of Minho), one of the best Portuguese specialists in education, Maria José Brites (Lusófona University of Porto, Portugal) and Stephane Chaudron (European Commission Joint Research Centre), who provided us with data collection tools and advice, Jackie Marsh (Sheffield University, UK), who signed the forward of this book and who led, between 2015 and 2018, the COST DigiLitEY action, a project with researchers from 36 countries, focused on the digital practices of children aged 0–8 years, in which we were integrated.

Also in 2016, we were part of the team of experts of the 'Digital Citizenship Education' project, of the Council of Europe, which allowed us to have contact with dozens of researchers and other experts from Europe and beyond. Regular discussion with external researchers allowed us to publicize the project, increase the team's resilience, and receive inputs that proved decisive in the direction the project took. Since the end of 2019, the project also benefits from the monitoring carried out by the Calouste Gulbenkian Foundation, through a team of academics who monitor the activities and support the team in measuring the impact of the project. This monitoring, which requires regular and detailed reports, implies a reflection on practices, methodologies and results that makes the Digital Citizenship Academy more effective and more sustainable.

5 - *Partnerships and visibility of the project*: the Caneças project has gained progressive visibility, first in the community, especially after the publication of the first edition of the school newspaper in December 2016, but also among political, cultural and social decision makers, since we presented the project at the Odivelas Municipal Education Council in January 2017. The newspaper then reached the page of the Directorate-General of Education and the following issues were already distributed in the community. Outside the community, the project reached many teachers during training sessions for teachers and even journalists.

In 2017, we joined the project created 'Media Literacy and Journalism' developed by the Journalists Union, with the support of CENJOR, Portugal's national training center for journalists, the Ministry of Education and the Presidency of the Republic. In November, we collaborated in the training of 78 journalists and journalism teachers in the area of Media Literacy. In 2018, a training was designed for Middle and Secondary School teachers, which would eventually be accredited by the Ministry of Education. Thirty of those journalists trained were then accredited as teacher trainers in the area of Media Literacy. In 2019 they trained 100 teachers across the country, and in 2020 they trained about 70 more, 23 of them in the Azores Archipelago.

In 2019, we adapted the training course for preschool and primary school teachers, which was accredited at the end of the year, so the two projects became associated, due to having common interests and sharing the same training workshop. The Caneças School District began to rely on journalists and their training center. In 2018, for example, as we were unable to design the school newspaper, we requested the support of the training center, which gave us the facilities to be able to do so.

Still in 2019, we presented both projects in the United States at a conference of the National Association for Media Literacy Education held at the now defunct Newseum in Washington D.C.. The correspondent from RTP, the Portuguese public TV made a report that was broadcast in Portugal on July 1st. The visibility became national. More recently, in June 2021, RTP did a report about disinformation at the Artur Alves Cardoso School, in which the students were the main actors. The report was broadcast in a major information program, and the national visibility increased.

Internationally, the project's visibility is centered on international conferences and scientific publications, and it has been publicized in several countries, from the United States to Australia, and from Brazil to Georgia, as well as several European countries. The Caneças project was also highlighted by the Council of Europe (Richardson and Milovidov, 2017). Further, in 2019, a teacher from the Artur Alves Cardoso School went to Florence to participate in a conference and mark the entry of the Caneças School District into the Democratic School Network of the Council of Europe. This participation was an essential milestone of the project that undoubtedly contributes to its continuity.

6.4 Making the Case-Study Replicable: The Methodological Level

After six years in the field, the Caneças project, currently titled 'Digital Citizenship Academy' will be replicated in the countryside of Portugal, 200 kilometers from Lisbon, in the municipality of Proença-a-Nova, a rural area with around 7100 inhabitants. This process began in April 2021, during an online monitoring meeting of the project. The proposal was presented to the teachers, who showed their availability to collaborate, including in the teacher training activities.

We then proposed to the Calouste Gulbenkian Foundation this new area of the project, which does not implicate extra funding, and the proposal was accepted. Then we asked the Directorate-General of Education to organize a teacher training course in Proença-a-Nova, replicating those that were implemented between September and December 2020. The proposal was accepted, and we contacted the Councilor of Education of Proença-a-Nova City Council, who organized a meeting with the board of Proença-a-Nova School District.

After the first meeting, in which we presented the project and the conditions for its realization, the school management requested summarized information to share with preschool, primary school and 2nd cycle teachers. We prepared this information, which the teachers analyzed in May. They later met on June 2nd with the administration and about 25 teachers who expressed interest. To work, a class must have a minimum of 12 elements and a maximum of 15, because the teachers do not want a totally face-to-face training, but a hybrid one, with half of the sessions online, which is perfectly possible according to the Ministry of Education's regulation approved in 2020.

We communicated to the teachers our intention to structure the project following Burns, Coke and Schweidler's (2011, p. 8) guidelines, which implies identifying a problem, resources and solutions, structuring and implementing a plan that will be evaluated periodically ("Action level"), while identifying a research question, which will be answered according to a given methodology to be implemented, from which data will emerge, which will be analyzed, and the results reported ("Research level"). In concrete terms, the following tasks will follow:

1. Workshop registration for teachers on the website of the Directorate-General of Education
2. Collection of data to characterize the teachers, their digital practices and their perceptions of their students' digital uses and practices (the template used in Caneças will be reused)
3. The training workshop will be distributed over three months, based on the work developed in Caneças, using materials already produced as well as new ones, depending on the interest of teachers and the needs identified (existing templates will be used for workshop planning, evaluation sheets for teachers, students and trainer, as well as for the teachers' report)
4. In a joint effort with the management of the Proença-a-Nova School District, the students of the teachers enrolled in the training will be identified, in order to send informed consent documents to their parents or caregivers (the template used in Caneças will be reused)
5. Application of a questionnaire of demographic information to the families who agree to participate (the template used in Caneças will be reused)
6. Pre-test questionnaires on social and emotional competences (Calouste Gulbenkian Foundation template)
7. Evaluation of the activities developed and possible publication of a book of best practices
8. Co-design of an intervention plan adapted to the context, with the data collected from the families
9. Implementation of the intervention plan (in conjunction with the methodology defined in the Research level)
10. Weekly project monitoring (online, via Zoom)
11. Application of post-test questionnaires on social and emotional competences (Calouste Gulbenkian Foundation template)
12. Analysis of results
13. Evaluation of the intervention plan and eventual renewal
14. Reporting of results

Once the conditions for applying the model followed in Caneças are verified, we will follow the same methodological option that we followed in Caneças, because we believe it adapts to different contexts. The essential part of the project will consist of knowing the terrain well and identifying a problem that the community wants to see solved, always involving the children in this resolution from the beginning and in an effective way, with them participating in decisions, taking initiatives, being assisted by adults.

References

Burns, J., Cooke, D., & Schweidler, C. (2011). *A short guide to community based participatory action research*. Los Angeles: Advancement Project.

Frau-Meigs, D., O'Neill, B., Soriani, A., & Tomé, V. (2017). *Digital citizenship education: Overview and new perspectives*. Strasbourg: Council of Europe.

Hart, R. (1992). *Children's participation from tokenism to citizenship*. Florence: UNICEF Innocenti Research Centre.

Huber, J., & Reynolds, C. (2014). *Developing intercultural competence through education*. Strasbourg: Council of Europe. Accessed from: https://rm.coe.int/developing-intercultural-enfr/16808ce258

Palaiologou, I. (2016). Children under five and digital technologies: Implications for early years pedagogy. *European Early Childhood Education Research Journal, 24*(1), 5–24.

Richardson, J., & Milovidov, E. (2017). *Digital citizenship education: Multi-stakeholder consultation report*. Strasbourg: Council of Europe.

Sefton-Green, J., Marsh, J., Erstad, O., & Flewitt, R. (2016). *Establishing a research agenda for the digital literacy practices of young children: A white paper for COST action IS1410*. Accessed from: http://digilitey.eu

CHAPTER 7

Lessons Learned and Moving Forward

Based on facts learned, it is our conviction that the Digital Citizenship Academy is a sustainable community-project. Firstly, all 29 participants who attended the 2020 training courses expressed the will to continue creating and implementing workshops until December 2022. Secondly, the plan for 11 new workshops for future implementation point to a continuity of work. Thirdly, even under very difficult conditions provoked by the Covid-19 pandemic, they managed to implement six new STEAM and Media Literacy activities after the school reopened in March 2021, and which they concluded in July. This resilience is fully in line with what they expressed in the final reports of the training courses, foreseeing the continuity of the work developed:

1. *Antecamera of future practices*—"Given continuity (…) by dramatizing the story, motor games, working on the area of world knowledge (farm animals …) " (W5); "The Workshop on vertical maternities (…) will continue (…) in the area of sciences and the emotional development of students" (W6); "Give continuity to the study of the human body, particularly about the organs that compose it and their functioning" (W14).
2. *Pedagogical strategy*—"To continue this workshop in the form of energizing Christmas songs" (W1); "to use the computer pedagogically to create a playful and interactive environment" (W13); "The phases

planned for this workshop pave the way for building new mathematical board games" (W15).

3. *Production of reusable resources*—"The instruments produced could be used in the weekly music activities" (W1); "Adaptation of the same characters for other stories" (W4); "Building stories orally, adapting them to the characters created" (W8); "Adaptation of the game [Electronic *Quizz*] to other subject areas (…), taking advantage of the electrical circuits and developing new cards" (W9).

4. *Means of sharing with other peers*—"If possible, they will present their work in the other 3rd grade class of the school" (W8); "Use of the electronic Quizz game by the 2nd grade class, when they will deepen this content, still in this school year" (W9).

5. *Social intervention through the media*—"Get response from the mayors (…) and the Parish Council presidents (…) and future improvements arising from the students' proposals" (W11); "publish news (…) in the newspaper 'O Cusco' this year" (W11); "arrange an interview with the President of the Parish Council and (…) spend a day with the President and from there make a report" (W11).

6. *Community involvement*—"After the session/interview, new activities were developed: "Cheetah Dress" session with the dresses of Mrs. Lurdes, Mrs. Lurdes' sister and the cousin of the grandmother of a student in the class" (W17); "Each student brought a square of fabric with a story (…) that we kept in a box that we called story chest" (W17).

7. *Replication and validation of the workshop*—"It would be interesting to extend it to other kindergarten classrooms and other children, in order to identify previous ideas regarding the phenomena addressed and compare them with the results of this workshop" (W3); "This workshop has the potential to be replicated, improved and continued, for example in the form of a school newspaper, digital" (W16).

The workshops were the origin of transdisciplinary activities, as happened in the 2nd cycle: "All the students made interviews with an older person to know what life was like when they were younger (food, education …)" (W17). These continuities are in many cases enhanced by the children: "Is the workshop finished? For us yes, but our creativity and that of the children is not exhausted here, as it was conceived because it is always possible to "upgrade" our imagination" (W3).

This willingness of children to continue to be involved in activities that associate Media Literacy and STEAM was also noted by the teachers: "In general, the students liked the workshop very much and wanted to participate in more workshops" (W9) "workshops like this one" (W13) or more workshops (W15). In the evaluation sheets applied to the children in the participating schools (Artur Alves Cardoso, Fontes de Caneças and Castanheiros), some of them made proposals for future workshops, such as:

- "He wanted us to make a tree and put things on it that were important to us, but it had to be a big tree to fit everyone's" (2nd grade, 1st grade);
- "Doing the Whole World " (2nd grade);
- "Making a rocket, a mini rocket" (4th grade, 1st grade);
- "A game, about healthy eating" (4th grade);
- "Making a robot" (4th grade);
- "We created a train circuit with the carriages with letters to form words. Then, while the train was running, we would read the words formed" (4th grade);
- "Take a visit to the ancient monuments of Caneças (2nd cycle);
- "Fashion show with cheetah dresses for the girls and hats for the boys" (2nd cycle);
- "Make an exhibition in the school and a newspaper" (2nd cycle);
- "Blogging" (2nd cycle);
- "Making a video to show what we did (2nd cycle);
- "Doing interviews with grandparents" (2nd cycle).

The next steps must still be defined, but they are sustainable due to the funding of the Digital Citizenship Academy project by the Calouste Gulbenkian Foundation, through the Knowledge Academies Program. This funding has made it possible to acquire materials and resources according to the needs identified, such as digital devices (e.g. computer, tablets), scientific equipment (e.g. microscope with projector), routers for Internet access and others that will overcome identified limitations.

Training needs have also been identified (e.g.: use of digital equipment, robotics, journalism), so short training sessions are being organized. Finally, the working groups were reformulated, and now have more members and with diverse scientific backgrounds, as well as agreed-upon methods of, currently, at-a-distance monitoring and follow-up.

The teachers also have a sense-making practices eBook and are available to participate in future training courses, as trainers and/or collaborators, which is key to the replicability of the Digital Citizenship Academy. There are three key pieces of information learned from the teacher training courses, which now serve as advantages for the next cohort:

1. *Conditions*—the teachers overcame difficulties by supporting each other and focusing on frequent joint reflection among themselves and with the students, through interdisciplinary dialogue, the use of their own resources, and the involvement of families and other community members.
2. *Practices*—the workshops were based on the children's interests, centered on practical and real situations, and for which proposals were sought in an interdisciplinary approach.
3. *Evaluation*—the children valued the participation in the workshops and wanted more. They enjoyed working in groups and creating "new things," having fun while doing it, and learned, not only scientific content, but also technical skills, social skills and even ways to intervene socially.

This project plans to move forward. The path is laid out, as is evident from what has been discussed in this book.

As an ongoing means of looking at the work of Media Literacy Education and Digital Citizenship Education, our main role, as a team, is to continue working, monitoring and improving, to reach new destinations that will be, sooner or later, new starting points, but more importantly to continue the work of teacher education in this area, which has demonstrated to be vital to the continued growth of our civic society. The work never stops.

Appendixes

Appendix A: Workshop Sheet of the "Digital Citizenship Academy" Project

1 - Title

2 - Target Audience

3 - Keywords

4 - Purpose

5 - Essential Learning/Profile of the Student Leaving Compulsory School
   -
   -

6 - Learning objectives (what the children should be able to do at the end of the workshop)

7 - Activity description

7.1 - Faculty prerequisites

7.2 - Materials and resources required (including links and recommended readings);

8 - Resources to be used in the assessment of student learning

8.1 - Resources to be used in the evaluation of the developed workshop

NOTE: The workshop sheet may have attachments.

Appendix B: STEAM/Media Literacy Workshop – structure of the final report

(a) The report should be three to five A4 pages (Trebuchet MS, size 12, 1.5 spaced), identified and not bound.
(b) May have attachments (photo, videos on CD, sentence record, student products);
(c) It is developed in group, but presented individually.

Title
Fulfillment of the planning stages
(a) From when to when it happened
(b) Contact hours with students related to the workshop
(c) Fullfilled/not fullfilled
(d) Strengths
(e) Possible constraints
(f) Strategies adopted for problem solving
Workshop evaluation strategy
(a) By the teachers:
(b) By participants/students:

Title
Results (a) Reached (b) Not reached + justification
Post-training workshop sustainability proposals (a) Continuity of the workshop (next phases) (b) Reuse of materials and equipment purchased for the project
Annexes a) Workshop form b) Presentation c) Links (to outputs created within the workshop, if any) d) (In)formative sheets e) Other documents used

Appendix C: Workshop evaluation form for preschool children_A

 AGRUPAMENTO DE ESCOLAS DE CANEÇAS
Educação Pré Escolar

Activity assessment … …. _____

NAME_____
DATE_____

Draw a picture about the activity you participated in.

AGRUPAMENTO DE ESCOLAS DE CANEÇAS
Educação Pré Escolar

WHAT DID I LIKE THE MOST ON THIS ACTIVITY? ☐   WHAT DID I LIKE THE LEAST ON THIS ACTIVITY? ☐

NAME: _____
DATE: ___/___/_____

APPENDIX C | 195

Workshop self-assessment	😊 😐 ☹

During rehearsals:

- I was attentive	😊 😐 ☹
- I behaved appropriately	😊 😐 ☹
- I participated with interest	😊 😐 ☹
- I collaborated in what I could	😊 😐 ☹

During the activity:

- I was quiet	😊 😐 ☹
- I helped my classmates	😊 😐 ☹
- I obeyed the rules	😊 😐 ☹
- I liked to participate	😊 😐 ☹
- I learned new things	😊 😐 ☹

Appendix D: Workshop evaluation form for preschool children_B

Name: _____
Workshop title: _____
Date: _____ School: _____

I am ☐ 🧑 ☐ 👧
I'm _____ years old

You enjoyed participating in the workshop (please tick one option out of the three below)
Not at all ☹ More or less 😐 A lot ☺

Paint according to the caption: 1 = Not at all ☹; 2 = More or less 😐; 3 = A lot ☺

I enjoyed working in groups with my classmates	☹	😐	☺
I learned new things	☹	😐	☺
I helped my classmates solve problems	☹	😐	☺
I didn't give up in the face of hardship	☹	😐	☺

I felt that my opinions mattered to my classmates	☹	😐	☺
I worked, but I also had fun	☹	😐	☺
We created something new	☹	😐	☺
I would like to participate in more workshops like this	☹	😐	☺

Now draw a picture (on the back of this sheet) that shows what you have most enjoyed learning during this activity.

Thanks for your participation!

Appendix E: Workshop evaluation form to be filled out by primary school children

Name: _____
Workshop title: _____
Date: _____ School: _____
Indicate your gender: ☐ Female ☐ Male
Indicate your age: _____ years   Indicate   your year of schooling: _____
_____

It is important to reflect on the way you have done your work and the learning you have gained.

1 - Did you enjoy participating in the workshop (check one of the three options below)?
☐ Not at all ☐ More or less ☐ A lot

2 - Evaluate the following items according to the scale: 1 = Not at all; 2 = More or less; 3 = A lot

	Circle the number you choose		
I enjoyed working in groups with my classmates	1	2	3
I learned new things	1	2	3
I helped my classmates solve problems	1	2	3
I didn't give up in the face of hardship	1	2	3
I felt that my opinions mattered to my classmates	1	2	3
I worked, but I also had fun	1	2	3
We created something new	1	2	3
I would like to participate in more workshops like this	1	2	3

3- How did this Workshop come about?
_____

4- Put in chronological order the phases of this workshop mentioned below.
    A -_____
    B-_____
    C-_____
    D-_____

Correct order: _____

5- Of everything you learned in the workshop, what was the most important thing you learned? Why was it important?
_____
_____
_____
_____

6- Do you have other ideas for a new work to develop after this workshop ...
_____
_____
_____
_____

Thanks for your participation!

Appendix F: Workshop evaluation form to be filled out by teachers

Workshop title: _____
Date: _____ School: _____
Number of participants: _____ _____ Male _____ Female
Age of participants: _____ Year of schooling: _____

To what extent did the workshop meet your expectations?
☐ Not at all ☐ Partially ☐ Very Much ☐ Completely

Rate each of the following items according to the scale: 1 = Not at all / 4 = Completely

	Circle the chosen option	Comments
The objectives of the workshop were achieved	1 2 3 4	
Students have developed competences referred to in the "Student Profile."	1 2 3 4	
Students developed socio-emotional skills	1 2 3 4	

	Circle the chosen option	Comments
The opinions of each student were respected in the group work	1 2 3 4	
Students were resilient in the face of difficulties	1 2 3 4	
There was mutual help in solving problems	1 2 3 4	
Students worked, but also had fun	1 2 3 4	
This workshop has potential for replication	1 2 3 4	

Appendix G: Initial questionnaire for parents

Digital Citizenship Academy - Parents (1)

This **questionnaire is** intended for **parents of pre-school and primary school students**. Please answer each question, choosing the option or options that best reflect your opinion.

The answers are confidential and anonymous. Thank you for your cooperation.

PART I

1 - Age: _____

2 - Gender:
　　　　　　☐ Male　　　　☐ Female

3 - Place of residence: _____

4 - Higher academic qualifications:

☐ 1st Cycle (4th Year)　　☐ Secondary (12th Year)　　☐ Master's Degree

☐ 2nd Cycle (6th Year)　　☐ Degree　　☐ PhD

☐ 3rd Cycle (9th Year)　　☐ Post-graduation　　☐ Other. Which one?

5 - Profession: _____

6 - NET monthly income of your household (in euros):

☐ Up to 600　　☐ Between 1501 and 2000　　☐ Between 3001 and 4000

☐ Between 601 and 1000　　☐ Between 2001 and 2500　　☐ More than 4000 euros

☐ Between 1001 and 1500　　☐ Between 2501 and 3000　　☐ I'd rather not answer

7 - Indicate the age of your child (_____) and the grade he or she is attending:

☐ 3 years old room　　☐ 6 years old room　　☐ 3rd Year CEB

☐ 4 years old room　　☐ 1st Year CEB　　☐ 4th Year CEB

☐ 5 years old room　　☐ 2nd Year CEB

8 - In addition to yourself and the child we are referring to, please indicate how many people make up your household and their ages.

　　　　　　　　　　　　　　　Who are they and how old are they?

APPENDIX G | 205

☐ A   ☐ Four   _____
☐ Two   ☐ Five   _____
☐ Three   ☐ More than five _____

PART II

B1 - Which of these resources do you usually have access to at home and how often?

	Less than 1 day/week	1 day week	2 days week	3 days week	4 days week	5 days week	6 days week	Every day	Never
Television	☐	☐	☐	☐	☐	☐	☐	☐	☐
Smartphone	☐	☐	☐	☐	☐	☐	☐	☐	☐
Internet	☐	☐	☐	☐	☐	☐	☐	☐	☐
Radio	☐	☐	☐	☐	☐	☐	☐	☐	☐
Newspapers/magazines	☐	☐	☐	☐	☐	☐	☐	☐	☐
Tablet	☐	☐	☐	☐	☐	☐	☐	☐	☐
Laptop	☐	☐	☐	☐	☐	☐	☐	☐	☐
Desktop	☐	☐	☐	☐	☐	☐	☐	☐	☐
Social media	☐	☐	☐	☐	☐	☐	☐	☐	☐

B2 - If you use online social media, which ones do you use the most:

☐ Facebook   ☐ Snapchat   ☐ Instagram
☐ Twitter   ☐ YouTube   ☐ Tik Tok
☐ LinkedIN   ☐ Other(s). Which ones? _____

B3 - If you are an Internet user, which of the following activities do you do there? (You can tick more than one option)

☐ Sending / receiving electronic mail messages (email)
☐ Contact with friends (in general)
☐ Read press releases via Facebook
☐ Search for travel information
☐ Use instant messaging programs (Ex: Messenger)
☐ Search information about your city
☐ Search for information on public services
☐ Search for health information
☐ Make / receive phone calls (Ex: Skype)
☐ Consult libraries / encyclopedias (e.g. Wikipedia)
☐ Search TV show's information
☐ Searching for a job
☐ Search for information on courses / training
☐ Search the housing market
☐ Search for political / trade union / association information

☐ Contact TV or radio programs
☐ Maintaining your own blog
☐ Participate in *online* courses
☐ Others. Which ones?_____

PART III

C1 - Which of the following media does your child have access to at home and how often does he/she use them, either alone or together with relatives.

		Never	<2d/week	3/5d/week	7d/week
1.	Newspapers or magazines in paper format	☐	☐	☐	☐
2.	Television	☐	☐	☐	☐
3.	Internet	☐	☐	☐	☐
4.	Radio programs	☐	☐	☐	☐
5.	Online social media (e.g. Facebook)	☐	☐	☐	☐
6.	Videos on YouTube	☐	☐	☐	☐
7.	Videos or movies available (on DVD, CD...)	☐	☐	☐	☐
8.	Blogs or photoblogs	☐	☐	☐	☐
9.	Interactive digital games	☐	☐	☐	☐

C2 - Of the following resources, which ones does your child use, at home or outside (e.g. associations, free time...) and how often?

		Never	<2d/week	3/5d/week	7d/week
1.	Computer (desktop/laptop) with internet access	☐	☐	☐	☐
2.	A camera (excluding mobile phone)	☐	☐	☐	☐
3.	A smartphone	☐	☐	☐	☐
4.	A tablet	☐	☐	☐	☐
5.	A mobile phone (not smartphone)	☐	☐	☐	☐
6.	A game console	☐	☐	☐	☐
7.	Television in their room	☐	☐	☐	☐
8.	Radio/MP3/MP4	☐	☐	☐	☐

C3 - How or from whom did/does your child learn how to use the equipment you use?

☐ Parents   ☐ Friends   ☐ Family members   ☐ School   ☐ Extracurricular

C4 - Of the equipment your child uses, which is the preferred one?_____
☐

C5 - How much time per day does your child use this equipment...
☐

		Up to 1 hour	1 to 2 hours	2 to 4 hours	> 4 hours
1.	On a normal weekday	☐	☐	☐	☐
2.	On a normal weekend day	☐	☐	☐	☐

C6 - How often do you develop these activities together with your child?

		Never	<2d/week	3/5d/week	7d/week
1.	We watch TV	☐	☐	☐	☐
2.	We a...				

3. We play online video games	☐	☐	☐	☐
4. View my online social media profile	☐	☐	☐	☐
5. We read a newspaper/magazine	☐	☐	☐	☐
6. We go to the movies	☐	☐	☐	☐
7. We practice sports (football, athletics...)	☐	☐	☐	☐
8. Other outdoor activities. E.g.: _____	☐	☐	☐	☐
9. We read books	☐	☐	☐	☐

C7 - Do you usually talk with your child about the use of Internet and/or social media (e.g. Facebook, YouTube, online game platforms...) and the practices that he/she develops there? (If you answer "Never", go to question C9).

Never	Some days	Many days	Every day
☐	☐	☐	☐

C8 - If you talk to your child about the Internet and/or social media (e.g. Facebook, YouTube, online gaming platforms...), how often do you address topics such as:

	Never	<2d/week	3/5d/week	7d/week
1. Limits of use (time/places of use...)	☐	☐	☐	☐
2. The risks associated with the use	☐	☐	☐	☐
3. Age as a reason for limitations in use	☐	☐	☐	☐
4. Encourage practice (e.g., Internet searches while doing homework)	☐	☐	☐	☐
5. The advantages in using these media	☐	☐	☐	☐
6. Encouraging access to adapted content the age of the student	☐	☐	☐	☐
7. Risks of online gaming	☐	☐	☐	☐
8. Advantages of online gaming	☐	☐	☐	☐

C9 - Regarding the use of Internet and/or social media (e.g. Facebook, YouTube, online gaming platforms...) in your family context...

	Totally disagree	Disagree	Agree	Strongly agree
1. We have clear and defined rules	☐	☐	☐	☐
2. The rules are the same for everyone	☐	☐	☐	☐
3. The rules were imposed by the adults	☐	☐	☐	☐
4. Rules were negotiated with the child(ren)	☐	☐	☐	☐
5. Those who do not follow the rules are punished for it	☐	☐	☐	☐
6. The rules have evolved over time	☐	☐	☐	☐
7. Home technology equipment is equipped with parental control systems	☐	☐	☐	☐

C10 - Considering the use of social media/digital technologies (e.g. Facebook, YouTube, online gaming platforms...) by your students...:

	Totally disagree	Disagree	Agree	Strongly agree
1. They are concerned about the risks they are exposed to (e.g. contacting strangers...)	☐	☐	☐	☐
2. The use of technologies has positive effects on family relationships	☐	☐	☐	☐

3. Children learn school content	☐	☐	☐	☐
4. Children learn content that interests them, not related to school	☐	☐	☐	☐
5. My students have felt uncomfortable in online social media	☐	☐	☐	☐

C11 - How do you position yourself in relation to the statement: "I am well informed about the risks my child is exposed to when using the Internet and/or social media?

Strongly disagree	Disagree	Agree	Strongly agree
☐	☐	☐	☐

C12 - Have you ever used any of the following addresses or services on Internet safety? (You can tick more than one option)

☐ Internet Segura.pt Help Line
☐ Safe Kids on the Net
☐ Seguranet
☐ Reporting of Internet sites
☐ Others. Which ones? _____
☐ No

C13 - Would you like more information about the risks students are exposed to when using the Internet?
☐ Yes ☐ No (if you answered "No", go to question D1)

C14 - How would you like to have access to this information? (You can pick several options)
☐ Through pamphlets or Support manuals sent by the School
☐ Via email from the School
☐ Via an online newsletter that I can subscribe to
☐ Through a website on online safety
☐ Through the newspapers and/or magazines I buy Through a CD
☐ From Information I can download from the Internet
☐ Other. Please specify

PART IV

D1 - Do you talk to your child's teachers about your child's use of the Internet and/or social media? (If you answer 'Never', finish your questionnaire)

Never	Some days	Many days	Every day
☐	☐	☐	☐

D2 - If you talk to teachers of your child(ren) about children's media use, how often do you address the following issues:

	Never	A few days	Manydays	Every day
1. The prohibition or limitation of certain practices (e.g.: time of use, places of use...)	☐	☐	☐	☐
2. Prohibiting or limiting access to certain content	☐	☐	☐	☐
3. Who decides the prohibition or the limit	☐	☐	☐	☐
4. The manner in which the prohibition or limit is established (advice, rule,	☐	☐	☐	☐

	prohibit use)				
5.	Prohibition/restriction on grounds of age	☐	☐	☐	☐
6.	The prohibition of the child having certain equipment	☐	☐	☐	☐
7.	The encouragement of certain practices (e.g. research)	☐	☐	☐	☐
8.	Encouraging access to certain content	☐	☐	☐	☐
9.	The encouragement of access according to the age of the child	☐	☐	☐	☐
10.	Encouraging the child to have certain equipment	☐	☐	☐	☐

D3 - If you talk to your child's teachers about children's use of media, how often is each of the following resources mentioned?

		Never	A few days	Many days	Every day
1.	All screens in general	☐	☐	☐	☐
2.	Television	☐	☐	☐	☐
3.	Videos and Movies	☐	☐	☐	☐
4.	Video Game Consoles	☐	☐	☐	☐
5.	Computer	☐	☐	☐	☐
6.	The Internet	☐	☐	☐	☐
7.	Tablets	☐	☐	☐	☐
8.	Mobile phones or smartphones	☐	☐	☐	☐

D4 - When you talk to your child's teachers, how do you usually rate each of the following equipments according to the risks and opportunities their use represents for the children? Only rate those mentioned in question D3.

		Good equipment	Bad equipment
1.	All screens in general	☐	☐
2.	Television	☐	☐
3.	Videos and Movies	☐	☐
4.	Video Game Consoles	☐	☐
5.	Computer	☐	☐
6.	The Internet	☐	☐
7.	Tablets	☐	☐
8.	Mobile phones or smartphones	☐	☐

Thank you very much for your cooperation.

Appendix H: Initial questionnaire for teachers

FCT Fundação para a Ciência e a Tecnologia
MINISTÉRIO DA CIÊNCIA, TECNOLOGIA E ENSINO SUPERIOR   Portugal

<u>**Media Literacy in Pre-school and Primary School**</u>

This <u>**questionnaire**</u> is part of a project supported by FCT – Foundation for Science and Technology (SFRH/BPD/77874/2011), focused on pre-school and primary school, namely on students, their teachers and their parents.

It aims to collect data on media use habits and perceptions of media use by <u>**pre-school and primary school teachers**</u>. It is organized into two parts: the first part aims to collect data to characterize the respondents. The second aims to obtain data on the research topic. Please answer each question by choosing the option or options that best reflect your opinion.

Your answers are confidential and anonymous. Do not write your name or anything that identifies you anywhere on the questionnaire.

We appreciate you answering **ALL** questions.

Thank you for your cooperation.

Vitor Tomé

PART I

1 - Mark your age group:

☐ Up to 25 years   ☐ From 36 to 40   ☐ From 51 to 55

☐ From 26 to 30   ☐ From 41 to 45   ☐ From 56 to 60

☐ From 30 to 35   ☐ From 46 to 50   ☐ More than 61

2 - Indicate your gender:

☐ Male   ☐ Female   ☐ Neutral

3 - Indicate your grouping: _____

4 - Mark the age group(s) or year/years of school you are teaching:

☐ 3 years old room   ☐ 1st Year CEB

☐ 4 years old room   ☐ 2nd Year CEB

☐ 5 years old room   ☐ 3rd Year CEB

☐ 6 years old room   ☐ 4th Year CEB

5 - Indicate your length of service:

☐ Up to 5 years   ☐ From 16 to 20 years old

☐ From 6 to 10 years old   ☐ From 21 to 25 years old

☐ From 11 to 15 years old   ☐ More than 25 years

6 - Indicate your highest academic degree:

☐ Bachelor's Degree ☐ Master's Degree
☐ Degree   ☐ PhD
☐ Post-graduation   ☐ Other. Which one?

6.1 - If you marked 'Other', please indicate which:
_____

7 - You have children, or other children living with you, who attend pre-school or primary school:

☐ Yeah, preschool. ☐ Yeah, primary school. ☐ No

PART II

B1 - Please indicate how often you use each of the following media:

	Less than 1 day/week	1 day week	2 days week	3 days week	4 days week	5 days week	6 days week	Every day	Never
Television	☐	☐	☐	☐	☐	☐	☐	☐	☐
Internet	☐	☐	☐	☐	☐	☐	☐	☐	☐
Social media online (e.g. Facebook)	☐	☐	☐	☐	☐	☐	☐	☐	☐
Radio	☐	☐	☐	☐	☐	☐	☐	☐	☐
Newspapers	☐	☐	☐	☐	☐	☐	☐	☐	☐
Magazines	☐	☐	☐	☐	☐	☐	☐	☐	☐

B2 - If you use online social media, which ones do you use the most:

☐ Facebook   ☐ Snapchat
☐ Twitter   ☐ YouTube
☐ LinkedIN   ☐ Other(s). Which one(s)?

B2.1 - If you ticked 'Other', please indicate which:
_____

B3 - If you are an Internet user, how do you normally access this media? (You can tick several options). If you do not use the Internet, go to question B5.

☐ Personal computer   ☐ Mobile phone
☐ Family computer   ☐ *Smartphone*   ☐ Other
☐ School computer   ☐ Tablet

B3.1 - If you ticked 'Other', please state which:

B4 - If you are an Internet user, which of the following activities do you do there? (You can tick several options)
- ☐ Sending / receiving electronic mail messages (email)
- ☐ Contact with friends (in general)
- ☐ Read press releases via Facebook
- ☐ Search for travel information
- ☐ Use instant messaging programs (Ex: Messenger)
- ☐ Search information about your city
- ☐ Search for information on public services
- ☐ Search for health information
- ☐ Make / receive phone calls (Ex: Skype)
- ☐ Consult libraries / encyclopedias (e.g. Wikipedia)
- ☐ Search TV show's information
- ☐ Search for information on courses / training
- ☐ Search the housing market
- ☐ Search for political / trade union / association information
- ☐ Contact TV or radio programs
- ☐ Maintaining your own blog
- ☐ Participate in *online* courses
- ☐ Other(s). Which one(s)? _____

B5 - Focusing on the use of media (e.g. Internet, television, radio, newspapers...) by students of pre-school and/or 1st cycle of basic education...

	Totally disagree	Disagree	Agree	Strongly agree
1. Media have pedagogical potential	☐			
2. Students learn school content there that is useful to them in school		☐	☐	☐
	☐	☐	☐	☐
3. Pupils learn non-school content there, according to their interests	☐	☐	☐	☐

B6 - Tick how often you use the following media resources in your teaching activities with your students.

	Never	Some days	Many Days	Every day
1. Newspapers or magazines in paper format	☐	☐	☐	☐
2. Online newspapers and magazines	☐	☐	☐	☐
3. Television programs (on a television)	☐	☐	☐	☐
4. Online TV shows	☐	☐	☐	☐
5. Available videos/films (on DVD, CD...)	☐	☐	☐	☐
6. Videos or movies available online	☐	☐	☐	☐
7. Radio programs (on a radio)	☐	☐	☐	☐
8. Radio programs (online)	☐	☐	☐	☐
9. Online social media (e.g. Facebook, ...)	☐	☐	☐	☐
10. Blogs or photoblogs	☐	☐	☐	☐

11. Wikipedia pages	☐	☐	☐	☐
12. Interactive digital games	☐	☐	☐	☐
13. Other	☐	☐	☐	☐

B6.1 - If you ticked 'Other(s), please state which: _____

B7 - Tick the resources used in your classroom and who uses them, whether they are from the school, yours or your students.

	I use	Students use	Both use	No
1. Computers in the school ICT room	☐	☐	☐	☐
2. School computer, with internet access	☐	☐	☐	☐
3. Projector connected to a computer	☐	☐	☐	☐
4. Interactive whiteboard	☐	☐	☐	☐
5. Camera (excluding the one on the mobile phone)	☐	☐	☐	☐
6. A video camera (excluding the one on the mobile phone)	☐	☐	☐	☐
7. A tablet	☐	☐	☐	☐
8. A mobile phone or a smartphone	☐	☐	☐	☐

B8 - Do you usually talk to your students about their use of social media (e.g. Facebook, YouTube, online gaming platforms) and the practices they develop there? (If you answer 'Never', go to question 10).

Never	Some days	Many days	Every day
☐	☐	☐	☐

B9 - If you talk to your students about social media (e.g. Facebook, YouTube, online gaming platforms), how often do you address topics such as:

	Never	A few days	Many days	Every day
1. Limits of use (e.g.: time of use, places of use...)	☐	☐	☐	☐
2. The risks associated with the use	☐	☐	☐	☐
3. Age as a reason for limitations in use	☐	☐	☐	☐
4. Encourage practice (e.g., Internet searches while doing homework)	☐	☐	☐	☐
5. The advantages you have in using these media	☐	☐	☐	☐
6. Encouraging access to adapted content the age of the student	☐	☐	☐	☐
7. Risks of online gaming	☐	☐	☐	☐
8. Advantages of online gaming	☐	☐	☐	☐

B10 - In your opinion, how many of your students use social media (e.g. Facebook, YouTube, online gaming platforms)?

No	Up to one quarter	Between ¼ and one-half	More than half	Between one-half and three-quarters	All
☐	☐	☐	☐	☐	☐

B11 - How do you position yourself in relation to the statement: "I am well informed about the risks students are exposed to when using the Internet and/or social media?

Strongly disagree	Disagree	Agree	Strongly agree
☐	☐	☐	☐

B12 - Have you used any of the resources on Internet safety? (You can tick several options)

☐ Internet Segura.pt Help Line
☐ Safe Kids on the Net
☐ Seguranet
☐ Reporting of Internet sites
☐ Others. Which?_____
☐ No

B13 - Would you like more information about the risks students are exposed to when using the Internet and/or social media?

☐ Yes   ☐ No (if you have answered "No", go to question B15)

B14 - How would you like to have access to this information? (You may check several options)

☐ Through pamphlets or support manuals sent by the School
☐ Via email from the School
☐ Via an online newsletter that I can subscribe to
☐ Through a website on online safety
☐ Through the newspapers and/or magazines I buy
☐ From Information I can download from the Internet
☐ Other. Please specify

B15 - Do you usually talk to parents of your students about the Internet and/or social media by the students/children? (If 'Never' go to question B19)

Never	Some days	Many days	Every day
☐	☐	☐	☐

B16 - If you talk to parents about their children's use of the Internet and/or social media, how often do you address the following issues?

	Never	A few days	Many days	Every day
1. The prohibition or limitation of certain practices (e.g.: time of use, places of use...)	☐	☐	☐	☐
2. Prohibiting or limiting access to certain content	☐	☐	☐	☐
3. Who decides the ban or the limit	☐	☐	☐	☐
4. The manner in which the prohibition or limit is established (advice, rule, prohibit use)	☐	☐	☐	☐
5. The prohibition/limit depending on the age of the child	☐	☐	☐	☐
6. The prohibition of the child having certain equipment	☐	☐	☐	☐
7. The encouragement of certain practices (e.g. research)	☐	☐	☐	☐
8. The encouragement of access to certain content	☐	☐	☐	☐
9. The incentive of access according to the age of the child	☐	☐	☐	☐
10. Encouraging the child to have certain equipment	☐	☐	☐	☐

B17 - If you talk to parents about their children's use of the Internet and/or social media, how often do they mention each of the following resources.

	Never	A few days	Many days	Every day
1. All screens in general	☐	☐	☐	☐

	□	□	□	□
2. Television	□	□	□	□
3. Videos and Movies	□	□	□	□
4. Video Game Consoles	□	□	□	□
5. Computer	□	□	□	□
6. The Internet	□	□	□	□
7. Tablets	□	□	□	□
8. Mobile phones or smartphones	□	□	□	□

B18 - When you talk to parents and guardians, how do you usually classify each of the following equipment, according to the risks and opportunities that the use represents for the children? Only rate the ones you mentioned in question B17.

	Good equipment the	Bad equipment
1. All screens in general	□	□
2. Television		□
	□	
3. Videos and Movies	□	□
4. Video Game Consoles	□	□
5. Computer	□	□
6. The Internet	□	
7. Tablets	□	□
8. Mobile phones or smartphones	□	□

B19 - Focusing on pre-school and/or primary school students, the Internet and/or social media...

	Totally disagree	Disagree	Agree	Strongly agree
1. Promote better collaboration between students				□
2. Allow students to share their work with wider audiences	□	□	□	□
	□	□	□	
3. Stimulate students' creativity and personal expression	□	□	□	□
4. Distract students from school work more than help them academically	□	□	□	□
5. Promote learning by connecting learners with content that interests them	□	□	□	□
6. Provide content that prompts students to become more engaged with school content	□	□	□	□
7. Provide content that broadens learners' worldview and perspectives	□	□	□	□

B20 - The following aspects are frequently identified as obstacles to the effective use of Internet and/or social media at school, in pedagogical situations. What is your level of agreement with each of them?

	Totally disagree	Disagree	Agree	Strongly agree
1. Resistance from teachers and management			□	□
2. Constraints arising from lack of time to use media and digital technologies	□	□	□	□
	□	□		
3. The pressure on teachers to prepare students	□	□	□	□

for assessments				
4. Lack of resources or access to media for students	☐	☐	☐	☐
5. Teachers' lack of willingness, knowledge and training to use them in the classroom	☐	☐	☐	☐
6. The lack of technical support (repairs, problem solving...) in schools	☐	☐	☐	☐

Thank you very much for your cooperation.

Index

Artur Alves Cardoso School 179–180
   journalism 119, 123–124, 128, 130, 133, 135–137, 145, 147, 150–151, 155–162, 176
   Kindergarten 2
   Primary School 2
   teacher community work 113–114
autonomy 81–83, 85, 100, 104, 115

basic education 28, 31, 76–77, 83, 93, 109
being online 19
best practices
   community-based project 121
   digital literary practices 173
   dissemination 111
   media literacy and STEAM activities 51, 164, 166, 168, 171
   teacher training 59, 175, 178, 181
bullying 63, 70–71, 73, 128, 131–134, 137, 161, 176
butterfly model 13–14
   learning outcomes 14
   values, attitudes, skills and knowledge 14

Calouste Gulbenkian Foundation 1, 3, 48, 60, 154, 156, 158–159, 175, 178–181, 185
Caneças School District 2, 4, 9–10, 56–57, 68, 77, 112, 114, 175, 179–180
   school newspaper and video services 129–130, 145–146, 156–157, 1591–61, 166–167
Chinese shadow theater 80–81, 86, 88, 97
citizen empowerment 16, 35, 123
   childhood education 33
collaboration 8, 19, 21, 24, 26
   community-based action research 128, 138–139, 145, 147, 175–176, 178
   teacher training 72, 82–85, 98–99, 115–116
Committee of Ministers of the Council of Europe 20
communication 14, 18–21, 24, 26, 42, 97–98, 104, 107, 153, 155, 158–159, 172, 176
community- based participatory action research project [CBPAR] 35
community-based project organization aims and goals 50–51

contextual references 50
critical analysis skills 49–50
data collection methods 53–54
empowerment of school children 51–52
families 56–57
four phases 47
municipal counties 55–56
outcome development 52–53
planning 48–49
preschool and primary school teachers 55
questionnaires 54–55
competences 14, 21, 25, 27, 29–30, 85, 96–98, 100–101, 103–104
 Competence 3 and 4, 21
 OECD on 22–25
 Portugal Education policy 27–29
 in STEM and STEAM 21
 UNESCO on 25–26
compulsory education 27, 30, 95–96
cooperation 17, 19, 24, 26, 50, 84–85, 99, 107, 115, 203, 212
Council of Europe
 citizenship project 178, 180
 on competence 13, 19–21, 23, 25–27
 teacher training 130, 173
Council of European Union 20
 on eight key competencies 21
Council of the European Union 26
Covid-19 pandemic 10, 76–77, 81–82, 112, 160, 163–165, 183
creativity 15–21, 24, 33, 83, 85, 95, 100, 102, 153, 157, 184
critical thinking 17, 20, 23–26, 83, 85, 127
cultures 14, 22–23, 26–29, 102, 104, 120, 143
curriculum 17–18, 23, 27, 31, 60, 136, 139, 144

data collection 48, 51, 53, 55–56, 77, 112, 181
democratic participation 1, 4, 49, 51, 59, 61, 120, 151, 153–154
digital citizenship, media literacy and STEAM 18–19

Digital Citizenship Academy 1, 18, 107, 113, 155–156, 158–159, 161, 1661–67, 179–180, 183, 185
 key concepts 13
 study of social and emotional skills 24

Digital Citizenship Education 1
 definition 14
 formal and informal learning contexts 20
 in Odivelas Municipality 2
 international conferences in European countries 2
 key concepts and domains 1, 3, 19
 key domains 19
 Ministerial Declaration on Education for Citizenship recommendation 20–21
 objectives 1–2
 teacher training courses 2
 ten domains 19–21
Digital Citizenship Education for Democratic Participation of young people
 Leonardo Coimbra Training Center. 61
 media literacy, classroom practices 65–66
 online hate speech analysis 61
 structure 61
 teacher training course 61–62
 topics and objectives 62–63
 training assessment 66–67
 work assessment, teachers 63–65
digital literacy 62, 120–123, 127, 172–173
 young children 32–33
digital media 50–52, 60–61, 66–67, 108–9
 community-based projects 125–126, 146, 152–153, 162–163, 173
dissemination 15, 33, 36–37, 80, 111, 143, 152, 154, 163, 165, 178
diversity 23, 25, 32, 95, 102, 120

education, sociocultural phenomenon 33–34
educators 7, 25, 33, 131, 144
empathy 14, 19, 24–25, 29, 99, 149, 153
ethics 16, 19, 76, 153
EU Kids Online 32, 37

European Commission 16
  global education proposal points 26
European countries 2, 8, 55, 130, 132, 180
  young children, online practice 32
European Cultural Convention 20
European Union 18, 21, 26–27, 54, 60, 166
evaluation 3–4, 26, 28
  community-based projects 156, 164–166, 171
  teacher training, 83, 85, 91–92, 97–98, 105, 107, 110–111, 114
expression 18, 79, 102, 145–146, 150
  artistic 102, 104
  freedom of 15
  physical-motor 145–146

families 2–3, 32–35
  community-based projects 120–121, 123–125, 127–129, 13
  training courses 52–56, 69–70, 82, 115–16
final reports
  antecamera 183
  community involvement 184
  conditions and practices 186
  evaluations 186
  future proposals 185
  Media Literacy and STEAM 184–185
  on workshop 184
  pedagogical strategy 183–184
  peer sharing 184
  reusable resources 184
  social intervention through media 184
  training needs 185

games 16, 32, 55, 80, 86–88, 96, 103, 125, 129, 137–138, 157
  computer equals 137
  digital 125–126
  electronic 115–116
  electronic quizz 184
  mathematical 80, 88
  motor 183
  new mathematical board 184
  traditional 147

geometric solids, learning objectives 78–80, 85–86, 88, 90, 96, 103, 116
Global Kids Online 32
guardians 52, 54, 124–125, 143, 162

human rights 14–15, 25, 28, 127, 131–132, 138, 144, 168

ICT 31, 60, 68, 70, 73, 75, 137–138, 145
inclusion 19, 29, 38, 66, 80, 153, 171
informal contexts 15, 26, 34, 65, 122, 156
information) literacy 19
interaction 28, 55, 99, 104, 122, 176
interdisciplinarity 82, 84, 107, 111, 137
Internet 37, 54, 63–64, 70, 74–75
  community -based projects 124–125, 127, 129, 140, 152–153, 162–163, 168–169
intervention plan 3–4, 119–21, 123, 127–28, 136–37, 145, 148–50, 159, 163, 165, 168, 173–74, 177, 181
interviews 53, 55, 87, 90, 94, 121, 124, 136–37, 145, 150, 177–78, 184–85

journalism and media literacy pedagogical practices
  activities development, teachers 77–80
  assessment of teacher's work 83
  chain improvements 82
  children's interest 83
  children, individualized support 81
  collaboration between students 82
  conjuncture 81
  constraints and strategies 80
  contents 77
  cooperation and collaboration 84
  cycles covered 76–77
  data collection 77
  drawings 88
  families and community support 82
  formats 76
  fostering interdisciplinarity 84
  games and experiments 88
  interdisciplinarity 82
  Journalistic text 88

learning with playing 84
media products, categories 86–87
models, solar system examples 88
musical instruments 88
number of trainees 77
physical conditions 80
Powerpoints 87
practical and real situations 83–84
product exhibition 88
reflection and monitoring 81
resources 81
slideshows 87
social intervention 84
software/ hardware strategies 88
teachers, use of technology 81
training course 76
use of teacher resources 82
working beyond hours 82
workshop plans and
   evaluations 84, 88–95
journalists 6, 62, 79, 90, 111, 128, 154, 168, 179

kindergartens 54, 65, 68, 70–72, 84, 112, 114–115, 138–140, 149
knowledge 14–15, 22–23, 25, 27, 30–31, 54, 65–66, 75, 84–85, 98–100, 107, 115–116, 151, 156, 173–174

Ladder of participation (Hart) 39
learning 16, 18–19, 21, 25–26, 84–85, 94, 107, 116
   community-based project 125, 131–32, 152–53, 157–58, 163, 166–167, 198–199
Leonardo Coimbra Training Center 56, 61, 66–67, 75, 175
local community 1, 27, 34, 51, 55, 60, 69, 73, 109, 115–16, 123

mathematics 13, 16, 20–21, 23, 68, 70, 73, 84, 87–88, 96–97, 150, 155
media financing models 19
media literacy
   active participation 19
   areas of competencies 15–16
   consumer awareness 19
   e- Presence and communication 19
   empowerment spiral 16
   ethics and empathy 19
   formal and informal learning
      context 15–16
   health and well-being 17
   key domains 19
   knowledge of media access 19
   learning and creativity 19
   learning challenges 16
   privacy and security 19
   rights and responsibilities 19
   together with STEAM 18
   training course 2–3
   use of technology 17
municipality 3, 47, 55–56, 61, 72–73, 112, 120, 129, 135, 175, 180
OECD (Organization for Economic Cooperation and Development) 16, 18, 22–24, 26, 72, 101, 137, 144, 158

OECD 16
   Big 5 model 24
   global competence and learning compass 22–24
   global education proposal points 26
   on curriculum development 23
offline 13–14, 17, 26, 120, 144, 177
online school newspaper 2
online 17, 19, 55, 115, 120, 141, 144, 168, 174, 177

parents 3–4, 34, 47–56, 64, 66, 73–74, 203
   community-based projects 119–20, 124–29, 133–36, 138–39, 141–48, 150–54, 157–60, 162–63, 165, 174, 176–77
participants 35, 55, 62–63, 68, 70–72, 75, 77–79, 106, 112, 114, 201
participatory- research approach
   action level 36
   bottom- up and top-down strategies 37

community-based projects 36
genuine participation levels 38–39
Hart's model of youth participation 39
informing, consultation and placation 35
levels of participation 35
manipulation and therapy 35
media literacy and digital citizenship education 36
non-participation levels 38
partnership, delegated power and citizen control 35
research level 36
2012 and 2015 in Portugal 34
types of project 35–36
use of social networks by young children 34–35
pedagogical practices
　aesthetic and artistic sensitivity/ awareness 102, 104
　area of competence 96–104
　body awareness and mastery 104
　critical and creative thinking 99, 104
　information and communication 104
　interpersonal relations 100, 104
　languages and texts 104
　LM/ STEAM relation 97–104
　manipulative activities 103–104
　personal development and autonomy 100–101, 104
　reasoning and problem solving skills 98–99
　science-based decision-making 103–104
　two training courses 96
　well-being, health and environment 104
Portuguese Education Policy
　core values, attitudes and skills of students 95
Portugal, educational policy
　areas of competences, curriculum 30
　citizenship education 27–29
　compulsory schooling concepts 30
　media literacy 27, 31
　preschool, primary and secondary levels 28–29
　SPECS 31
　STEAM 27, 31
post-test questionnaires 112, 158–159, 164–165, 181
PowerPoint 65, 79, 82, 86, 88, 95, 98, 115–116, 141
preschool education
　creativity through play 18
　development of socio-cultural practices., 17
　interest in use of technology 17
　learning potentials 18
　postdigial activities 18
　STEAM 17–18

primary school
primary school 2, 27–28, 48–50, 61, 67–68, 72–73, 76–77, 93, 100–101, 108, 111–114, 211
　journalism 123–124, 128–130, 137–139, 141–142
　teachers 1, 5, 51–56, 59–61, 64–65, 70–72, 76, 112–113, 120, 177, 179
problem solving 2, 15–16, 18, 21, 23, 33, 95, 98, 104, 155, 158
Profile of Students upon leaving Compulsory Schooling 101
project evaluation
　case study replication 180–181
　results 2015–2020 171–174
　sustainability plan 175–180

questionnaires 53–56, 67, 70, 73, 105, 107, 111, 133–34, 151, 160, 176–177, 203, 211

reflection 24, 29, 74, 81, 96–97, 105, 129, 179
rights online 19

school newspaper, media education
　activities development, teachers 69–71
　assessment of teacher's work 71–75

course rules 66–67
goals 67
journalism, objectives 67–68
Leonardo Coimbra Training Center 67
teacher distribution by age group 68–69
trainee enrollment 68
training assessment 75
science 1–2, 6, 8, 13, 15–16, 20–21, 23, 27, 30, 47–48, 86, 88, 97, 138, 175
smartphones 55, 63–64, 125–26, 162
social intervention 15, 19, 26, 30, 63, 74, 84–85, 95, 136, 172, 184
social media 4, 34, 50, 52, 54, 61
social networks 34, 49, 60, 162
STEAM— Science, Technology, Engineering, Arts and Mathematics
    access and inclusion 19
    active participation 19
    areas of competency 17
    consumer awareness 19
    e-presence and communication 19
    ethics and empathy 19
    five central aspects 17–18
    health and well- being 19
    journalism 97–103, 105, 115–116
    key concepts and domains 13, 19
    learning and creativity 19
    linking arts with 16
    Makerspaces 17–18
    privacy and security 19
    project- based learning methodology 16
    rights and responsibilities 19
    training course 2–3
    use of technology 17
    whole school approach 155, 159, 161
    with media literacy 18–19
Sustainable Development Goals 2030 23, 25
sustainability 14, 29, 80, 84, 173
    environmental 30, 96, 150

teacher training 10, 55–56, 59–60, 62, 108–111, 114
    digital citizenship (2016–2020) 59–61
    media literacy 59–61
    whole-school approach 130, 133, 159, 161, 164, 166, 171, 174–175
Technology Portuguese Foundation 1, 6, 47–48, 120, 128
television xii, 32, 64, 124, 126, 155, 157
trainer 62, 106–11, 166, 168, 177, 181, 185
training courses 3, 75, 80, 85, 111–114, 116, 159, 172–174, 176, 183, 185
    assessment 105
    continued teacher training 108–110
    five types of positive aspects 106–107
    teachers' distribution 112–116
    trainees' perspective 105–106
    trainer's perspective 107–111
training workshops 31, 103, 116, 165, 179, 181
transmedia literacy 15
transversal 27–28, 74, 97–98, 101
TV News services 70, 73–74, 147, 156–157, 165–166, 168

UNESCO 15–16, 18, 25–26, 49–50, 60, 65, 85
    global citizen education perspective 25–26
    infodemic and disinfodemic 15
United Kingdom
    digital technology 54, 178
    young children, online practice 32

video games 125, 157, 162–163
video news 2

well-being 19–21, 24, 28, 101, 104
whole- school approach
    action vs research level 120–121
    co-designing 127–128
    contributions by funding 154–159
    cooperation, establishment of 137–139
    Covid-19 163–167
    digital citizens 120
    evaluation of activities 136–137
    family context 162–163

focus group results 145–150
hypothesis 121–122
improvement proposals 142–145
informal context 122–123
interactive situation 123–124
intervention strategy 120–121
media use, teacher perceptions 124–127
parents intervention 150–154
pre- test questionnaires 159–162
project development 128
project perceptions (from april 2016 to june 2017) 139–142
school newspaper publication 129–136
teachers' assessment of the intervention plan 136
training, impact on 136
working groups 66, 69, 77, 79, 85, 108–109, 111, 115, 123, 185
workshop phases
  content 94
  social intervention 95
  social skills 95
  technical skills 94–95
workshop sheets
  Digital Citizenship Academy 189–190
  pre-school children, evaluation form 193–195, 197–198
  primary-school children, evaluation form 199–200
  questions for parents 203–210
  questions for teachers 213–218
  STEAM/media literacy 191–192
  teachers, evaluation form 201–202
workshops 76–80, 82–89, 91–98, 100–106, 108–10, 112, 114–16, 143, 155, 160, 183–86, 189–93, 197–202

xylophones 86, 91

young children 8, 13, 37, 49, 66, 121, 173, 177
  digital use and practices 32–33
  online practices 31–32
  television use 32

CRITICAL ISSUES FOR LEARNING AND TEACHING

Shirley R. Steinberg
General Editor

Minding the Media is a book series specifically designed to address the needs of students and teachers in watching, comprehending, and using media. Books in the series use a wide range of educational settings to raise consciousness about media relations and realities and promote critical, creative alternatives to contemporary mainstream practices. *Minding the Media* seeks theoretical, technical, and practitioner perspectives as they relate to critical pedagogy and public education. Authors are invited to contribute volumes of up to 85,000 words to this series. Possible areas of interest as they connect to learning and teaching include:

- critical media literacy
- popular culture
- video games
- animation
- music
- media activism
- democratizing information systems
- using alternative media
- using the Web/internet
- interactive technologies
- blogs
- multi-media in the classroom
- media representations of race, class, gender, sexuality, disability, etc.

- media/communications studies methodologies
- semiotics
- watchdog journalism/investigative journalism
- visual culture: theater, art, photography
- radio, TV, newspapers, zines, film, documentary film, comic books
- public relations
- globalization and the media
- consumption/consumer culture
- advertising
- censorship
- audience reception

For additional information about this series or for the submission of manuscripts, please contact:
  Shirley R. Steinberg
  msgramsci@gmail.com

To order other books in this series, please contact our Customer Service Department:
  peterlang@presswarehouse.com (within the U.S.)
  orders@peterlang.com (outside the U.S.)

Or browse online by series:
  www.peterlang.com

www.ingramcontent.com/pod-product-compliance
Lightning Source LLC
Chambersburg PA
CBHW061711300426
44115CB00014B/2645